T0144555

PARADATA AND TRANSPARENCY IN VIRTUAL HERITAGE

Digital Research in the Arts and Humanities

Other titles in the series

Art Practice in a Digital Culture
Edited by Hazel Gardiner and Charlie Gere
ISBN 978 0 7546 7623 2

Digital Research in the Study of Classical Antiquity
Edied by Gabriel Bodard and Simon Mahony
ISBN 9 780 7546 7773 4

Paradata and Transparency in Virtual Heritage

Edited by

ANNA BENTKOWSKA-KAFEL, HUGH DENARD and DREW BAKER
King's College London, UK

ASHGATE

Published by
Ashgate Publishing Limited
Wey Court East
Union Road
Farnham
Surrey, GU9 7PT
England

Ashgate Publishing Company
Suite 420
101 Cherry Street
Burlington
VT 05401-4405
USA

www.ashgate.com

British Library Cataloguing in Publication Data
Paradata and transparency in virtual heritage. – (Digital research in the arts and humanities)
 1. Metadata. 2. Interpretation of cultural and natural resources–Data processing. 3. History–Research–Methodology. 4. History–Data processing. 5. Three-dimensional imaging. 6. Imaging systems in archaeology. 7. Virtual reality in archaeology.
 I. Series
 907.2-dc22

Library of Congress Cataloging-in-Publication Data
Paradata and transparency in virtual heritage / [edited] by Anna Bentkowska-Kafel, Hugh Denard, and Drew Baker.
    p. cm. – (Digital research in the arts and humanities)
  Includes bibliographical references and index.
      ISBN 978-0-7546-7583-9 (alk. paper) – ISBN 978-1-4094-3761-1 (ebook)
1. Cultural property–Digitization. 2. Interpretation of cultural and natural resources. 3. Visualization-Data processing. 4. Digital media. 5. Digital images. 6. Virtual reality. I. Bentkowska-Kafel, Anna. II. Denard, Hugh. III. Baker, Drew.
  CC135.P364 2011
  363.6'9--dc23

2011022579

ISBN 9780754675839 (hbk)
ISBN 9781409437611 (ebk)

Printed and bound in Great Britain by the
MPG Books Group, UK.

To Harold Short,
Director of the Centre for Computing in the Humanities, King's College London,
the champion of unconventional thinking, innovative research and collaboration,
on his retirement
Editors

PART IV   CONCLUSION

List of Figures and Tables

Figures

Tables

List of Plates

The colour plates are located between pages 134–5.

1   Left: Plan of medieval Southampton based on the Southampton Terrier of 1454 (Lawrence Arthur Burgess (ed.), *The Southampton Terrier of 1454* (London: HMSO, 1976))
     Right: Plan derived from combined sources: 1454 Terrier (green), archaeology (red); cartography (blue) and inferred data (magenta) © Matt Jones, 2008

2   Visualization of Southampton as it might have looked in 1454. © Matt Jones, 2008

3   Visualization of Piet Mondrian's studio at 5 rue de Coulmiers, Paris. South wall view with and without easel. © Ryan Egel-Andrews, 2009

4   Computer simulation of the House of the Vettii, Pompeii, under electric light (left) and as illuminated by olive oil lamp (right). © Kate Devlin

5   Fourteen different versions of visualizations for the same data flow field, after Mary J. McDerby, *Introduction to Scientific Visualization*, Training notes (Manchester: University of Manchester Research Computing Services, 2007). Reproduced with kind permission

6   Photogrammetric photo-sequences of the Athena Lemnia statue demonstrating the effectiveness of the random pattern. The sequence consists of 21 photos, the first eight are shown. The second row shows the reconstruction quality from the dense matching: blue indicates that a reliable depth value is available for the respective pixel, yellow means very low quality

7   The final step: aligning the resulting meshes from the eight image sequences, then fusing them together. This involves a rough manual alignment, followed by numeric refinement. The ICP algorithm has only a small radius of convergence, so considerable experience is required to perform the alignment and select good feature points

8   Cybernetic map of the Castiglion Fiorentino Museum by Eva Pietroni. Reproduced courtesy of Eva Pietroni, CNR ITABC

9   Virtual archaeological reconstruction of the House of Livia in Rome where every artefact has affordances such as Space, Time, Use, Type and Similarity assigned. Affordances may be activated and examined by the users as they interact with the model

mainly on medieval and Early Modern visual culture in Western Europe, and the use of advanced ICT methods in documentation and interpretation of art. She has published on digital iconography and digital iconology, the evidential value of the digital image and the impact of interactive computer graphics on representation and interpretation of art and architecture of the past. She has been involved in a number of computer-based art projects hosted by the Courtauld Institute of Art in London and the Department of Digital Humanities, King's College London, including the JISC 3D Visualisation in the Arts Network, 3DVisA <http://3dvisa.cch.kcl.ac.uk>, and the British Academy project, *Corpus of Romanesque Sculpture in Britain and Ireland* <http://www.crsbi.ac.uk>, of which she is Associate Director. She has been a committee member and editor for CHArt, Computers and the History of Art <http://www.chart.ac.uk>, since 1999.

Mark Carnall is the curator of the Grant Museum of Zoology and Comparative Anatomy University College London. He is a palaeobiologist and curates the historic teaching collection, founded in 1828. Recently, he has been working to catalogue the collection, recording specimens with a 3D laser scanner, as well as using other new technologies to bring the relatively hidden collection to a wider audience. As well as a lifelong interest in natural history and science communication, Mark grew up with video games and the internet and is particularly interested in applying these technologies to keeping museums pertinent, innovative and engaging to public audiences.

Hugh Denard (BA, Trinity College Dublin; MA, PhD, Exeter) lectures in the Department of Digital Humanities, King's College, London, where he is Associate Director of the King's Visualisation Lab and programme director of the MA in Digital Culture and Technology. He is editor and joint coordinator of The London Charter for the Computer-based Visualization of Cultural Heritage, an initiative arising out of a symposium convened by the AHRC 'Making Space' project that he co-directed, and which was designed to develop a methodology for tracking and documenting the cognitive process in 3D visualization-based research. In 2006–2009 he directed the JISC-funded 3D Visualisation in the Arts Network, which supports arts and humanities academics in the use of 3D visualization technologies. Other current projects include: the AHRC 'Body and Mask in Ancient Theatre Space' project, the 'Villa at Oplontis' project, funded by the Leverhulme Trust and the Eduserv 'Theatron 3' project.

Kate Devlin is a Lecturer in the Department of Computing at Goldsmiths, University of London. Her research is interdisciplinary, applying computer graphics and perception analysis to archaeology. She has a PhD in Computer Science from the University of Bristol, and an MSc in Computer Science and a BA in Archaeology from Queens University, Belfast.

Ryan Egel-Andrews received his BA in History of Art from University College London and in 2009 completed the MA in Digital Humanities course based at the Department of Digital Humanities, King's College London. His MA dissertation involved a visualization of one of Piet Mondrian's studios in Paris and is concerned with the application of 3D-modelling technologies to art-historical research.

Maurizio Forte is Professor of World Heritage at the School of Social Sciences, Humanities and Arts, and Director of the Virtual Heritage Lab at the University of California, Merced. His research interests include virtual reality, GIS, spatial technologies, 3D documentation, virtual reconstruction of archaeological landscapes and epistemology of the virtual. Prior to this appointment he was Head of Research for the Italian National Research Council's (CNR) programme, 'Virtual Heritage: Integrated Digital Technologies for Knowledge and Communication of Cultural Heritage through Virtual Reality Systems' and Senior Scientist at CNR's Institute for Technologies Applied to the Cultural Heritage (ITABC). He is also Vice-President of the international, non-profit Virtual Heritage Network and Professor of Virtual Environments for Cultural Heritage at the University of Lugano. He holds a PhD in Archaeology from the University of Rome, 'La Sapienza'. He coordinated archaeological fieldwork and many research projects internationally. He has published widely, authoring and editing numerous books. His *Space, Place, Time* (co-edited with S. Campana and C. Liuzza) and *Cyber-Archaeology* are forthcoming from BAR-Archaeopress, Oxford. He created the Virtual Museum of the Scrovegni Chapel <http://www.vhlab.itabc.cnr.it/giotto/> and the Virtual Museum of the Ancient Via Flaminia <http://www.vhlab.itabc.cnr.it/flaminia/>, the latter being a virtual collaborative environment for cultural heritage in Europe. 'Building Virtual Rome' <http://www.itabc.cnr.it/buildingvirtualrome> and 'ArcheoVirtual' <http://www.vhlab.itabc.cnr.it/archeovirtual/eng/index.html> are his two recent international exhibitions of virtual archaeology.

Sven Havemann is a scientist at the Institut fur ComputerGraphik und WissensVisualisierung, Technische Universitat, Graz, Austria. He has a degree in Computer Science from the University of Bonn (1998) and a PhD from the Technical University of Braunschweig (2005). He has developed a novel approach to the generative representation of 3D shapes and is the author of the Generative Modelling Language (GML). He has been active in projects at the national (V3D2) and European levels (FP5 Cultural Heritage project, CHARISMATIC) and is the sub-area coordinator for visualization and rendering in the EPOCH Network of Excellence, under the EU Sixth Framework Programme, with almost a hundred partners in the area of cultural heritage. He was a lead researcher in DAVE, a novel CAVE installation at the Technical University of Braunschweig. His main research interests are shape representations and geometric modelling with a focus on interactive techniques. He has published twenty papers in international journals and conference proceedings, and serves as a reviewer for the conferences Eurographics and VAST, as well as specialist journals in the area of computer graphics.

Sorin Hermon received his PhD in Archaeology from the Ben-Gurion University of the Negev, Beer-Sheva, Israel, in 2003, where he also taught. He has participated in several excavations mainly of prehistoric sites in Israel, some of which he also directed. From 1999 to 2008, he was a Senior Researcher at VAST-Lab, PIN, University of Florence. He is now a Scientific Research Coordinator at the Science and Technology for Archaeological Research (STAR) Centre at the Cyprus Institute. His other interests include knowledge transfer and design of cognitive technologies adapted for collaborative research, education and communication of cultural heritage, such as visualization, collaborative and knowledge management tools. He has published some twenty scientific articles in edited books, conference proceedings and journals. The subjects of his publications include the use of visualization (mainly virtual reality and 3D modeling) in the research and communication of cultural heritage; theoretical and methodological aspects of research in archaeology; reports and investigation of archaeological sites and the application of fuzzy logic concepts in the humanities. He is the author of *Socio-Economic Organisation of Calcolithic Societies in Southern Levant* (Archeopress), editor of *Academic Curricula for Digital Heritage. A Proposal* (Archaeolingua) and co-editor of *VAST 2008, 9th International Symposium on Virtual Reality, Archaeology and Cultural Heritage, Eurographics Symposium Proceedings*, Eurographics, Germany.

Matt Jones graduated from Southampton University in 2007 with a distinction in Archaeological Computing, following a first class honours bachelor's degree in History. His MSc dissertation was concerned with digital visualization of the city of Southampton in 1454, based on the surviving document of that year, *Southampton Terrier*. The computer model was intended for display at the Museum of Archaeology in Southampton. He is the winner of the 3DVisa Student Award 2007, run by the JISC 3D Visualisation in the Arts Network.

Mark Mudge received his BA in Philosophy from New College of Florida (1979). He has worked as a professional sculptor and has been involved in photography and 3D imaging for over twenty years. In 2002, he co-founded Cultural Heritage Imaging, a non-profit corporation based in California, in which he serves as President. He is a co-inventor of Highlight Reflectance Transformation Imaging. He has published twelve articles related to cultural heritage imaging and serves on several international committees.

Franco Niccolucci is Professor at the Science and Technology for Archaeological Research (STAR) Centre at the Cyprus Institute. Between 1974 and 2008, he taught at the University of Florence. He has a degree in Mathematics and has been involved in the applications of Information Technology to Archaeology and Cultural Heritage for more than ten years. He is a founder of the VAST series of international conferences on applications of Virtual Reality to Archaeology and Cultural Heritage, which he launched in 2000. He has chaired or co-chaired several international events on the subject, and is a co-founder and co-chairman of The London Charter. He has been a scientific coordinator of several projects funded by the European Union. He has published widely on ICT applications to archaeology and cultural heritage. He authored and edited several books and articles.

Sofia Pescarin has a degree in Archaeology and a PhD in History and Computing. She is a researcher with the Virtual Heritage Lab (VHLab) at the Instituto per le Technologie Applicate ai Beni Culturali (ITABC), Rome. She is also a national coordinator of research in the area of virtual heritage, for the Consiglio Nazionale delle Ricerche (CNR), promoting integrated digital technologies for the understanding and communication of cultural heritage through virtual reality systems. She has been a technical director of the Virtual Museum of the Scrovegni Project. In 2006, she participated in the EPOCH Network of Expertise Centres; chaired the fourth Italian Workshop on Archaeology and Open Source; and co-chaired the international conference 'From Space to Place' on remote sensing in archaeology, organized by CNR ITABC and Siena University. She is the Scientific Director of the Italian School of Virtual Archaeology <http://www. archeologiavirtuale.it> and Director of Archeovirtual <http://www.archeovirtual. it>. She is a recipient of the E-Content Award Italy for the project Virtual Rome, which she coordinated. Her book, *Reconstructing Ancient Landscape* was published by Archaeolingua in 2009.

Daniel Pletinckx has extensive experience in system design, quality assurance, digital image processing and synthesis, 3D and virtual reality, acquired in a fifteen-year career in private industry. He was chief consultant on the Ename 974 project, Belgium, and co-founded the international Ename Center for Public Archaeology and Heritage Presentation. He is Director of Visual Dimension bvba, offering advice to a number of major European organizations on innovating and optimizing the use of ICT technology in cultural heritage and tourism. Visual Dimension also specializes in novel and efficient digitization of cultural heritage sites and objects, and in the virtual reconstruction of lost historical buildings and landscapes. He is a founding member of the European Sixth Framework Programme's IST EPOCH Network of Excellence, which deals with optimizing the use of ICT in Cultural Heritage, and acted as Coordinator for Integration Activities. He coordinates the 3D activities of the CARARE project, which adds 3D and georeferencing capabilities and content about archaeology and monuments to *Europeana*.

Donald H. Sanders PhD, has a multidisciplinary background, as an architect and an archaeologist, having worked amidst the dirt and stones, but now strictly amongst pixels. He owns and presides over two companies in the US specializing in virtual heritage. Learning Sites, Inc., with its roots dating back to 1993, builds virtual ancient reconstructions for scholars, educators and students. The Institute for the Visualization of History, Inc., is a not-for-profit educational organization, founded in 2001, which expands the chronological and geographical scope of Learning

Sites and provides still more accessibility to the vast potential of interactive 3D environments for documentation and teaching, research and display, publication and broadcast.

Martin J. Turner is currently the Visualization Team Leader within the Research Computing Services at the University of Manchester, UK. He gained his PhD in the Computer Laboratory, at Cambridge University, on Image Coding. His research interests cover a broad range of subjects such as visualization, computer graphics and mathematical topics associated with image and signal creation, analysis, processing and presentation. His teaching has covered all academic levels from undergraduate to postgraduate as well as within external courses, involving the Royal Air Force and British Gas. He is an Honorary Lecturer within the School of Computer Sciences at the University of Manchester. Research in these fields has resulted in a short-term Fellowship with British Telecom and the book *Fractal Geometry in Digital Imaging*, co-authored with J.M. Blackledge and P.R. Andrews (Academic Press) as well as some seventy-five other publications. Key activities and grants cover both local and nationally funded high-end visualization services as well as commercial contracts. He is a member of the British Computer Society (BCS), the Optical Society of America (OSA), the Institute of Mathematics and its Applications (IMA), and the Institute of Electrical and Electronics Engineering (IEEE), and is executive Member and Treasurer of the Eurographics UK Chapter.

Series Preface

Paradata and Transparency in Virtual Heritage is volume nine of *Digital Research in the Arts and Humanities.*

Each of the titles in this series comprises a critical examination of the application of advanced ICT methods in the arts and humanities. That is, the application of formal computationally based methods, in discrete but often interlinked areas of arts and humanities research. Usually developed from Expert Seminars, one of the key activities supported by the Methods Network, these volumes focus on the impact of new technologies in academic research and address issues of fundamental importance to researchers employing advanced methods.

Although generally concerned with particular discipline areas, tools or methods, each title in the series is intended to be broadly accessible to the arts and humanities community as a whole. Individual volumes not only stand alone as guides but collectively form a suite of textbooks reflecting the 'state of the art' in the application of advanced ICT methods within and across arts and humanities disciplines. Each is an important statement of current research at the time of publication, an authoritative voice in the field of digital arts and humanities scholarship.

These publications are the legacy of the AHRC ICT Methods Network and will serve to promote and support the ongoing and increasing recognition of the impact on and vital significance to research of advanced arts and humanities computing methods. The volumes will provide clear evidence of the value of such methods, illustrate methodologies of use and highlight current communities of practice.

Marilyn Deegan, Lorna Hughes, Harold Short
Series Editors

AHRC ICT Methods Network
Centre for Computing in the Humanities
King's College London
2012

About the AHRC ICT Methods Network

The aims of the AHRC ICT Methods Network were to promote, support and develop the use of advanced ICT methods in arts and humanities research and to support the cross-disciplinary network of practitioners from institutions around the UK. It was a multi-disciplinary partnership providing a national forum for the exchange and dissemination of expertise in the use of ICT for arts and humanities research. The Methods Network was funded under the AHRC ICT Programme from 2005 to 2008.

The Methods Network Administrative Centre was based at the Centre for Computing in the Humanities (CCH), King's College London. It coordinated and supported all Methods Network activities and publications, as well as developing outreach to, and collaboration with, other centres of excellence in the UK The Methods Network was co-directed by Harold Short, Director of CCH, and Marilyn Deegan, Director of Research Development, at CCH, in partnership with Associate Directors: Mark Greengrass, University of Sheffield; Sandra Kemp, Royal College of Art; Andrew Wathey, Royal Holloway, University of London; Sheila Anderson, Arts and Humanities Data Service (AHDS) (2006–2008); and Tony McEnery, University of Lancaster (2005–2006).

The project website (<http://www.methodsnetwork.ac.uk>) provides access to all Methods Network materials and outputs. In the final year of the project a community site, 'Digital Arts and Humanities' (<http://www.arts-humanities.net>) was initiated as a means to sustain community building and outreach in the field of digital arts and humanities scholarship beyond the Methods Network's funding period.

Acknowledgements

The authors and editors are grateful to the AHRC ICT Methods Network, EPOCH; PIN, Prato, Italy and King's Visualisation Lab, King's College London, for co-sponsoring the expert seminar, 'Making 3D Visual Research Outcomes Transparent', held at the British Academy on 23–5 February 2006. The ideas discussed in this seminar have influenced subsequent developments in international research and led to collaboration between some of the contributors to this volume.

Mark Carnall would like to thank his colleagues at University College London who helped to foster the research into digital culture, including Professor Stuart Robson, Mona Hess and Sally MacDonald. He also wishes to thank David Richards and Dr William Birkin, who have worked with Mark for many years conducting research with many 'digital natives' and intercultural interactions.

Kate Devlin's research was carried out with the support of the University of Bristol and Goldsmiths, University of London.

Maurizio Forte and Sofia Pescarin wish to thank the Virtual Heritage Lab team at the CNR, Rome, who worked on the Appia Antica and Via Flaminia projects: Eva Pietroni, Claudio Rufa, Carlo Camporesi, Marco Di Ioia, Fabrizio Galeazzi, Alessia Moro, Augusto Palombini, Valentina Vassallo and Lola Vico; colleagues at CNR ITABC directed by Paolo Salonia; the Soprintendenza Speciale per i Beni Archeologici di Roma; and the CINECA Visit Lab team, in particular Antonella Guidazzoli, Luigi Calori, Francesca Delliponti, Tiziano Diamanti and Silvano Imboden.

Sven Havemann wishes to thank the Gipsmuseum of the Institut für Archäologie Universität Graz for permission to reproduce photographs of plaster casts.

Matt Jones was able to base his visualization of medieval Southampton on data obtained courtesy of Oxford Archaeology, from their recent excavations in the French quarter.

Mark Mudge of Cultural Heritage Imaging, California, US, extends his thanks to his colleagues and collaborators, including Carla Schroer, Marlin Lum, Claudia Willen and Michael Ashley, a member of the CHI Board of Directors and Chief Architect of the Media Vault Program at the University of California Berkeley (UCB). He also wishes to thank Steve Stead and Martin Doerr, central authors of the Conceptual Reference Model produced by the International Council of Museums' (ICOM) Documentation Committee (CIDOC).

Daniel Pletinckx's paper has benefited from the support of the European Commission under the Community's Sixth Framework Programme, Contract no. 2002–507382. The author wishes to thank Marie-Claire Van der Donckt, the curator of the Provincial Archaeological Museum Ename, and Dirk Callebaut of the Flemish Heritage Institute, who directed the excavations at Ename, for making the 3D visualization of Ename, from 1020 to 1780, possible. The project provided an opportunity to learn about many new issues and methodologies for 3D visualization. These visualizations continue to play an important role in the Provincial Archaeological Museum in Ename. Daniel Pletinckx is also grateful to Anna Bentkowska-Kafel, Hugh Denard and Drew Baker, of King's College London, for providing valuable feedback on the concept and text of his paper; as well as Professor Richard Beacham, Professor Franco Niccolucci and many other 3D visualization specialists, who have been the driving forces behind The London Charter, which plays a crucial role in setting standards and quality measures for 3D visualization. Further thanks are due to Peter Sterckx for offering access to his thesis at the KU Leuven, on the 3D visualization of Horst castle in Belgium, which shows the implementation and feasibility of interpretation management for large-scale projects. Joyce Wittur of the University of Heidelberg provided insights into her ongoing PhD work. She discussed the 3D visualization process and its implementation within the cultural heritage community. Daniel Pletinckx also wishes to thank Luc Van Gool for his encouragement in developing the Interpretation Management tool under the EPOCH Common Infrastructure work package, and Peter Sterckx, Joyce Wittur and colleagues on the projects mentioned in his chapter for the use of their images.

Plate 5 in Martin Turner's chapter is reproduced with kind permission from Mary J. McDerby, from her training notes titled *Introduction to Scientific Visualization* and produced by the University of Manchester Research Computing Services in 2007.

Note on the Text

All publications in English are presumed as published in London unless otherwise stated. Abbreviations and acronyms used are explained on p. xxix. Definitions of specialist terms are provided in the Glossary on p. 259.

Disclaimer

The articles in this collection express the views of the authors and not necessarily those of the editors.

Abbreviations and Acronyms

2D	two-dimensional
3D	three-dimensional
3ds Max®	3DStudioMax, 3D visualization software by Autodesk®
3DVisa	3D Visualisation in the Arts Network, UK (2003-2006)
AHRC	Arts and Humanities Research Council, UK
AI	Artificial Intelligence
AL	Artificial Life
BAR	British Archaeological Reports
BRDF	Bidirectional Reflectance Distribution Function (see also SVBRDF)
CCH	Centre for Computing in the Humanities, King's College London, UK. Now named the Department of Digital Humanites.
CGI	Computer-Generated Imagery
CGIs	Computer-Generated Images
CHArt	Computers and the History of Art
CHI	Cultural Heritage Imaging, California, US
CIDOC	Comité International pour la Documentation de l'ICOM
CRM	Conceptual Reference Model, guidelines for the exchange of information between cultural heritage institutions produced by CIDOC (ISO 21127:2006)
CRT	Cathode Ray Tube
CVRO	Cultural Virtual Reality Organisation
DCC	Digital Content Creation
DEM	Digital Elevation Model (see also DTM)
DIKW	Data, Information, Knowledge, Wisdom
DSS	Decision Support System
DTM	Digital Terrain Model (see also DEM)
DVD	Digital Versatile Disc
EAI	External Authoring Interface
EPOCH	European Research Network of Excellence in Open Cultural Heritage
EPSP	Excitatory Postsynaptic Potential
FMV	Full Motion Video
FRBR	Functional Requirements for Bibliographic Records
GIS	Geographic Information System
GML	Generative Modelling Language
GPS	Global Positioning System

ICOM	International Council of Museums
ICOMOS	International Council on Monuments and Sites
ICP	Iterative Closest Point
ICT	Information Communications Technology
IFLA	International Federation of Libraries and Archives
IMLS	Institute of Museum and Library Services
INAH	Instituto Nacional de Antropología e Historia, Mexico
IPSP	Inhibitory Postsynaptic Potential
ISO	International Organization for Standardization
ISS	Interpretation Support System
JISC	Joint Information Systems Committee
KVL	King's Visualisation Lab, King's College London, UK
LCD	Liquid Crystal Display
LCSL	London Charter in Second Life
mpeg	Moving image format established by the Moving Picture Experts Group
MVP	Media Vault Program
NuME	Nuovo Museo Elettronico, Centro Gina Fasoli, University of Bologna
PIP	Personal Interactive Panel
PTM	Polynomial Texture Mapping
R&D	Research and Development
RGB	Red, Green and Blue
RTI	Reflectance Transformation Imaging
SAI	Scenegraph Architecture Interface
STAR	*State of the Art Reports* published by Eurographics
STARC	Science and Technology for Archaeological Research Centre, Cyprus Institute
SVBRDF	Spatially-varying Bidirectional Reflectance Distribution Function, a six-dimensional variant of BRDF
UCB	University of California Berkeley, US
UCMP	University of California Museum of Paleontology
VASIG	Virtual Archaeology Special Interest Group
VAST	International Symposium on Virtual Reality, Archaeology and Cultural Heritage (since 2000)
VH	Virtual Heritage
VLE	Virtual Learning Environment
VR	Virtual Reality
VRE	Virtual Research Environment
VRML	Virtual Reality Modelling Language
WWD	*Walking with Dinosaurs*

Chapter 1

Introduction

Anna Bentkowska-Kafel and Hugh Denard

Computer-generated images (CGIs) are widely used and accepted in the world of entertainment but the use of the very same visualization techniques in academic research in the Arts and Humanities remains controversial. The techniques and conceptual perspectives on heritage visualization are a subject of an ongoing interdisciplinary debate. By demonstrating scholarly excellence and best technical practice in this area, this volume is concerned with the challenge of providing intellectual transparency and accountability in visualization-based historical research. Addressing a range of cognitive and technological challenges, the authors make a strong case for a wider recognition of 3D visualization as a constructive, intellectual process and a valid methodology for historical research and its communication.

Heritage visualization is considered here as a process of representing knowledge about space, time, behaviour, sound and light, and other elements that constitute cultural environments. What can visualization-based research processes uniquely achieve? Representing ideas and phenomena verbally can achieve heightened analytical power and precision at a conceptual level. Similarly, visual representations of ideas and phenomena can enable synthesis of potentially vast amounts of varied information with graphical precision, and can provide intuitive interfaces that facilitate understanding of spatial, temporal, acoustical and other data. Digital technologies offer flexible analytical tools, both sensory and semantic, for the study and representation of the past, but the digital techniques – it is argued here – are only useful and valid if interpretative frameworks and processes are published.

Intellectual transparency of visualization-based research, the pervading theme of this volume, is addressed from different perspectives, reflecting the theory and practice of a variety of disciplines. The contributors – archaeologists, historians, computer scientists, ICT practitioners and a palaeobiologist – emphasize the importance of reliably documenting the process of interpretation of historical materials and hypotheses that arise in the course of research. The discussion of this issue, which pertains to all aspects of the intellectual content of visualization, is centred around the concept of 'paradata'. The term is borrowed from other disciplines that rely on recording information processes. Paradata document the process of interpretation so that the aims, contexts and reliability of visualization methods and their outcomes can be properly understood. Paradata may be seen as a digital equivalent to *scholia*, as well as an addition to the traditional critical apparatus for describing the process of reasoning in scholarly research. The failure to provide this kind of intellectual transparency in the communication of historical content may result, among others, in visual products that only convey a small percentage of the knowledge that they embody; thus making research findings highly resistant to peer review and further discussion. It is argued therefore that an amount of paradata sufficient to provide genuine intellectual accountability should be published alongside other research outcomes and sustained beyond the lifespan of the technology that underpins visualization.

Visualization of cultural heritage is no longer limited to the representation of bricks and mortar, but now also encompasses intangible cultural heritage, such as dance, drama, skills and crafts. Our capacity to capture and process all dimensions of human culture increasingly benefits from developments in intuitive computing. While scope for experimentation remains considerable, the need for widely recognized, robust theoretical and methodological frameworks is urgent. Bearing in mind that our knowledge of the past is partial and uncertain, the authors address the following questions:

- With no fundamental *technological* difference between visualizing structures that still need to be built and structures that have existed, what are the *methodological* differences?
- How can the process of interpretation of material evidence be conveyed, particularly in areas where data are questionable, incomplete or conflicting?
- How can computer models and other visualization outputs be made open to further investigation, particularly as and when new evidence and enhanced tools become available?
- What are the limits of visual representation; what tools are available, or need to be developed, to convey information about levels of empirical certainty in hypothetical reconstructions?
- What is the value, in different contexts, of simplified and inexpensive visualization versus expensive and photo-realistic modelling of heritage?

This volume arises out of the internationally coordinated attempts to establish core principles and guidelines for computer-based visualization of cultural heritage known as The London Charter (<http://www.londoncharter.org>), in which the editors and a number of contributors are centrally involved. Several papers included here were originally presented at the expert seminar, Making 3D Visual Research Outcomes Transparent, co-sponsored by the AHRC ICT Methods Network; European Commission Research Network of Excellence in Open Cultural Heritage (EPOCH); Il Pin Scrl - Polo Universitario (PIN), Prato, Italy and King's Visualisation Lab, King's College London and held at the British Academy on 23–25 February 2006. The report on this seminar can be found at <http://methodsnetwork.ac.uk/activities/act1.html>. The papers presented at the British Academy are complemented by texts commissioned for this volume. The London Charter has been recognized by the AHRC Methods Network Activities

Evaluation Report (March 2008) as 'probably one of the potentially most far reaching outcomes of any of the Methods Network events', and also constitutes a major outcome of the EPOCH Network (<http://www.epoch-net.org>). The most up-to-date text of the Charter (Version 2.1, February 2009), which incorporates feedback from a community-wide consultation, is introduced and published in full in this volume. Together, the papers provide the context for The London Charter and respond to it, demonstrating the depth of intellectual concerns and the wide-ranging application of its principles.

The international contributors to this volume are recognized experts in their fields. They are actively engaged in academic research in various areas of cultural heritage and have published extensively on numerous aspects of computer-based visualization. Much of this experience reflects contribution to important visualization projects and international collaboration between subject and technology specialists, academic and heritage organizations, and commercial sectors. They are joined by two representatives of the new generation of researchers, both recent graduates, of MSc in Archaeological Computing and MA in Humanities Computing respectively. Their discussion of the decision-making process involved in computer modelling is indicative of the implementation of new ICT-based pedagogy. Their work is also exemplary of emerging interdisciplinary research practice that combines different subject areas, but is no longer dependent on collaboration and may be carried out by a single researcher. The chapter by the curator of a zoological collection serves as a reminder of just how wide-ranging the notion of cultural heritage is; it also illustrates the interdisciplinary sharing of knowledge that is now possible through the application of digital technologies. A commentary on the variety of approaches presented by the contributors to this volume is offered in the conclusion. The latest developments in digital visualization of cultural heritage are discussed in the wider context of historical research and established practices and theories of heritage conservation.

This volume may appeal to the widespread, international audience that has interests in computer-based visualization and the digitally enabled study of cultural heritage. It has much that will be of value to archaeologists, educators and professionals – from content creators to curators – within the cultural heritage sector, and to historians of every hue, whether they are themselves actively engaged in the application of digital visualization technologies, or merely fascinated by the continuing capacity of emerging technologies to alter the way in which we see and interact with the world.

All illustrations in this book are reproduced in colour on the companion blog, <http://visualizationparadata.wordpress.com>, which consists of additional visual material and links.[1]

Similarly to other volumes in the AHRC ICT Methods Network series, this book presents current developments in advanced digital methodologies in the arts

---

1   Any changes to the blog's location (URL) will be posted to The London Charter website, <http://www.londoncharter.org>.

and humanities, and is solely dedicated to the issue of intellectual transparency of visualization-based research. Select applications of digital visualization were covered earlier in the series, in the volume *The Virtual Representation of the Past*, which also introduced the aims of The London Charter and its debt to previous work.[2] This volume, however, is unique in the breadth of the discussion of intellectual content enabled by visualization.

---

2   Richard Beacham, '"Oh, to make boards to speak! There is a Task!" Towards a Poetics of Paradata', in Mark Greengrass and Lorna Hughes (eds), *The Virtual Representation of the Past* (Ashgate, 2008), pp. 171–7.

PART I
Conventions and Emerging Standards

Chapter 2

Defining our Terms in Heritage Visualization

Richard C. Beacham

The Paradox of Paradata

Paradata according to The London Charter, which figures prominently in this volume, is

> Information about human processes of understanding and interpretation of data objects. Examples of paradata include descriptions stored within a structured dataset of how evidence was used to interpret an artefact, or a comment on methodological premises within a research publication. It is closely related, but somewhat different in emphasis, to 'contextual metadata', which tend to communicate interpretations of an artefact or collection, rather than the process through which one or more artefacts were processed or interpreted.[1]

Paradox is 'a statement or proposition that seems self-contradictory or absurd but in reality expresses a possible truth'.[2] So what might be thought of, in our context here, as paradoxical about paradata? We can approach this by briefly considering two terms conveniently uttered in the quotation from Blanche Dubois in Tennessee Williams's work of 1947, *A Streetcar Named Desire*: 'I don't want realism; I want magic.' She goes on to say, by way of defining 'magic': 'Yes, yes, magic. I try to give that to people. I do misrepresent things. I don't tell truths. I tell what ought to be truth.'[3]

So when one speaks about the (possibly paradoxical) quality of paradata, and their role in the 3D modelling and documentation process, whose nature and methodology one is concerned to make transparent, where does 'realism' or 'magic' come in, and what might be the relationship between them?

Magic is 'the art of producing illusions as entertainment by the use of sleight of hand, deceptive devices'.[4] One should perhaps usefully bear in mind Arthur C. Clarke's Third Law: 'Any sufficiently advanced technology is indistinguishable

---

1   The use of the term 'paradata' has been proposed by my colleague, Drew Baker, who discusses it in his contribution: see Chapter 14. For The London Charter, see Chapter 7 and <http://www.londoncharter.org>; see pp. 259–61 for the definitions of terms used in version 2.1 of The London Charter.

2   *Random House Dictionary* (2009).

3   Tennessee Williams, *A Streetcar Named Desire* (New York, 1947), Scene 9.

4   *Random House Dictionary* (2009).

from magic.'[5] And its corollary: 'any technology distinguishable from magic is insufficiently advanced'.[6] Is this a proposition that those working in the area of 3D visualization, need to take to heart? And if so, does such an aspiration serve to further underscore the central importance of paradata, to enable those viewing the results of visualization to be able to discern facts from fiction, or magic from realism?

The final term to be considered here is realism. Amongst various choices, perhaps the definition most appropriate to the topic here would be: 'treatment of forms, colours, space, etc., in such a manner as to emphasize their correspondence to actuality or to ordinary visual experience'.[7] Alternatively, for a working definition of realism, one might turn to the 1951 US Popular Culture TV series *Dragnet*. It began with the announcement: 'The story you are about to see is true. Only the names have been changed to protect the innocent.' As its protagonist, Sergeant Joe Friday, famously said: 'All we want are the facts, ma'am, just the facts.'[8]

Looking at History

The relationship between realism and magic is not always, as one might think at first, a straightforward dichotomy of opposites, but can also involve a rather more subtle cognitive blending of various and ostensibly incongruent mental conceptions (and visual perceptions). This blending itself has an extensive history in the history of history or more accurately, in historiography.

The writing of history from the very beginning, as pointed out and practised by Herodotus (who has been called both the 'Father of History' and the 'Father of Lies'), was to a significant degree itself a form of creative writing. Often he gives several alternative but incompatible versions of the same event, with a nod towards what we might now term 'paradata'. In effect, 'This is what they say, but in my opinion it is just one of those tall stories of the Egyptians.'[9]

Antiquity is itself an imagined construct. A great 'Lost Continent' populated by cultural, aesthetic and imaginative notions and associations, cluttered with current and accumulated histories, and – to use a plain word – scholarly 'make-believe'. One visits that Continent via the mind's eye (or the computer screen) bearing an enormous amount of cultural 'luggage': lots of steamer trunks and extravagant

---

5   Arthur C. Clarke, 'Hazards of Prophecy: The Failure of Imagination', in *Profiles of the Future* (New York, 1962).

6   Ibid., p. 36.

7   See <http://dictionary.reference.com/browse/realism>.

8   *Dragnet*, dir. Jack Webb, from 1951. See <http://en.wikipedia.org/wiki/Dragnet_(series)>.

9   Herodotus, *Histories*, trans. George Rawlinson (1996). A typical formulation of his approach is in Book 1, chapter 5: 'Whether this latter account be true, or whether the matter happened otherwise, I shall not discuss further.'

hatboxes. One returns too, in the company of ghosts; rather like persistent holiday acquaintances that cannot be shaken off.

The greatest of these encumbrances is history itself; indeed the very 'idea of history'. One definition of realism according to *Webster's Dictionary* is, 'Fidelity to nature or to real life; representation without idealization, and making no appeal to the imagination; adherence to the actual fact.' Such a characterization is cognate to the view asserted by Leopold von Ranke in the nineteenth century that history was first and last dependent upon objective facts: 'das Ding an sich' (the thing itself); 'wie es eigentlich gewesen' (as it essentially was); a phrase which the post-positivist know-it-alls (adamantly insisting that in facts they know nothing) – cannot hear without smiling, or use without blushing.[10] In the 1920s, R.G. Collingwood, as he so ingeniously merged history into philosophy, asserted instead that the idea of history was indeed a history not of pure facts, but of thought, and consequently could not remain untouched by the imagination. He saw 'the objective fact as the inseparable correlative of the subject's thought'.[11] Such thought is generated in the first instance by one's reaction upon perceiving the facts:

> In perception we are immediately aware of our object, which is a concrete and therefore historical fact: perception and history are identical. But the immediacy of perception does not exclude mediation; it is not abstract immediacy (sensation) but implicitly contains an element of mediation (thought)... History is thus as a specific form of experience, identical with perception.[12]

As Collingwood went on to point out, thought, in facing the facts, seeks of course to make sense of them, and ultimately to tie them together into comprehensive knowledge and understanding.[13] This was essential; otherwise the contemplation of historical events risks becoming mere entertainment.

> Take away the conception of a universal history in which every special history finds its place and its justification, and you have committed the first and deepest sin against history, you have confused it with art: you have denied it any concern with truth and made it a mere thing of the imagination.'[14]

---

10   Leopold von Ranke, *Geschichte der romanischen und germanischen Völker von 1494 bis 1514* (Leipzig, 1874), p. vii. The full quotation is: 'Man hat der Historie das Amt, die Vergangenheit zu richten, die Mitwelt zum Nutzen zukünftiger Jahre zu belehren, beigemessen: so hoher Ämter unterwindet sich gegenwärtiger Versuch nicht: er will blos zeigen, wie es eigentlich gewesen.' Translation by Richard Beacham: 'The task, commonly attributed to History, is to judge the past, to instruct the present, for the benefit of the future: such a noble role is not claimed for this essay: it aims simply to show how it actually was.'

11   Robin G. Collingwood, *Speculum Mentis* (Oxford, 1924), p. 287.

12   Ibid., pp. 204–5.

13   Ibid., p. 235.

14   Ibid., p. 235.

Looking at Looking

Collingwood confessed early in his career: 'I have found in my historical inquiries that I can never determine the exact truth about any historical fact, but have to be content with an account containing a large and unverifiable amount of what I know to be conjecture.'[15] This brings one face to face with the sort of issues that one confronts in fashioning virtual reconstructions of historical artefacts, and by extension with the role such initiatives as The London Charter may play in helping both to raise awareness of and to address them. Three-dimensional visualization might in an ideal form aspire to depict 'wie es eigentlich ausgesehen hat' (as it essentially appeared). However, just as Collingwood could identity no pure fact, untouched by conjecture, the same is true of the efforts to identify the facts, as they are conveyed visually, of spatial structures and their appearance.

One is aware how easily – and how often – some practitioners (occasionally even established and reputable scholars) have been tempted by the publicity and hype of virtual reality as an element of popular culture to slip into what might be called the 'P. T. Barnum syndrome', in which scholarship takes second place to showmanship.[16] Such visualizations are produced and launched with media hype, articles in the press and the like, and in the process questions of accuracy and the scholarly basis for such visualizations are too often displaced by their undeniably compelling 'magic'. Although scholarship of this dubious sort may draw attention (and even vital funding) to those creating the visualization, ultimately it carries the risk of discrediting the reputation of visualization-based research which must be protected if such visualizations are to be perceived and taken seriously by scholars as the extraordinarily valuable 'publications' they undoubtedly have the potential to be.

Seneca described

> the 'arts of entertainment (*ludicrae*) which give amusement to the eye and ear
> [...] Amongst these you may count the engineers (*machinatores*) who contrive a
> structure that soars up by itself, or floors that rise silently into the air, and many
> other unexpected devices such as objects that fit together which come apart, or
> things separate which automatically join together, or objects which stand erect
> then slowly collapse. The eyes of the ignorant are astonished by such things.[17]

Scholars who have pursued such aspects of 'show business' in the field of computer-based visualization are at least in the company of a venerable tradition.

---

15   Robin G. Collingwood, 'Some Perplexities about Time', in *Outlines of a Philosophy of Art* (Oxford, 1925), p. 146.

16   The American Phineas Taylor Barnum (1810–91) was a man of show business and circus. He had many other talents, but is best known for his hoaxes.

17   Seneca, *Epistulae Morales*, 88.22, in *Epistles*, trans. Richard M. Gummere, Loeb Classical Library, vol. 76 (Cambridge, MA, 1991), p. 349.

Cicero also called attention to the particularly compelling and seductive nature of visualization even for those with what he called '*oculos eruditos*' (educated eyes): 'You stand gaping spell-bound [...] when I see you gazing and marvelling and uttering cries of admiration, I judge you to be the slave of every foolishness'.[18]

Making Space

It is essential that scholars, to paraphrase The London Charter's preamble, seek to establish what is required for 3D visualization to be, and to be seen to be, as intellectually rigorous and robust as any other research method. Transparency is crucial if 3D visualization is to 'mature' as a research method and acquire widespread acceptance within subject communities. In particular, it must be possible for those communities to evaluate the choice of a given visualization method, and how it has been applied in a particular case without having to rely exclusively on the 'authority claims' of the author, however eminent, experienced (or media-savvy) they might be. A significant amount of work has been done in this area, and there is now an extensive bibliography on this and related issues.

At the same time that 'reality' is conscientiously pursued using such guidelines and principles as The London Charter as a major 'reality checking' instrument, it is important that a due regard and openness are retained – if not to the expectation of 'magic' – then at least to the appearance of new and surprising discoveries that work in this still relatively unexplored realm of 3D visualization may uncover.

As in any field of research (and particularly, as has been noted, in the case of history), one must be prepared from time to time to loosen one's moorings from the strictest (and safest) readings of the texts, or interpretation of the physical evidence, to see where one might possibly intimate new insights and, in the process, create new knowledge. The knowledge one needs fully to understand the ancient phenomena one presumes to discuss is rare – there are vast black holes and vacuums. It is important to remember that such vacuums do *not* mean that 'nothing' was there: something was. Joined up, or even lateral thinking (and the new forms of knowledge that they can enable), very often in the absence of direct connections and absolutely safe conjunctions of meaning, requires some imaginative leaps in the dark; always as securely as possible, and with safety nets in place (qualifications, an indication where fact ends and hypothesis begins, etc.). It may be, of course, that the fleeting fact we are trusting to find on the opposite trapeze will not join hands with us, and we will plunge like Icarus into the sea. But just as often we may actually, as we leap out into the dark, almost magically find something there to catch and hold us, and even dazzle the eyes of the onlookers.

---

18   Cicero, *Paradoxa Stoicorum*, 5.38.2, in *On the Orator*, trans. Harris Rackham, Loeb Classical Library, vol. 349 (Cambridge, MA, 2004), p. 289.

Chapter 3

Scientific Method, *chaîne opératoire* and Visualization: 3D Modelling as a Research Tool in Archaeology[1]

Sorin Hermon

Introduction

As straightforwardly defined by Clive Gamble, archaeology is 'simply the study of the past through material remains' in order to gain most of the available knowledge about the past.[2] Basic archaeological research analyses the remains of products of human activity in the past, unearthed during excavations, collected during surveys or identified through various remote sensing techniques. At a very first stage, these are divided by type of material (pottery, bone, stone, etc.) and subjected to a classification process. This process is based on the degree of visual resemblance between objects and a detailed attribute analysis, and checked against relevant typologies. Objects are compared with other remains. Consequently, chemical, statistical and/or spatial analyses are used, alongside an examination of historical sources, in order to obtain as accurate a description of the subjects under investigation as possible.

The natural and anthropogenic contexts of finds are also examined, as well as the relationships between artefacts and their surroundings. The next step is concerned with the interpretation of the findings within a given theorctical framework and according to the aims of research. These may involve understanding the cultural history of an archaeological culture, the socio-economic organization of a human group, the human occupation of an area and its relationships with the environment, as well as an analysis of historic events, settlement patterns and movements of population, social behaviour, etc. Thus, remains of material culture are analysed from three basic perspectives: material (the relationships with the environment), social (within the frame of the human society) and ideational (how and what human ideas and beliefs they embed).[3]

---

1   This chapter is a much revised and expanded version of the paper presented at the seminar Making 3D Visual Research Outcomes Transparent, co-sponsored by the AHRC ICT Methods Network; EPOCH; PIN, Prato, Italy and King's Visualisation Lab, King's College London, held at the British Academy on 23–25 February 2006.

2   Clive Gamble, *Archaeology: The Basics* (London, 2001), p. 15.

3   Ibid.

Commonly, this process of data reading yields sets of alpha-numerical data, which are visualized in 2D as tables, maps or graphs, reflecting the results of the classification processes, attribute analyses, comparisons or statistical analyses. Much has been written and a lot of intellectual effort has been dedicated in the past to the definition of theoretical frameworks of archaeological data interpretation. Less importance has been given to the way we look at the data. This process is normally theory laden, that is dictated by the research questions and adopted theoretical framework. It is argued here that the processes of data interrogation can be furthered through the application of scientific data visualization and 3D modelling at the very early stages of data acquisition, interrogation and interpretation. This method may greatly contribute to a better understanding of the archaeological remains under investigation.

Scientific Method and 3D Visualization

Scientific visualization is a graphical representation of data in order to gain deeper understanding and new insights, allowing the researcher to study the material in ways previously impossible. As various researches in education, cognitive psychology and related disciplines point out, there is a positive relationship between the visualization tools and the way we perceive information: the better the visualization tool, the better the explanation and understanding.[4] Some known advantages of data visualization, and 3D visualization in particular, are:

1. A lot of data (of different nature) may be compressed into one picture.
2. Correlations between different quantities, both in space and time, may be represented visually.
3. New structures of data and patterns invisible in 2D representations may be revealed.
4. A visual expression of concepts, ideas or hypotheses may be provided.
5. Alpha-numerical data (resulting, for example, from attribute analyses) may be combined with visual data (images, plans, pictures, maps or drawings) into a single visual representation.
6. A visual comparison between archaeological data and a visual representation of data interpretation is made possible.

Scientific method consists of a set of procedures enabling one to ascertain, by combining observation and logical processing, whether a particular solution to a particular problem is correct. The basic steps of this method are as follows:

---

4   Ruth B. *Ekstrom,* John W. *French and* Harry H. *Harman, Manual of Kit of Factor-Referenced Cognitive Tests* (Princeton, 1976).

1. Define research questions.
2. Gather information and resources.
3. Form hypothesis.
4. Perform experiment and collect data.
5. Analyse data.
6. Interpret data and draw conclusions.
7. Formulate new hypotheses.
8. Publish results.

Scientific method is a basic research methodology widely applied in archaeology. Since the 1950s, scientific method has been regarded as reliable and open to verification, thus fulfilling science's social mission to inform.[5] The scientific method can be integrated with 3D visualization (see Figure 3.1).

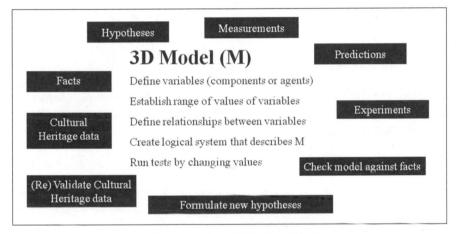

Figure 3.1   The scientific method and 3D visualization

The facts gathered in order to demonstrate the validity of the hypotheses may be integrated into a 3D representation, thus virtually recreating the archaeological context under analysis. The variables, or components, that will make up the base of the 3D model should also be included. Relationships between the variables will define the nature of the 3D model as a representation of the archaeological context under examination. The hypotheses may be visualized in 3D at this stage, and a visual comparison between the hypothesis and the facts may be performed. A logical system, which describes the relationships between the variables and the range of values for each variable, will allow experiments to be performed, measurements to be taken and results to be predicted.

5   Henry Mehlberg, 'The Range and Limits of the Scientific Method', *The Journal of Philosophy*, 51, 10 (1954): 285–94.

It is also normally expected that 3D visualization and interrogation of the archaeological context would lead to the formulation of new questions and hypotheses. The experiments may be performed using archaeological contexts created virtually. By changing the values of selected variables and relationships between variables, different tests may be carried out in order to identify the critical proofs of the existence of a given archaeological context.

An important additional benefit of 3D visualization is the possibility of testing the validity of archaeological 'facts'; such an experiment may lead to the isolation of incorrect data by identifying whether values of archaeological data are true in a given context.

Using a processualist approach, 3D visualization can serve as a means for the application of a 'middle-range theory',[6] connecting the research questions under analysis to the 'facts' (archaeological data). Moreover, the 3D visualization may reconstruct the history of an artefact,[7] or visually reconstruct the 'narrative[8] and its meaning, by choosing the relevant components, or variables, of the 3D model.

3D Visualization and Scientific Method: An Example

The starting point of the scientific method is the formulation of hypotheses. In the example chosen here, it is a historical description implying the existence of a mausoleum:

1. C. Plinius Secundus, *Naturalis Historia, xxxvi.19 – Namque et Italicum (labyrinthum) dici convenit, quem fecit sibi **Porsenna rex Etruriae sepulcri causâ, simul ut externorum regum vanitas quoque ab Italis superetur. Sed cum excedat omnia fabulositas, utemur ipsius M. Varronis in expositione ejus verbis: Sepultus est, inquit, sub urbe Clusio**; in quo loco monumentum reliquit lapide quadrato: singula latera pedum lata tricenûm, alta quinquagenûm; inque basi quadratâ intus labyrinthum inextricabilem; quo si quis improperet sine glomere lini, exitum invenire nequeat. Supra id quadratum pyramides stant quinque, quatuor in angulis, in medio una: in imo latae pedum quinûm septuagenûm, altae centum quinquagenûm: ita fastigatae, ut in summo orbis aeneus et petasus unus omnibus sit impositus, ex quo pendeant exapta catenis tintinnabula, quae vento agitata, longe sonitus referant, ut Dodonae olim factum. Supra quem orbem quatuor*

---

6   Lewis R. Binford, *In Pursuit of the Past. Decoding the Archaeological Record* (London, 1983).

7   Gamble, *Archaeology.*

8   Ian Hodder, *Reading the Past. Current Approaches to Interpretation in Archaeology* (3rd edn, Cambridge, 2003).

pyramides insuper, singulae exstant altae pedum centenûm. Supra quas uno solo quinque pyramides; quarum altitudinem Varronem puduit adjicere.[9]

2. The archaeological remains *in situ* are inexistent – no traces whatsoever indicate the location of the monument.

3. A geological survey of the area has demonstrated an abnormal amount of copper on a hill where presumably the mausoleum was erected.

4. Although much smaller, similar structures are not uncommon in the same period and area (for example the Alba Longa tomb and the mausoleum of Augustus).

Calculation and Socio-Historical Analyses

1. The author of the above historical text, Gaius Plinius Secundus, known as Pliny the Elder (23–79), quotes an earlier historian, Marcus Terentius Varro, adding that the mausoleum was probably destroyed in a fifth-century BC earthquake, and in any case, '*Fabulae Etruscae tradunt eandem fuisse, quam totius operis: adeo vesana dementia quaesisse gloriam impendio nulli profuturo. Praeterea fatigasse regni vires, ut tamen laus major artificis esset* …'. It may be assumed in this case that, if Pliny the Elder went to such lengths to account for what is possibly a legend, some kind of monument might have existed. The disappearance of material evidence, Pliny adds, was probably caused by the earthquake and the re-use of stones and bronze.

2. A calculation of the necessary amount of the building material (mainly stone and bronze) may indicate the time and labour invested in their procurement and the construction.

---

9   English translation by John Bostock and H.T. Riley of this extended excerpt reads: '[…] of the Cretan Labyrinth and of that in Italy not a vestige is left. As to this last, which Porsena, King of Etruria, erected as his intended sepulchre, it is only proper that I should make some mention of it, if only to show that the vanity displayed by foreign monarchs, great as it is, has been surpassed. But as the fabulousness of the story connected with it quite exceeds all bounds, I shall employ the words given by M. Varro himself in his account of it: "Porsena was buried," says he, "beneath the city of Clusium; in the spot where he had had constructed a square monument, built of squared stone. Each side of this monument was three hundred feet in length and fifty in height, and beneath the base, which was also square, there was an inextricable labyrinth, into which if any one entered without a clew of thread, he could never find his way out. Above this square building there stand five pyramids, one at each corner, and one in the middle, seventy-five feet broad at the base, and one hundred and fifty feet in height. These pyramids are so tapering in their form, that upon the summit of all of them united there rests a brazen globe, and upon that a petasus; from which there hang, suspended by chains, bells, which make a tinkling when agitated by the wind, like what was done at Dodona in former times. Upon this globe there are four other pyramids, each one hundred feet in height; and above them is a single platform, on which there are five more pyramids," the height of which Varro has evidently felt ashamed to add; but, according to the Etruscan fables, it was equal to that of the rest of the building.'

3. A geological survey of the area may indicate a possible location for such a massive construction, measuring almost 90 sq m at its base and approximately 190 m high. Pliny explicitly locates the mausoleum 'beneath the city of Clusium' (modern Chiusi).
4. A historical analysis of the geo-politics of the area that would have justified the existence of such a monument.
5. Potential impact of such a structure on the environment and the inhabitants of the area (for example the sound of the bronze bells).

Predictions and Experiments

When interpreting the historic text and checking it against the surviving monuments of the same period, several possible interpretations may lead to different reconstructions of the mausoleum (see Figure 3.2). Each of them can be further analysed against static laws, and according to the different measurements defined above. These analyses will indicate a range of possible structures that might have existed, according to the most reasonable values of parts of the 3D model. For example, one may question how such a large bronze disc could have been cast, lifted and anchored on the supporting four pyramids. Moreover, given its calculated weight, how strong were the pyramids and, generally, the foundation of the entire structure.

Several other experiments may be carried out. Bearing in mind the hilly surroundings of modern Chiusi and considering the necessary access routes for transporting the building materials, where could it have been located and what was the visibility of the mausoleum?

Figure 3.2   Hypothetical 3D models of the mausoleum described by Pliny, *Nat. Hist.***, xxxvi.19**

New Hypotheses and Validation of Archaeological Data

As has been shown elsewhere, creating a 3D model invariably leads to the formulation of new research questions.[10] Adding the third dimension enhances the archaeologist's sensory stimulation, thus enabling enhanced input in a manner closer to a natural interpretation of the subject. By visually analysing the 3D model, one may identify features that do not fit into the picture, such as, in the example shown in Figure 3.2, the upper parts of the supporting pyramids. Moreover, the virtual reconstruction allows comparison between 'what is possible' according to the reconstructed model and the 'facts'. A possible discrepancy requires re-evaluation both of the model and the archaeological data.

Chaîne opératoire and 3D Visualization

3D visualization can be applied alongside other research methodologies, including the analysis of remains of material culture through the reconstruction of the processes that transform natural matter into cultural matter. Understanding this process ultimately leads to the better understanding of a society, its individuals and the culture in which they operated. This relationship between culture, technique and society, and its use for studying archaeological cultures has been extensively described in the past.[11] The concept of *chaîne opératoire*, or the operative chain, was primarily designated to describe this relationship and was applied mostly to the study of prehistoric societies.[12]

---

10   Sorin Hermon and Peter Fabian, 'Virtual Reconstruction of Archaeological Sites – Some Archaeological Scientific Considerations', in Franco Niccolucci (ed.), *Virtual Archaeology*, Proceedings of the VAST Euroconference, Arezzo 24–26 November 2000. BAR International Series 1075 (Oxford, 2002), pp. 103–108. Sorin Hermon, Franco Niccolucci and Andrea D'Andrea, 'Some Evaluations on the Potential Impact of Virtual Reality on the Archaeological Scientific Research', in *VSMM 2005: Proceedings of the Eleventh International Conference on Virtual Systems and MultiMedia*, Ghent, Belgium, 2005, pp. 105–14. Sorin Hermon, 'Reasoning in 3D: A Critical Appraisal of the Role of 3D Modelling and Virtual Reconstructions in Archaeology', in Bernard Frischer and Anastasia Dakouri-Hild (eds), *Beyond Illustration: 2D and 3D Digital Technologies as Tools for Discovery in Archaeology*, BAR International Series 1805 (Oxford, 2008), pp. 36–45.

11   Marcel Mauss, 'Les techniques et la technologie', *Journal de psychologie normale et pathologique*, 41 (1941): 71–8. Claude Lévi-Strauss *Structural Anthropology* (New York, [1958] 1976), André Leroi-Gourhan, Gérard Bailloud, Jean Chavaillon and Annette Laming-Emperaire, *La Préhistoire* (Paris, 1966). Pierre Lemmonier 'The Study of Material Culture Today: Towards an Anthropology of Technical Systems', *Journal of Anthropological Archaeology*, 5 (1986), pp. 147–86.

12   Eric Boëda, Jean-Michel Geneste and Liliane Meignen, 'Identification de chaînes opératoires lithiques du Paléolithique ancien et moyen', *Paleo*, 2 (1990): 43–80. André Leroi-Gourhan, *Le geste et la parole. I – Techniques et langage* (Paris, 1964). Jacques Pelegrin, Claudine Karlin and Pierre Bodu, 'Chaînes opératoires: un outil pour

Two basic mechanisms shape an operative chain: *conceptual knowledge* (*connaissance*) – the mental representation of ideal forms – and *procedural knowledge* (*savoir faire*) – memorization of operational modes.[13] In general terms, conceptual knowledge deals with our hypotheses (what we would like to find, or what we have in mind), and procedural knowledge deals with the research process.

The main stages of this research methodology are:

1. Acquisition: what raw materials were used and what were their procurement strategies.
2. Production: how these raw materials were modified and adapted in order to obtain the products under investigation.
3. Shaping: how and what kind of objects have been produced.
4. Utilization: how these objects have been used.
5. Discard: where, why and how these objects were rejected and what happened to them afterwards (taphonomic or preservation processes).

In general terms, the chain of operation is a framework that focuses on describing:

- What happened: the archaeological event under investigation;
- How it happened: description of the process that shaped the event;
- Why it happened: the factors that enabled the event to occur.

As illustrated in Figure 3.2, by reconstructing virtually 3D visualization is particularly relevant to stages 3 to 5. Virtual reconstruction gives our assumptions a visual meaning, based on the relevant observations and our acquired knowledge. Relevant in this context is the possibility of applying 3D visualization as a comparison meter between the *connaissance* and *savoir faire* implied in the construction of the structure. Both may be achieved, among others, by visually analysing the model and juxtaposing it with mental models of the subject under investigation that we may have.[14]

---

le préhistorien', in J. Tixier (ed.), *Technologie Lithique* (Paris, 1988), pp. 55–62. See also Nicolle Pigeot, 'Technical and Social Actors: Flint Knapping Specialists and Apprentices at Magdalenian Etiolles', *Archaeological Review from Cambridge*, 9 (1990): 126–41. Nicolle Pigeot, 'Réflexions sur l'histoire technique de l'homme: de l'évolution cognitive a l'évolution culturelle', *Paleo*, 3 (1991): 167–200.

13   Jacques Pelegrin, 'Reflection sur le comportement technique', in *L'Apport des sols d'habitat à l'étude de l'outillage technique*, ed. M. Otte (Oxford, 1985), pp. 72–91. Jacques Pelegrin, 'Les savoir-faire: une très longue histoire', *Terrain*, 16 (1991): 106–13.

14   Kenneth Craik, *The Nature of Explanation,* (Cambridge, 1943). J. Oakhill and A. Garnham (eds), *Mental Models in Cognitive Science* (Mahwah, NJ, 1996).

Conclusion

We are witnessing constant growth in the number of 3D VR models concerned with archaeological reconstruction. The purpose of the majority of such projects has been communication or education rather than scientific use in archaeological research.[15] This chapter aimed to demonstrate how 3D visualization can be applied to archaeological research, independently of the theoretical approaches or the research questions involved.

Three-dimensional visualization is an efficient method of visualizing a large amount of data originating from different sources, thus enabling visual problem-solving.[16] Because it is possible to visualize both concepts and ideas (translated into a quantifiable and measurable geometric language) and archaeological 'facts', visualization is an ideal means for validating hypotheses, running tests, performing predictions and simulating behaviour under different circumstances and processes in a given period. Consequently, it is possible visually to differentiate between an observation (based on the archaeological 'facts') and theoretical statements (the hypothesized archaeological reality). In other words, 3D visualization enables the connection between the world based on our intuition, previous knowledge or imagination, and the 'world of science', that is what we observe, measure and quantify.[17] Moreover, this connection can be quantified, allowing a scientific analysis of the 3D model, as has been described elsewhere.[18]

Three-dimensional visualization is also a good tool for analysing virtually recreated cultural material in its presumed 'real' context, both in a given historical moment and over a longer period. It also allows visual juxtaposition of the fragmentary archaeological evidence and the researcher's mental model of this reality with the reality reconstructed virtually. In this sense, 3D visualization and its outcomes (such as 3D models and virtual reality worlds) serve as an interactive, multi-disciplinary research platform. A 3D model can be seen as an

---

15   Sorin Hermon, 'Reasoning in 3D: A Critical Appraisal of the Role of 3D Modelling and Virtual Reconstructions in Archaeology', in Bernard Frischer and Anastasia Dakouri-Hild (eds), *Beyond Illustration: 2D and 3D Digital Technologies as Tools for Discovery in Archaeology*, BAR International Series 1805 (Oxford, 2008), pp. 36–45, available at <http://www.iath.virginia.edu/~spw4s/Beyond/BAR/Hermon.pdf>.

16   Sorin Hermon, Franco Niccolucci and Andrea D'Andrea, 'Some Evaluations on the Potential Impact of Virtual Reality on the Archaeological Scientific Research', in *VSMM 2005 – Proceedings of the Eleventh International Conference on Virtual Systems and MultiMedia* (Ghent, 2005), pp. 105–14.

17   See also Meurig W. Beynon, 'Computational Support for Realism in Virtual Environments', in *Proceedings of the 11th International Conference on Human-Computer Interaction (HCII 2005)*, vol. 10, *Internationalization, Online Communities and Social Computing: Design and Evaluation*, Las Vegas, NV, 22–27 July 2005, available at <http://www2.warwick.ac.uk/fac/sci/dcs/research/em/publications/papers/084/>.

18   See Hermon and D'Andrea, 'Some Evaluations on the Potential Impact of Virtual Reality on the Archaeological Scientific Research'.

expression of the acquired knowledge of the subject, combining the understanding of archaeological data with inference (the information derived from analysing such data), thus visually communicating the cognitive process of archaeological reasoning. The behaviour of a virtually reconstructed archaeological environment can be analysed and quantified when its components change. When relationships between the components are defined and able to simulate the behaviour of real environments, it is possible to test the behaviour of the virtually created (archaeological) world, and critically examine both the archaeological data under investigation and the hypothesized past as reconstructed by the researcher. Various possible archaeological realities may be scientifically visualized and compared.

By representing the entire *chaîne opératoire* of archaeological research we make visible the process of scientific reasoning that led to the construction of the 3D model and the virtual archaeological environment. This process includes presenting the 'raw data' and the building of a 3D model whose components have modifiable values and which is a quantitative evaluation of the credibility of interpretation. The entire scholarly work will become transparent and open from the points of view of critical, archaeological and historical evaluation as well as those of the computer sciences.

Chapter 4

Setting Standards for 3D Visualization of Cultural Heritage in Europe and Beyond

Franco Niccolucci

Introduction

In a paper published in 2002, co-authored by Bernard Frischer, Nick Ryan, Juan Antonio Barceló and myself, important questions pertaining to the application of virtual reality (VR) in archaeology were addressed.[1] Of these, perhaps the most important was the use of VR for the creation of models reconstructing objects, monuments, sites or landscapes that have been either partially or totally modified, or destroyed. The paper in question grew out of discussion during the first International Symposium on Virtual Reality, Archaeology and Cultural Heritage (VAST), which was held in 2000 and dealt, in a synthetic way, with issues deemed by the scientific community as acutely relevant to the field. In brief, the paper refers to an analogous process in philology, as described in Maas 1958.[2] The interpretative and reconstructive processes of modelling are summarized as 'recensio, examinatio, and divinatio'. The goal is therefore to verify the remains, establish if they can be considered original and reconstruct the missing elements. This approach ought to be recorded in the final report in the form of an introduction, where the reconstruction data are also laid out and evaluated in terms of their quality and relevance. Data lacunae, additions and conjectural elements should be indicated in the body of the report. Philological notes should be provided in the form of an apparatus criticus, showing the variants selected by the author for the purpose of text reconstruction. The paper underlines the importance of standardization in the field of cultural VR and proposes 'political' actions to promote initiatives in favour of this approach.

Since the publication of this paper, as often happens, the research activities of its co-authors split. Nevertheless, the thesis it proposed has exerted a strong influence on several initiatives on both sides of the Atlantic. Notable among these

---

1   Bernard Frischer, Juan A.Barceló, Franco Niccolucci and Nick Ryan, 'From CVR to CVRO: The Past, Present, and Future of Cultural Virtual Reality', in Franco Niccolucci (ed.), *Virtual Archaeology. Proceedings of the VAST Conference, Arezzo, Italy*. BAR International Series 834 (Oxford, 2002), pp. 7–18.

2   Paul Maas, *Textual Criticism*, trans. Barbara Flower (Oxford: Clarendon Press, 1958).

by the Ename Charter, fostered by the group in charge of the Ename project,[8] there had been no attempt to standardize and define the criteria for assessing reliability until The London Charter was made available online in 2006. A further problem has been the lack of standards and clarity in communicating the validity of reconstructed elements to end-users. Consequently, the 'philological approach' espoused by the authors of the paper quoted at the beginning of the chapter has not yet been put fully into effect. The following questions now arise:

- *Utility*: can 3D models and virtual reconstructions be useful for academic research, or are they just a means of communicating information to the public?
- *Autonomy*: how autonomous is the archaeologist in the creation of reconstruction models? Is their dependence on technicians, programmers and 3D modellers only temporary and due to a lack of software for independent work; or is it structural and caused by the diversity of the competences required to manipulate 3D visualization? In other words, can we expect, and possibly advocate, that in the future archaeologists will be enabled to create their own 3D reconstructions in the same easy way they now write their papers using a word processor, without the assistance of a professional typist?
- *Validity*: what information ought to be introduced into the model so that it is philologically correct? And how is such information to be incorporated?
- *Uncertainty*: is there a way to define and represent uncertainty in a reconstruction, in a manner objective enough to be communicated?
- *Temporality*: is there a way to introduce temporal change?
- *Standardization*: are there technological standards that offer interoperability and the inclusion of an *apparatus criticus*, philological signs, uncertainty, changes over time, and all the information and meta-information needed for a 3D model?

This chapter attempts to offer some answers to these questions. The discussion of uncertainty and temporality has already been presented and will be the subject of future work.[9] For the other questions, it is needless to say that the answers presented here do not pretend to be definitive, but a mere starting point for further discussion and debate.

---

8   The Ename Charter is available on <http://www enamecharter.org>.
9   Sorin Hermon and Franco Niccolucci, 'A Fuzzy Logic Approach to Reliability in Archaeological Virtual Reconstruction', in Franco Niccolucci and Sorin Hermon (eds), *Beyond the Artifact. Digital Interpretation of the Past* (Budapest, 2006).

Three-Dimensional Models and Archaeological Research

There is a moment during an excavation when a spatial pattern of archaeological findings begins to emerge, and trench interpretations begin to coalesce into a broader explanatory scheme. Whether at the level of individual buildings, settlements or regions, the process of archaeological excavation and interpretation entails the 'reading' of extant remains, the subtraction of chronologically irrelevant features, such as superimposed strata, and the supplementation of missing elements in a way that best explains, to the mind of the excavator, the complex under scrutiny. During this process, simple tools such as the Harris Matrix (stratigraphy) and phase plans (2D distribution of remains) come in handy. Both are codified representations of archaeological findings, intelligible through academic and field training. Such tools do not, however, permit volumetric representation, except in an implicit way (for example, schematically, in the form of axonometric plans) and only from a fixed point of view. Undoubtedly there is at work here a symbolic language that is too elementary to handle the complexities of the 3D world, but that is adequate when supplemented by the educated imagination of the professional archaeologist.

These tools have been universally accepted by the academic community: researchers may investigate the schemes used by the discoverer, and check their interpretation and approve the conclusions, or discover mistakes and propose alternative solutions. This acceptance allows shortcuts in scientific reasoning as well as in scientific communication, without infringing the validity of the conclusions. It guarantees the scientific status of the result, by disclosing the information necessary to evaluate each step of the reconstructive process. Dante called this approach 'provando e riprovando' – that is 'arguens pro et contra', 'experimenting and confirming' – when describing the geometer's approach to mathematical problems;[10] Galileo adopted these words for the motto of his Accademia del Cimento. Formal procedures ensure good scientific standards by eliminating the 'black box' of intuition, which often creates pretty pictures without documentation; they allow – even force – us to record the reasons for each decision, to share them with the scientific community, and to open them to peer reviewing.

Although it is widely accepted that 3D visualization technology is a substantial aid in communicating cultural heritage, its potential as a research tool is not acknowledged in the same way. A few examples will suffice to prove that in some cases 3D reconstructions are indeed indispensable.

The Maya site of Calakmul, located in a nature reserve near the Mexico and Guatemala border, includes a number of outstanding pyramids and other buildings. The site was inscribed on the UNESCO World Heritage List in 2002. The beautiful native flora is well preserved, although partly restored after the damage caused by archaeological excavations in this area. The presence of tropical trees and bushes severely hinders the accessibility and viewing of the

10   Dante, *Divine Comedy*, Paradise III.3.

architectural remains. The lack of open space demands considerable imagination even from a trained observer to understand the unintelligible spatial relationships between the various structures. Furthermore, the most important pyramid, known as Structure II, incorporates several earlier structures separated by tight passages. The Calakmul Project team from the Mexican National Institute of Anthropology and History (INAH), under the directorship of Ramón Carrasco, investigated the inner structures by excavating tunnels in the outermost structure and supporting the elevations of excavated areas.[11] Nevertheless, it is impossible fully to grasp the inner, oldest phase of the building. In a related VR project subsequent phases can be 'peeled off', like a virtual *matrioska*.[12] The model enables virtual visits to the site and the study of its architectural development; it also promotes a safer excavation approach.

Another aspect of archaeological research benefiting from computer visualization is the study of the astronomical alignment of ancient buildings, which would be difficult to pursue through other means.[13]

It is certainly the case that the creation and editing of 3D models are complex operations. They entail a close collaboration between archaeologists and technical specialists. Variations and changes of position and view slow down interpretation and make the project more costly. Above all, 3D modelling involves a mediating process between archaeology and technology, that is the transformation of archaeological interpretation to visual reconstruction and ideas into virtual representation. This adds a further mediation level between the past and its understanding. Those in charge of this operation – the modellers – may have their own preconceptions that may influence the final result.

The development of accessible and user-friendly modelling systems would help disseminate 3D and VR technologies more widely and beyond the current emphasis on spectacular, photo-realistic and fast visualizations. An EU-funded project, CHARISMATIC has moved in this direction.[14] The interface of CHARISMATIC provides tools for rapidly creating geo-referenced models of buildings using virtual 'bricks', similar to Lego blocks, subsequently covered with appropriate textures.

---

11   For a full report on Calakmul, see the two monographic issues of *Arqueologia Mexicana*, 2000 and 2005.

12   Rocio Ruiz-Rodarte, 'Augmented Reality for Museum Exhibits', *Proceedings of the Seventh International Workshop, PRESENCE 2004 (*ISPR, the *International* Society for *Presence* Research and MedICLab/UPV Spain, 2004), pp. 317–20. Rocio Ruiz-Rodarte, 'Museo Virtual de Calakmul', *Gaceta de Museos*, 33: 22–7.

13   See for example Emília Pásztor, Ákos Juhász, Miklós Dombi and Curt Roslund, 'Computer Simulation of Stonehenge', in Juan A. Barceló, Maurizio Forte and Donald H. Sanders (eds), *Virtual Reality in Archaeology*, BAR International Series 843 (Oxford: Archaeopress, 2000), pp. 111–14.

14   David Arnold, 'Economic Reconstructions of Populated Environments: Progress with the Charismatic Project', in Franco Niccolucci (ed.), *Virtual Archaeology*, Proceedings of the VAST Euroconference, Arezzo, Italy, 24–25 November 2000, Bar International Series 1075 (Oxford: Archaeopress, 2002), pp. 203–208.

Another tool developed by the EPOCH project 'City Engine', by Luc Van Gool and his team at ETH Zurich, offers the possibility of easy and fast visualization of urban models through the use of so-called procedural modelling.[15] In this case, the underlying model of the city consists of the description of its features in a formalized language. Both these applications are steps forward in the direction of the availability of libraries of components to be assembled for the creation of more complex structures, such as buildings or cities, and the description of the basic features and assemblage procedure by means of a formalized language. It is anticipated that this methodology will ultimately free users from the need to use skilled craftsmen laboriously to build the 3D models from scratch.

These two examples show the convergence of computing visualization research towards tools that allow re-use of basic components and flexibility in model construction, together with the possibility of experimenting alternative solutions before choosing the final interpretation.

These considerations give a positive answer to questions (1), utility, and (2), autonomy. However, the actual feasibility of archaeologists developing an autonomous tool anticipates the full availability of appropriate technological tools – in addition, perhaps, to an improved willingness amongst humanists to make use of them.

Question (3), validity, has inspired the formation of The London Charter. Nevertheless, the Charter is still only a guideline, and needs examples and case studies to develop operational procedures. Although this important component is still missing, the Charter is nevertheless an important step towards incorporating 3D visualization techniques into accepted methods of archaeological research.

In conclusion, a scenario where the archaeologist will use 3D model building software to support his reasoning is not science fiction. In the near future, such a tool will allow users to pick details from a digital library of architectonic parts to complete a volumetric reconstruction, validated according to the principles of statics. Incorporation of The London Charter principles in such tools will require the inclusion of annotations justifying every single choice. The next section illustrates, in a very preliminary way, how this might happen.

Developing Interpretive Decisions in 3D Reconstruction

The workflow for creating 3D models, as introduced by Niccolucci and Hermon, may be theoretically imagined as a linear process that is divisible into steps.[16] Each new step involves the addition of new detail that enhances the model.

---

15   Pascal Müller, Peter Wonka, Simon Haegler, Andreas Ulmer and Luc Van Gool, 'Procedural Modeling of Buildings', in *Proceedings of ACM SIGGRAPH 2006/ACM Transactions on Graphics*, 25, 3 (New York, 2006), pp. 614–23.

16   Hermon and Niccolucci, 'A Fuzzy Logic Approach to Reliability in Archaeological Virtual Reconstruction', pp. 11–17.

In the hypothetical example used in their paper, a partially preserved tower is reconstructed step by step (outline, windows, upper part, roof). The final reconstruction is the outcome of a sequence of intermediate models: M0 = existing remains, M1 = M0 + tower outline, M2 = M1 + windows, and so on.

The type of building used in that paper as an example makes this simple, linear approach possible and easy to explain. The process of reconstruction can be more complicated when there is a choice between, for example, a top with or without crenellation, and can then be represented as a sequence of decisions. In more complex cases, the modelling process can be represented as a decision tree, with some branches more articulated than others. In still more complex cases, certain branches might merge with others. For instance, choices relating to the reconstruction of one part of a settlement will affect the reconstruction of adjacent areas.[17] Here, instead of a tree, the reconstruction process will be a directed graph, in which the terminal nodes represent final (alternative) stages, that is alternative reconstructions. In other words, a reconstruction model goes through successive refinements. The overall process can be represented as a graph whose nodes correspond to sub-models with elementary details, or complex models of their own, being incorporated in a larger one. Thus, at the level of a city the focus is on building location and relationships. Subsequently, buildings are reconstructed in more detail (unless a simple volume representation suffices). Architectural elements such as windows may be added; they can be sketches or worked out later in even more detail. Alternatively, the city model may directly incorporate models of buildings created individually in a separate reconstruction process. The use of a formal procedure of reconstruction such as this guarantees the scientific status of the outcome by disclosing the information necessary to evaluate each step of the reconstructive procedure.

To further illustrate the suggested methodology, let us examine another example, based on a literary source and not on archaeological excavation. It may look too simple compared to real cases, but it is a good illustration of the methodology under consideration here.

The example concerns the reconstruction of the monumental tomb of Lars Porsenna (or Porsina), a legendary Etruscan king famous for having defeated the Romans. The history of this monument has been thoroughly described in Niccolucci and Cantone[18] to illustrate the use of visualization techniques for its modelling.

---

17   For consideration of 'dependency relationships between elements' see The London Charter, 4.1.

18   Franco Niccolucci and Francesca Cantone, 'Legend and Virtual Reconstruction: Porsenna's Mausoleum in X3D', in Martin Doerr and Apostolos Sarris (eds), *The Digital Heritage of Archaeology*, CAA 2002, Proceedings of the 30th Conference of Computer Applications and Quantitative Methods in Archaeology, Heraklion, Crete, April 2002 (Athens: Hellenic Ministry of Culture, 2003), pp. 57–62.

While there are numerous hypotheses concerning the location of this funerary mausoleum, no trace of it survives. We only have a controversial description by Pliny the Elder (C. Plinius Secundus, *Naturalis Historia* xxxvi.19), itself based on an earlier account by Marcus Terentius Varro:

> Sepultus sub urbe Clusio, in quo loco monimentum reliquit lapide quadrato quadratum, singula latera pedum tricenum, alta quinquagenum. In qua basi quadrata intus labyrinthum inextricabile; quo si quis introierit sine glomere lini exitum invenire nequeat. Supra id quadratum pyramides stant quinque, quattuor in angulis et in medio una, imae latae pedu quinum septuagenum, altae centenum quinquagenum; ita fastigatae ut in summo orbis aeneus et petasus unus omnibus sit impositus, ex quo pendeant exapta catenis tintinnabula, quae vento agitata longe sonitu referant, ut Dodonae olim factum. Supra quem orbem quattuor pyramides insuper singulae stant alta pedum centenum. Supra quas uno solo quinque pyramides quarum altitudinem Varronem puduit adicere; fabulae Etruscae tradunt eandem fuisse quam totius operis ad eas.[19]

The above text lends itself naturally to a linear model for the 3D reconstruction. In the past, it was the source for totally different reconstructions, as described by Niccolucci and Cantone.[20] For the sake of brevity, in the following description the Roman foot will be used as the unit of length: a Roman foot (*pes*) is equal to 29.57 cm, or, by approximation, there are 3 feet to 1 metre.[21]

---

19   '[Porsenna] was buried beneath the city of Clusium, in the spot where he had constructed a square monument, built of squared stone. Each side of this monument was 300 ft in length and 50 ft in height, and beneath the base, which was also square, there was an inextricable labyrinth, into which if any one entered without a clew of thread, he could never find his way out. Above this square building there stand five pyramids, one at each corner, and one in the middle, 75 ft broad at the base, and 150 ft in height. These pyramids are so tapering in their form, that upon the summit of all of them united there rests a brazen globe, and upon that a *petasus*; from which there hang, suspended by chains, bells, which make a tinkling when agitated by the wind, like what was done at Dodona in former times. Upon this globe there are four other pyramids, each 100 ft in height; and above them is a single platform, on which there are five more pyramids, the height of which Varro has evidently felt ashamed to add; but, according to the Etruscan fables, it was equal to that of the rest of the building.' Translation after <http://www.perseus.tufts.edu/cgi-bin//// ptext?lookup=Plin.+Nat.+36.19>. The *petasus* is a helmet of Greek origin, similar in shape to the British helmets used in World War I.

20   Niccolucci and Cantone, 'Legend and Virtual Reconstruction'.

21   Oswald Ashton Wentworth Dilke, *Mathematics and Measurement* (London, 1987), p. 26.

- According to Pliny, the monument consisted of the following components:
- Base: this is a parallelepiped with a square base, 300 ft long and 50 ft high. As regards the material, it must have been *petra foetida*, a local, yellowish limestone typically used by the Etruscans.
- First level: the source mentions dimensions of 75 ft per side and 150 ft in height; there were four pyramids in the corners and one at the centre. We do not know the number of sides, but it may be hypothesized that the pyramids had square bases given a necessary symmetry with the base and by analogy with other funerary monuments of the same period. But the phrase 'ita fastigatae ut in summum orbis aeneus [...] sit impositus' raises doubts: perhaps the pyramids were not straight but oblique, or the bases were not placed on the perimeter of the base but closer to its centre. In the alternative reconstructions one can: (a) vary the location of the pyramids with respect to the perimeter, bringing them closer, or moving them farther away; (b) vary the form of the pyramid from straight to oblique, with the edge nearest to the centre of the mausoleum as perpendicular to the base.
- *Petasus*: this is shaped like a disk of unknown thickness, superimposed onto the pyramids of the first level. In the past, the Pliny description has been interpreted as suggesting many separate disks placed atop the pyramids of the first level, but this reconstruction does not seem to reflect the source ('orbis aeneus et petasus unus omnibus sit impositus'), which suggests a single (*'unus'*) *petasus*. An estimated weight of the disk (c. 12,000 tons, assuming a thickness of 1 m) makes it improbable that its dimensions corresponded to those of the base. If the pyramid tops converged at the centre (*fastigatae*), a more feasible reconstruction of this feature would be obtained. An alternative reconstruction, perhaps more faithful to Pliny's description but still posing problems (means of support atop the pyramids), would be a bronze sphere (*orbis aeneus*) with a *petasus* lying on top of it, flat.
- Bells: Pliny does not give the number or their dimensions, but the fact that they ring when moved by the wind witnesses their lightness and mobility.
- Second level of pyramids: the positions of the pyramids depend on the dimension of the *petasus*. Moreover, Pliny does not give the dimensions of the base but only the height (100 ft). Assuming the dimensions of the *petasus* have been established, these pyramids could have the same proportions as the earlier ones and thus the side of their base would be 50 ft long.
- Last level: the reconstruction, as Pliny himself admits, is completely conjectural.

The above description is summarized in Table 4.1.

Table 4.1   Summary analysis of Pliny's description of the Porsenna Mausoleum, *Naturalis Historia* xxxvi.19

Step	Model	Detail Added	Comments
0	M0	Base	Certain (working hypothesis)
1	M1	First pyramid level	Assumption: square pyramids (see similar existing monuments) Alternatives: (i) straight pyramids or (ii) oblique ones; (iii) located close to the edge of the base or (iv) close to its centre
2	M2	*Orbis aeneus* and *petasus*	(a) Option 1 (disk): thickness of 0.6–3 ft; diameter (correlated to the preceding choice) of 105–210 ft b) Option 2 (sphere with disk lying flat on top): radius (correlated to the preceding choice) of 75–250 ft
3	M3	Bells	No information about number and size, but capable of ringing when moved by the wind, so sufficiently small and light
4	M4	Second pyramid level	Information available only concerns height; side to be determined according to underlying level
5	M5	Final pyramid level	No reliable information provided: reconstruction completely conjectural

The reconstruction process for Porsenna's mausoleum exemplifies the methodology for archaeological reconstructions, which can be described in general as follows:

- 3D models are built by assembling sub-models, using previously built components ('details') that in some cases may be very simple and elementary parts, in others complex models.
- 3D models are a function of time: that is, they refer to a precise time span.
- The assembly occurs in a sequential and discrete (possibly non-linear) way: (i) by incorporating a new detail into a 3D model (for example, adding a window to a building), or (ii) by combining two or more models to obtain a more general one (for example, combining buildings to obtain a model of a city). The time span of the assembly is the intersection of the time spans of the components.
- The assembly process can be represented as a directed graph whose terminal nodes constitute alternative reconstructions.
- The starting point of this process is empty, meaning that interpretation for the purpose of reconstruction starts by looking at the objective, actual archaeological remains. Clearly, however, archaeological findings are also the result of interpretation.

- Aggregating a detail to a model to generate the next step of the reconstruction, or combining models into a more general one, requires appropriate comments and justifications according to The London Charter.
- Alternate solutions may be considered when adding a detail to a model, generating a branch in the reconstruction process.
- The credibility of the model obtained after the insertion of a new detail is smaller than the one of the pre-existing model. Moreover, its trustworthiness is a function of time within the validity time span of the model.
- Embellishments – defined as unfounded but marginal details useful for conveying a sense of the whole or enhancing the expressiveness of the model – are legitimate, provided that: (a) they are not prominent in the reconstruction, (b) they do not suggest interpretations otherwise impossible, and (c) they are clearly recognizable or labelled as such. Embellishments have no effect on the overall credibility of the model.
- Point 8 above, that is the law of decreasing credibility of reconstructions, is counter-intuitive but true: any additional detail is risky and may jeopardize the overall credibility of the reconstruction. For example, anachronisms in the movie *Scipio Africanus* (dir. Carmine Gallone, 1937), as well as wristwatches, telephone poles on a Roman battlefield, and shoes of modern leather worn by a Roman legionnaire, completely undermine the historical value of that film. The same has recently happened with the beautiful, but inaccurate, architectural reconstructions of Rome in *The Gladiator* (dir. Ridley Scott, 2000).[22] Notably, adding erroneous details inadvertently is rather likely in Augmented Reality, which utilizes contemporary landscape images as background.
- Point 9 mitigates the strict reconstruction rules. Embellishments may, for example, include the addition of climate-appropriate plants, such as ivy on a wall; scene illumination, provided that it does not distort the monument; human figures at the correct scale and dressed in historically accurate clothing. The nice moustaches appearing on one of the earliest face reconstructions based on forensic methods[23] may also be considered as an embellishment of the scientifically based outcome, while the dark eyes appearing on the same reconstructed face are more likely to be another, relatively safe detail relying on the Mediterranean descent of the subject.

---

22   A detailed list of goofs is available at <http://207.171.166.140/title/tt0029526/goofs> for *Scipio Africanus* and at <http://www.imdb.com/title/tt0172495/goofs> for *The Gladiator*. However, neither movie claims to be a philological reconstruction.

23   Giuseppe Attardi, Marilina Betrò, Maurizio Forte et al., '3D Facial Reconstruction and Visualization of Ancient Egyptian Mummies using Spiral CT Data Soft Tissue Reconstruction and Texture Application', in Juan A. Barceló, Maurizio Forte and Donald H. Sanders (eds), *Virtual Reality in Archaeology*, BAR International Series 843 (Oxford, 2000), pp. 79–86.

Documenting the Reconstruction Process

The standard for heritage documentation is CIDOC-CRM (ISO standard 21127:2006), the Conceptual Reference Model developed within the International Committee for Museums (ICOM) International Documentation Committee (CIDOC).[24] CIDOC-CRM is a formal ontology intended to facilitate the integration, mediation and interchange of heterogeneous cultural heritage documentation. So far, its acceptance has not been as wide as it deserves; even so it is limited to museum collections. Archaeological excavation data have also employed CIDOC-CRM, with the ultimate goal of making them widely available in an international digital library of tangible heritage, but this is still work in progress. Architectural information is so far still untouched by such a standardization effort.

CIDOC-CRM is based on the concepts of entities (object attributes) and properties (relationships linking different entities). In its current version it lists 84 entities and 141 properties, but envisages the possibility of extensions related to specific domains. CIDOC-CRM is deeply influenced by its museum origin. Nevertheless, its flexibility and extendibility allow – or promise to allow – for further and more general applications. For example, in a working paper of 2007 by Doerr and LeBoeuf, the authors attempt to model Intellectual Processes within the Conceptual Reference Model.[25] The paper was produced in the framework of the harmonization work between CIDOC-CRM and Functional Requirements for Bibliographic Records (FRBR), created by the International Federation of Libraries and Archives (IFLA).

Another example is presented by D'Andrea and Niccolucci, where a 3D ontology is attached as an extension of CIDOC to create a new ontology for 3D cultural objects.[26] However, in this paper 3D graphics are presented as a visual attribute of the documentation, namely as a specification of the entity E36 Visual Item. Therefore, developing this logic further would lead one to consider reliability annotations as appendices to a specific graphic model. With this approach, annotations would be rather easy to introduce. They could be represented as a note extension to any graphic ontology, which could be ignored by graphic-unaware processors and considered for display and editing, or special visualization, by

24   For CIDOC-CRM see <http://cidoc.ics.forth.gr/>.

25   Martin Doerr and Patrick LeBoeuf, 'Linking CIDOC-CRM and FRBR', *Proceedings of the Conference on Intelligent Access to Digital Heritage*, National Library of Estonia, Tallin, 18–19 October 2007, available at <http://conference2007.kul.ee/failid/LeBoef_Linking_CIDOC_CRM_and_FRBR.pdf>.

26   Andrea D'Andrea and Franco Niccolucci, 'An Ontology for 3D Cultural Objects', in David Arnold, Marinos Ioannides, Katerina Mania and Franco Niccolucci (eds), *Proceedings of VAST2007, the Seventh International Symposium on Virtual Reality, Archaeology, and Intelligent Cultural Heritage* (Aire-La-Ville, 2003), pp. 203–10.

those compliant with The London Charter. For example, a note referring to the Porsenna case could be introduced in an X3D model[27] in this way:

<PhilologicalNote>

The first level is formed by five pyramids, four at the corners and one in the middle, see C. Plinius Secundus, Naturalis Historia, 36.19. The source does not state the shape of the pyramids. It may be assumed that they have a square base, as shown in paintings of the same period for other funerary monuments.

</PhilologicalNote >

The X3D processor could be instructed to ignore or to display (in a suitable form) the content of the PhilologicalNote element.

However, the philology of the reconstruction does not pertain to a graphic model developed using a specific technology. It is related to reconstruction in general, using *any* graphic tool. It seems therefore more appropriate to document it as a property of the object rather than a property of the graphic model. Of course, CIDOC-CRM does not include entities for philological notes, but some of its entities may be the anchor point for an extension, 'attaching' a specific philological ontology. For example, E73 Information Object or E31 Document might reasonably be used for this purpose, on one side being linked (through an appropriate property, as 'P67 refers to' or P70 documents) to the object and on the other to its reconstruction notes – and perhaps to the reconstruction itself.

Therefore, extending CIDOC-CRM to include the annotations envisaged by The London Charter seems a possibility, currently under development by the author. This will provide a standardized way to include philological annotations in the documentation of 3D reconstructions and thus allow to be incorporated in the scientifically accepted apparatus of the interpretation of the past.

---

27   X3D is an ISO standard (ISO/IEC 19775) defining a runtime system and delivery mechanism for real-time 3D content and applications running on a network. For further details see <http://www.x3d.org>.

Chapter 5

More than Pretty Pictures of the Past: An American Perspective on Virtual Heritage[1]

Donald H. Sanders

Introduction

The author has a multi-disciplinary background and has presented his views as a member of various constituent groups directly related to heritage visualization. He is an architect and an archaeologist (see Figure 5.1). Having worked amidst the dirt and stones, he now works strictly amidst the pixels. He is also the owner of two companies specializing in virtual heritage (see Figure 5.2): Learning Sites, Inc., with its roots dating back to 1993, builds virtual ancient reconstructions for scholars, educators, and students. The Institute for the Visualization of History, Inc. is a unique, not-for-profit educational organization founded in 2001, which expands the chronological and geographical scope of Learning Sites, and provides still more accessibility to the vast potential of interactive 3D environments for documentation, teaching, research, display, publication and broadcast.

Learning Sites and the Institute for the Visualization of History routinely work with archaeologists, other historians, museums, schools and governments to create vivid visualizations of past places and events. Over the years, one has seen enormous growth in the ways in which 3D computer technologies have been applied to the goals and problems of cultural heritage interpretation, documentation and preservation. Simply shaded massing models have given way to complexly lit and detailed virtual worlds. Yet virtual heritage is still not where it should be in many aspects of our results, and how it does what it does is still a mystery to many.

This chapter touches on the following topics:

- how archaeology has traditionally dealt with the evidence trail, with special focus on the use of images as documentation;
- how digital archaeology has changed the rules and how the discipline is trying to cope;

1   This chapter is a revised and expanded version of the paper presented at the seminar *Making 3D Visual Research Outcomes Transparent*, co-sponsored by the AHRC ICT Methods Network; EPOCH; PIN, Prato, Italy and King's Visualisation Lab, King's College London, held at the British Academy on 23–25 February 2006.

- how virtual heritage projects can solve many problems relating to data trails, allowing researchers to compare the evidence to the outcome, and to have virtual worlds become visual indexes to all the information, and thus more than pretty pictures of the past; and
- how my companies have handled some of these issues in our projects.

Topics in Detail

As an introduction, it is instructive to look back at how archaeologists typically work, and how images are normally used to maintain the evidence trail throughout the excavation process. In general, archaeologists pick a site, or develop a hypothesis about some problem and then find a site. We raise funds, establish some excavation strategies, hire a team and go off to dig. We lay out a grid, get out our trowels and scrape away. As we dig, we record our finds, the stratigraphy, and 3D contextual information. We document our progress in field notebooks describing in some detail what transpired, what we found, and perhaps what preliminary thoughts we have about the meaning of our finds. We might even add some drawings and photographs of objects, architectural features and soil changes.

When archaeologists publish their results, evidence-tracking may occur if a description of the excavation methods, strategies, and decision-making and analytical processes happens to be included. But some transparency has already been lost, once the final publication arrives. In order to really tie the results back to the evidence, one would have to read the final report with the daily logbooks in

Figure 5.1   Donald H. Sanders (left) as a conventional field architect working at Ancient Corinth (1972); and (right) giving an interview on Dutch television from inside the virtual reality model of the Northwest Palace at Nimrud (2000)

Figure 5.2   Sample renderings from various projects by Learning Sites and the Institute for the Visualization of History, Inc.

hand and have access to all the preliminary analyses from all the fieldworkers, all the photos and all the drawings.

Since this is usually not practical, what kinds of visual documentation traditionally accompany those weighty reports and how do they relate to the fieldwork, data collection and interpretation processes? First, a little background about architectural drawings as a means of presenting the evidence about a historical location (drawings are chosen as an example, because they are directly relevant to the process of creating virtual worlds). Ever since historians began purposely chronicling the built environment of the past through images, at least since the early thirteenth-century drawings of the French traveller, Villard de Honnecourt, the primary means of visualizing architecture has been via plans, sections and elevations.[2] This so-called sacred triad was first published as a set by

2   For a complete review of the work of this early chronicler of architecture, see the exhaustive research by Carl F. Barnes, Jr, including his comprehensive bibliography of Villard's portfolio and analysis of his life, now online at <http://www.villardman.net>;

Albrecht Dürer in 1527.[3] The main reason for this now centuries-old dependence on a few basic drawing types is the historically close relationship between the architectural profession and the archaeologists. In the eighteenth and nineteenth centuries architects supplied details of ancient monuments to architects for their new buildings, which were then being designed in the Neoclassical style. These building details were supplied in the formats needed most by architects, namely plans, sections, and elevations.[4] It was precisely at that time – throughout the nineteenth century – that our profession developed and matured, with excavations often led or co-directed by architects.

There has normally been no clearly stated connection between the published images in excavation reports and either the excavation or the delineation process. Whatever field notes or detailed measurements were taken in support of the final drawings they rarely became part of the published documentation. The results were just trusted as presented, as close enough. Each succeeding generation of archaeologists has continued to prepare and put forth drawings seemingly more accurate than the previous depictions of the remains. The level of trust on the part of researchers in the visualizations given rests primarily on the reputation of the delineator – something that is still very much a part of the discipline's acceptance of any visual surrogates.

Today, in the midst of the information revolution, archaeologists still rely too heavily on those same static, 2D representations of what is really a dynamic, behaviour-influencing 4D system. The idea that representing architecture in arbitrary frozen slices through its spaces can somehow provide meaningful insight into the actual use of the spaces or can possibly represent actual 3D reality, is simplistic and biased. It is simplistic, because the complexities of construction, the visual impact of decorative detailing, the nuances of lighting (see Figure 5.3), the behavioural issues of privacy, territoriality and viewsheds cannot even be studied,

---

the complete Villard portfolio of drawings is in the Bibliothèque Nationale, Paris, MS. Fr. 19093.

3   Eve Blau and Edward Kaufman (eds), *Architecture and Its Image: Four Centuries of Architectural Representation. Works from the Collection of the Canadian Centre for Architecture* (Montreal, 1989), p. 161.

4   See, for example, the drawings of the Tower of the Winds in James Stuart and Nicholas Revett (eds), *The Antiquities of Athens* (1762), and compare them to the details of the tower on St Pancras New Church, London, by William and Henry Inwood, architects [1818]. The full connections between the origins of archaeology, the Neoclassical movements of the time, and the design choices of European architects are a bit more complex, as further discussed in Donald H. Sanders, *Behavior and the Built Environment: An Interpretive Model for the Analysis of Architecture in an Archaeological Context and Its Testing on Material from the Aegean Bronze Age Site of Myrtos, Crete*, PhD thesis, Columbia University, Ann Arbor, 1985 and Donald H. Sanders, 'Architecture: The Neglected artifact', in E.B. French and K. A. Wardle (eds), *Problems in Greek Prehistory: Papers Presented at the Centenary Conference of the British School of Archaeology at Athens, Manchester, April 1986* (Bristol, 1988), pp. 489–98.

Figure 5.3   **Rendering of the interior courtyard of the House of Many Colours, Olynthus, Greece, from the Learning Sites virtual reality model**

let alone be understood, in two dimensions. The premise is biased, because this traditional approach to documenting and visualizing space relegates the study of architecture to the same level as the study of individual artefacts isolated from their context and societal function. This is not to diminish the study of pottery or stone tools, since they too could benefit from interactive 3D computer modelling, but the built environment is a fundamental modifier of human behaviour as well as an encapsulation and reflection of that behaviour.[5] Thus, in order truly to understand how buildings were erected, why they were erected, how they were used by real people, and in what condition they remained when excavated, it would seem more advantageous to recreate them and experience them in simulations of their original complexity, which means interactively in 3D.

The introduction of photography into archaeological record-keeping, publishing and evidence-tracking has only moderately altered our approach to the problems. Photographs give us perhaps a bit more of a realistic and direct connection between the actual evidence and the visualization. There are also subjective interpretations behind the choice of, for example, photographic angle, the time of day the photograph was taken, the type of lighting used, and the

---

5   Sanders, *Behavior and the Built Environment.*

degree of colour calibration or post-processing. Rarely do archaeologists publish these details.

Thus, the dependence on the codex and static 2D images has remained an unquestioned ingredient of archaeological reporting methods since the profession's inception. Excavation reports typically contain long descriptions of the fieldwork and its finds, a few charts, and only as many pictures – usually black and white – as printing costs or book length permits. Illustrations generally include pottery profiles, isolated views of a few artefacts or trenches, and token line drawings of key features. Architectural drawings persistently repeat, unquestioned, the plans, sections, and elevations used since our discipline's eighteenth-century origins.

Fast forward to today's vast array of digital tools (GIS, GPS, ground-penetrating radar, laser scanning, and virtual reality). The focus here will be on virtual reality (VR) to investigate how things have or have not changed. To put the discussion in context, one needs to evaluate what happens when a new technology is introduced into a well-established profession. For example, when the architect Imhotep introduced ashlar masonry – for the pyramid complex of King Djoser, at Saqqara, around 2800 BC – he designed stone walls *imitating* reeds and other plants, the traditional Egyptian building materials. His innovation relied upon visual forms rooted, so to speak, in the plant-based construction of his predecessors.

Further, when Formica™ plastic laminates were introduced to the general public in the 1920s and 1930s, the first textures applied to their surfaces were imitation wood colour or wood graining patterns; and the first places they were used were on furniture, countertops and car detailing.[6] That is, their location and visual vocabulary imitated wood, the previous technology. As with Imhotep's use of plant motifs, there is no inherent reason why this should be so, since both cut stone and Formica have qualities suitable for many applications and patterns totally unique to themselves. In each case, it took years before some alternative uses and motifs were explored. Both innovations became cloaked in the visual vocabulary of the previous technology. This is not to criticize; it just happens. So, too, our computer graphics often present data in ways that reproduce the look, the presentation mode and even the graphic style of our predecessor's visualization techniques. Once this pattern is recognized, virtual heritage professionals will have more freedom to apply the new technologies in ways that are not just digital replacements for traditional paper-based image types. The discipline's challenge is to use this now-not-so-leading-edge technology in ways that innovate, educate and elucidate.

When virtual reality was introduced into archaeology in the early 1990s, some of the concerns about its usefulness raised by the academic community were precisely the same as those that had been expressed by a previous generation of historians about the use of photography in archaeology in the mid-nineteenth

---

6   A brief history of the product's development can be found on the company's website: <http://www.formica.com/publish/site/na/us/en/index/content/about_formica/history/history. html>.

century. For example, it is cumbersome and difficult to learn; few people in the field know how to use it effectively; it is expensive to create useful results; and the images cannot be trusted by scholars.[7]

By the 1870s, archaeologists were finally beginning to see the benefits of photography for recording sites, excavations and artefacts with a level of accuracy and precision not previously possible, and making these images available to a wider audience in a reproducible format. The connection between the evidence and the disseminated results became a bit clearer, as not only increased realism was possible, but there was also a concomitant ability to document the excavation process (which of course became even easier later through the use of moving image and then digital video photography). Since the early 1990s, virtual reality has offered the same benefits to archaeology – and many more. VR can tailor visualizations to different end-users, reconstruct elements now lost, and, most importantly for the theme under investigation in this volume, link vast amounts of supporting documentation to interactive and customizable visuals. Even though a 3D computer model can be subject to the same subjective interpretations as drawings, the benefits of VR for cultural heritage leap far beyond those of any technology previously available. Much as photography did, VR is in the process of gradually becoming a standard indispensable tool for the discipline – but at present it is only emerging slowly from the early wood-grained Formica stage.

Archaeologists, modellers and the general public have come a long way from the initial enthusiasm of just being able to create virtual worlds. Yet, today, the process of building a virtual recreation of a historical place or event still demands skill, patience and hard work, and is rarely ever used innovatively – for example, as a visual index for all the documentation and analysis of the primary evidence – too often remaining a mere digital substitute for hand drawings. Can the connection between the source material and the interactive result be retained? Can the virtual environment become a window into history *and* a roadmap for accepting the path to the past? The discipline needs to realize that digital recreations of the evidence, in the form of cool worlds to explore (even if they offer unique insight into the past) are by themselves insufficient for convincing the discipline as a whole to adopt the technology.

---

7   Virtual reality was introduced nearly simultaneously through projects by English Heritage (Stonehenge, with Intel Corp. under the direction of Robert J. Stone), Carnegie-Mellon University (a virtual Egyptian temple, under the direction of Carl E. Loeffler), and a team that would eventually become Learning Sites (the Fortress at Buhen, Egypt, under the co-direction of Timothy Kendall, Bill Riseman, and Donald H. Sanders; see also below p. 45). For complaints about photography during its early use by archaeologists, see for example, Peter G. Dorrell, *Photography in Archaeology and Conservation* (Cambridge, 2nd edn, 1994), pp. 1–7; Jean-Claude Lemagny and André Rouillé (eds), *A History of Photography: Social and Cultural Perspectives*, trans. by Janet Lloyd (Cambridge, 1987), pp. 54ff; Eric Meyers (ed.), *The Oxford Encyclopaedia of Archaeology in the Near East* (Oxford, 1997), pp. 331–3.

One can restate the issues another way. Creating visual surrogates intended to reproduce life's experiences has been part of human activity for millennia. From its earliest known images in cave paintings, humankind has exhibited an innate drive to represent the world around it. In addition to visual images, theatre and literature have all offered views of other places, other experiences, other beliefs, and other times, to stimulate the imagination, to instil wonder about the fantastic, and to speculate about the spiritual. As technologies have changed, so have the means for stimulating the eye and the imagination, from mathematical perspective in the fifteenth century to motion pictures in the twentieth. People are fascinated by the illusion of *being there*.

Representation has also been used throughout human history to educate and entertain. Visualization is a recognized means of making data and concepts more easily comprehended and assimilated. Thus, instructional books are illustrated, and audiovisual materials are widely used in classrooms. Then along come computers and interactive 3D digital visualizations. Virtual reality is just another step in the age-old drive toward heightened visual experience based on reality.

Historian David Staley, Executive Director of the American Association for History and Computing, wrote that computer visualization when used 'to represent simultaneity, multidimensionality, pattern and nonlinearity with ... speed and efficiency' can do what 'prose cannot capture'.[8] Staley argues that the real impact of the computer has been as a graphics tool more than as a processor of words. The importance of 3D imagery lies in its ability to address longstanding concerns of historians who agree with the observation of the nineteenth-century writer, philosopher and social reformer, Thomas Carlyle, that 'Narrative is linear, Action is solid.'[9] Thus, the technical potential of computer graphics is that it can present a deeper and more richly rewarding history by giving a 3D solidity to past places and events, and at the same time that it can act as a repository for the images, words and objects that together define who we are and how we got here.

The London Charter initiative demonstrates that it has become as much about the methods as about the results. We must convince more than just ourselves that the value of virtual heritage is contained as much in the process as in the pretty pictures.

Examples

Although Learning Sites and the Institute for the Visualization of History strive to create virtual worlds that are as accurate and precise as the evidence allows, the goal has never been simply to reproduce the past, either as excavated or as reconstructed, as realistically as possible. Realism is not a necessary part of the game; believability, trustworthiness and credibility are the keys to the companies'

---

8   David J. Staley, *Computers, Visualization and History: How New Technology Will Transform Our Understanding of the Past* (Armonk, NY, 2002), p. 36f.

9   Ibid, pp. 38ff.

survival. The only way they have found to attain and retain the confidence of fellow historians is not to simply wow them with good-looking textures and interactivity (that has become a little old, since computer games and animated full-length movies can do it much better). Instead, the companies have tried to instil in our colleagues the sense that we are developing an entirely new paradigm for collocating the many diverse datasets that comprise their interpretation of the past. Ironically, the author had already set off down that path in his very first virtual world, back in 1993.

The virtual world of the Fortress at Buhen (located along the River Nile at the ancient Egyptian–Nubian border, see Figure 5.4) was created through a collaboration between a VR programmer, an architect, an archaeologist and a museum curator. The group's results were presented at many early VR conferences, including the First Annual Virtual Heritage Conference, held in Bath in 1995. Back then the collaborators recognized the value of linking supplemental text and image databases to specific objects, avatars and locations in the virtual world. Unfortunately, the data for that world were lost through a series of tragic events

Figure 5.4   Screen shots and a rendering from the Buhen virtual world, showing the avatar guide leading a virtual tour and accessing the linked information about the site from a virtual kiosk, one of several scattered around the virtual environment. Archaeological data and interpretations by Timothy Kendall, Bill Riseman and Donald H. Sanders

that took the life of the author's partner. The original data have only recently been recovered, and that project is slowly coming back to life.

Learning Sites' next exploration into creating direct links between the archaeological evidence and virtual recreations of an archaeological site came in 1998, with the beginnings of the Nemea Valley Archaeological Project (see Figure 5.5). The goal presented to Learning Sites by the field team was to reinvent the excavation report, by devising a means for publishing all the data from the excavations of the Bronze Age settlement of Tsoungiza, ancient Nemea, Greece: all the field notebook pages, all the photographs, all the drawings, all the descriptions and analyses and all the artefact databases. Learning Sites built a set of intertwined access points from a Java-based search engine to virtual recreations of trenches, to straight html pages, whereby users from different backgrounds (students, professionals, or the general public) could access and search any or all datasets from any other dataset. That is, the search engine linked the artefact databases with the locations of the objects in the virtual worlds and text descriptions; the objects in the virtual trenches linked to their database records, find notebook pages and phase descriptions. In this manner, anyone could find and collocate background evidence to test against our virtual recreations and the archaeologists' analyses.

In 1999, Learning Sites began to work on one of its most extensive virtual worlds, a recreation of the ninth-century BC Northwest Palace of King Ashur-nasir-

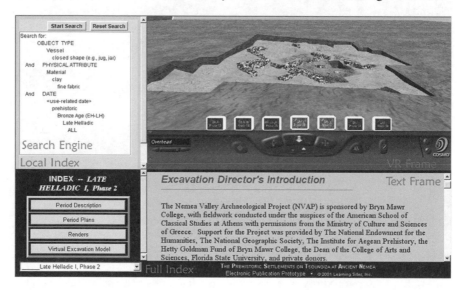

Figure 5.5   **Screen grab from the Nemea Valley Archaeological Project digital excavation report, interim version, showing the various data frames, including the cross-linked search engine, virtual recreation of one of the trenches, local and global indexes, and general text**

Figure 5.6   Sample renderings from the Northwest Palace at Nimrud (Assyria) virtual world; archaeological data and interpretations by Samuel M. Paley, Richard P. Sobolewski and Alison B. Snyder

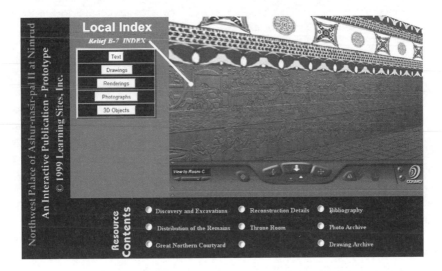

Figure 5.7   Screen grab from an interim version of the Northwest Palace, Nimrud, virtual world research resource, showing the links between objects in the virtual world, such as wall reliefs, and the reference items pulled from a linked database

pal II, at Nimrud, Assyria (present-day Iraq; see Figure 5.6). This is a long-term project that is still expanding. The goal here is to provide researchers with an experience that at once shows the Palace as the Assyrians would have seen it, and also provides from within the world access to information about the resources we relied upon to build it (see Figure 5.7). This supplemental data would include photos, drawings, video and text provided by the many museums around the world that hold sculptural and architectural pieces from the building, excavation notes from the long 160 years of work at the site, and descriptions and analyses from Assyriologists. The virtual world, in this case, is also being used to track on-going looting at the site, as well as to gauge the speed of deterioration of the remains now exposed to weather, gunfire and crowbars (see Figure 5.8).

In 2001, the Institute began to work on its first underwater site, a series of Arab trading vessel shipwrecks (see Figure 5.9) from Tantura Harbor, off Tel Dor, Israel. The results of this ongoing project will become a supplement to a traditional paper publication that will allow nautical archaeologists to virtually 're-dive' the site. There are no reconstructions. The goal is to build interactive 3D models of the wrecks and link each timber and artefact to the photos, drawings and field notes collected by the diving team (see Figure 5.10). This way it will be possible to test our virtual worlds directly against the primary evidence from the site. This approach will allow researchers to revisit underwater sites in ways otherwise impossible and still have access to data and interpretations normally not included in final reports.

In 2004, the Institute began another underwater project to aid a large archaeological team studying the last days of the coastal trading ship that sank off Kyrenia, Cyprus in the fourth century BC. This complex and long-term endeavour has the Institute's team virtually recreating the wreck with its hundreds of surviving artefacts in just the way it looked when it was discovered (see Figure 5.11). The virtual world will be used to help test a series of hypotheses about the way the cargo was originally arranged, the physics of how the ship sank and broke apart, and whether the resulting amphora scatter provides clues that can be used to analyse the shape of vessels in other wrecks for which the timber framing does not survive. As the modelling team progresses, each stage of the modelling and testing process is being recorded for use by the field team for their final publication analyses.

In 2005, the Institute was approached with a project about a different kind of ship: a wooden model found by Flinders Petrie in a (Nineteenth Dynasty) tomb at Gurob, Egypt. The goal of this project was to create interactive 3D computer models for a DVD accompanying a traditional paperbound book about the little ship. Continuing our tradition of providing researchers with links between the final graphics and the primary evidence, so that they could better judge the validity of the results, we added new features to the virtual models. Not only can researchers click on each piece of the ship model to bring up low-, medium and high-resolution photographs of the actual wooden fragments, but the Institute also programmed sliders that enabled users to change the physical appearance of the virtual reality

Figure 5.8   Photographs showing recent damage done to the reliefs and inscriptions at the Northwest Palace due to looting attempts, natural decay and gun battles

Figure 5.9   Rendering from our virtual recreation of the Tantura B shipwreck and a photograph of the remains

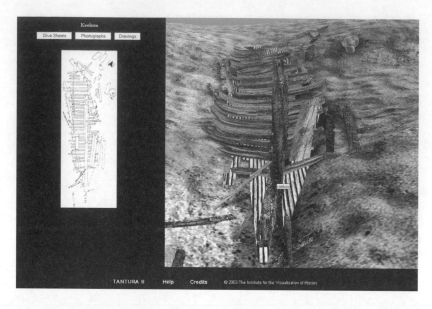

Figure 5.10 Screen grab from the excavation report digital supplement showing the virtual shipwreck, interactive plan and linked database information

Figure 5.11 Rendering from the Kyrenia shipwreck virtual world showing the remains of the ship as excavated

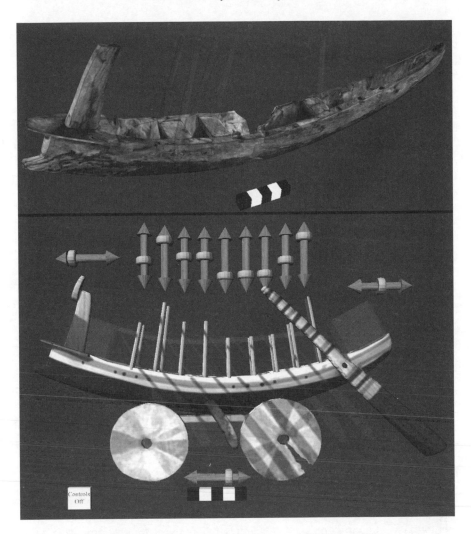

Figure 5.12   Screen grabs from virtual reality models of the Gurob ship. The upper image shows the main pieces of the ship reconstructed in its current condition; the lower image depicts a reconstruction of the original ship. The lower image also shows (in the lower left) the button that turns the sliders on and off, and the sliders that affect the positions of various elements of the ship

models of the ship (see Figure 5.12). Since the ship was found broken into many bits, scholars are unsure about its precise original configuration; there is room for alternate interpretations aside from the one that the publication will offer. Thus, the sliders allow users, upon evaluating the evidence presented in the book and from the photographs, to come to their own conclusions, thereby creating a direct relationship between the evidence, their analyses and the visualizations.

From very early on in the companies' use of VR, Learning Sites and the Institute heard from colleagues, students and friends that they wanted to know how virtual worlds were created. For them, Learning Sites assembled a 'how we build a virtual model' demo that moves through and describes the steps we take to go from published text and 2D images, through the 3D modelling and texturing phases, to the final generation of a virtual world. This demo provides archaeologists with a bit of an education and insight into how we work, and comes in useful at meetings, presentations to non-professionals and for students learning computer graphics. It is also important, because, like drawings, digital renders have a degree of separation between the actual remains and the final visualizations. This differs from photography or laser scanning, which provide a more direct translation of reality into a visualization. How textures are made and applied, what level of precision is built into the 3D model and what software package was used are all part of the process that affects the resulting imagery, and these steps and decisions need to be made clear to end-users if they are to trust the outcome.

One final example is in some ways the best but also the most vexing (see Figures 5.13–14). Learning Sites' so-called 'java panel' is the in-house attempt to utilize the digital medium to its fullest potential for designing an interface so that archaeologists can interact with their data and our virtual visualizations in an innovative yet familiar fashion. Without going into all the programming details of this research and development (R&D) project, the main features of the panel's functionality that are relevant to the themes under discussion here include: (1) a VR recreation of a building or site and links to and from it, and an interactive excavation plan for varied navigation and comparison of 2D to 3D image types; (2) links from 3D artefacts in the VR scene to full database records, photographs, drawings, detailed 3D models and analyses for direct comparison of the visualization of the objects to the evidence; and (3) an interactive time-slider that fades the as-reconstructed virtual model back to a model of the as-excavated architectural remains for direct one-on-one evaluation.

Learning Sites' next addition to this package would allow users to leave digital footnotes inside the virtual world as comments about their visit; a subsequent visitor could find the date, email address, time, and 3D viewpoint of the visitor's footnote, text comments, as well as links to adjunct images that the visitor wanted to leave. This would allow digital annotations of the virtual world on the fly and is the first of our planned efforts to allow dynamic additions to virtual worlds.

For many years, Learning Sites and the Institute have been pursuing alternative methods of linking evidence to results, and showing how we move from the as-excavated remains to the reconstructed virtual worlds. There are problems with

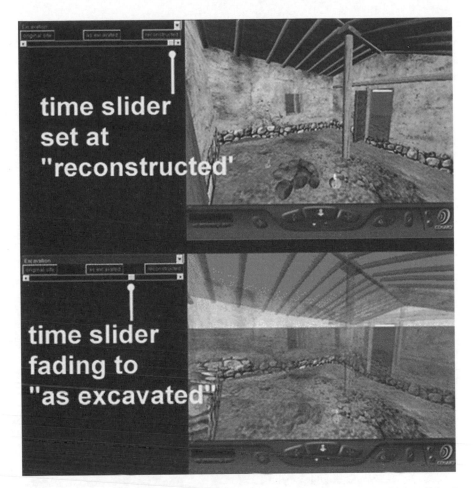

Figure 5.13 **Screen grabs from a 'java panel' showing how the 'time slider' works to change the virtual world, by fading away the as-reconstructed elements back to the as-excavated features, for direct comparison**

some of the approaches that could potentially harm efforts to continue such innovations. Many of our External Authoring Interface (EAI) and Java-based applets have run into difficulties as we began to port them up to WindowsXP running the newest browsers and latest VRML viewers. Although the applications run fine under old versions of browsers with the Cosmo VRML Player, they will not run under any of the newer, faster and more efficient VRML viewers, such as Contact (<http://www.blaxxun.com>), Cortona (<http://www.parallelgraphics. com>) or Octaga (<http://www.octaga.com>) in the new Web browsers. The author has been in communication with these companies regarding these issues, and their responses have been that they have no plans to implement fully the

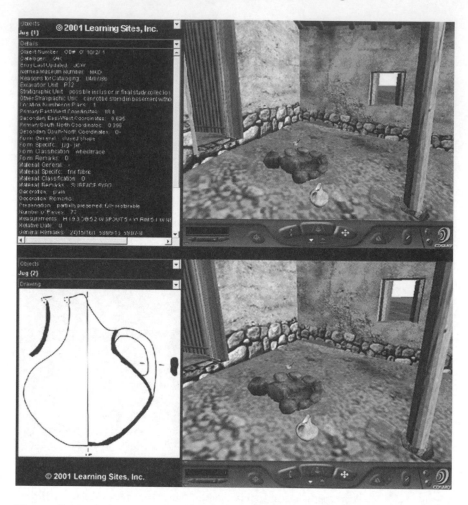

Figure 5.14 **Screen grabs from a 'java panel' showing how objects in the virtual world are linked to several databases containing text and image background information**

older or newer EAI specifications at this time, opting instead to wait for the Web 3D consortium to firm up specifications for the new Scenegraph Architecture Interface (SAI) and X3D. At this time, there are no X3D exporters for the popular 3D modelling programs, and no truly cross-platform X3D viewers. This is bad news for the future of VRML and the future of any efforts to continue to respond to requests to make virtual worlds more than pretty pictures.

In any case, the various approaches illustrated here begin to demonstrate that the discipline of virtual heritage can indeed go beyond the codex, beyond creating digital versions of plans, sections and elevations, that it can emerge from the wood-grained Formica phase and utilize 3D computer graphics in ways unique to the medium and not dependent on previous technologies. In doing so, virtual heritage practitioners can provide archaeologists with convincing software solutions that directly connect their excavated evidence with interactive visualizations.

Conclusion

There was one question put to the attendees of the first Virtual Heritage conference (mentioned above) held in Bath in 1995 that still resonates today. Virtual heritage: is it authentic or fantastic? This question gets to the heart of matter: can archaeologists and the general public trust our visualizations, and while we all strive for accuracy, what level of accuracy and precision is acceptable? Our approach, and that of most virtual heritage practitioners, has been to be as fastidious as the evidence permits, and only recreate the rest based on scholarly and studious investigation. The primary goals of virtual heritage are documentation, education and preservation, not games (though they may be part of the end result). However, this still begs the question: do we need standards for judging the integrity and accuracy of our creations?

The issue of defining standards of good practice in virtual heritage arose at another symposium held in Mussoorie, India in 2005.[10] After much consideration, participants broke off discussion because of the dizzying set of questions it raised, such as, what is a standard, who sets the standards, and how do we enforce standards? Does a standard become a standard because it is mandated and enforced, or because it just happens by having the vast majority of people simply choose to use it, for whatever reason? What are the minimum requirements for something to become a defined standard? Are standards meant to be broken as advances in the technology and applications outpace changes to the language defining the standard?

Looking ahead to what more can be done beyond standards, what do we envision about the future of virtual heritage and how will these changes affect the issues being tackled here? It seems likely that very soon virtual heritage worlds will be much more complex, real-time, networked environments updated and tracked globally. These worlds will contextualize not only places and objects, but also people and events. The entire historical fabric will be made available, including intelligent agents, people with real-time behaviours, vegetation, animals and climate. We will be able to include n-dimensional semantic networks linking vast complex datasets to the worlds via routines based on simulations and game engines. Intelligent site guides and virtual ancient inhabitants will be able to vocalize to each other and to our avatars the information we are now including only in the form of background text.

---

10   Indo-US Science and Technology Forum, 11–13 November 2005, Mussoorie, India; publication forthcoming.

Other current projects point the way toward the next major leaps in graphics technology, such as ubiquitous computing (anywhere, anytime), projection holographs, laser-plasma free-floating 3D models, an all 3D Internet (the Metaverse); floor-mounted 3D TVs, on-demand augmented reality, and on-demand 'world-boards' under development by IBM (handheld devices mixed with wearable systems with global access to information and location-aware 3D worlds).[11] Such devices will have universal statistically based translators for instant 'any language to any language' translations for multilingual access to voice, text and video.

This upcoming technology could generate the virtual time machine. Can we and do we want to visit the past as if we were first-hand observers of ancient events? We cannot change the past, but we can understand it more completely. How do we offer users of this crystal ball sufficiently transparent and comprehensible knowledge to trust, interpret and value such complex and malleable results? How much of our work can keep pace with the changing nature of the archaeological evidence constantly being recovered? How much of the success of our visualizations depends on the critical evaluation skills of our audience? We do not want to overly burden the user with tediously detailed and overly technical explanations of processes when it comes to technologies many still consider either fringe or at best frivolous.

It has not been easy to nudge cultural heritage specialists toward acceptance of new technologies, or to convince schools, museums and the general public that problems in software compatibility, changes in hardware specifications and cross-platform non-interoperablity are still minor distractions compared to the benefits that emerge from the use of interactive computer graphics. The virtual heritage discipline needs to move beyond just using 3D images because they are cool; it must integrate the process and the evidence and the decisions. If the discipline cannot take full advantage of all the technology can achieve, then its practitioners are still cutting stone in the shape of plants. Perhaps, as a single voice, the visualization community could send an edict to the cultural heritage community as a whole that a disservice is being done to colleagues, students and the public by not providing justification for the use of new media technologies. In that way perhaps we can increase trust in the adoption and full acceptance of the resulting visualizations, which, in turn, can instil greater confidence in the ability to produce believable interpretations of history rather than mere pretty pictures of the past.

---

11   Free-floating 3D models were demonstrated at SIGGRAPH, Boston 2006; the Metaverse at the Metaverse Roadmap Summit, held at the Stanford Research Inst., Menlo Park, California between 5–6 May 2006.

Chapter 6

A New Introduction to The London Charter

Hugh Denard

Introduction

The London Charter for the Computer-based Visualisation of Cultural Heritage was conceived, in 2006, as a means of ensuring the methodological rigour of computer-based visualization as a means of researching and communicating cultural heritage. Also sought was a means of achieving widespread recognition for this method.

In 2006, Beacham, Denard and Niccolucci published a concise account of the origins and rationale of The London Charter, concentrating on the issue of 'intellectual transparency'.[1] The lack of transparency had been identified, along with the epistemological problems posed by hyperrealism, as a burning issue by scholars from the mid 1990s.[2] An early introduction, subsequently reproduced on

---

1   Richard Beacham, Hugh Denard and Franco Niccolucci, 'An Introduction to The London Charter', in Marinos Ioannides et al. (eds), *The e-volution of Information Communication and Technology in Cultural Heritage*, Proceedings of VAST 2006 (Budapest, 2006), pp. 263–9.

2   Nick Ryan, 'Computer-based Visualization of the Past: Technical "Realism" and Historical Credibility', in Peter Main, Tony Higgins and Janet Lang (eds), *Imaging the Past: Electronic Imaging and Computer Graphics in Museums and Archaeology*, British Museum Occasional Papers, 114 (1996), pp. 95–108; Jonathan C. Roberts and Nick S. Ryan, 'Alternative Archaeological Representations within Virtual Worlds', in Richard Bowden (ed.), *Proceedings of the 4th UK Virtual Reality Specialist Interest Group Conference*, Brunel University, Uxbridge, Middlesex, November (1997), pp. 179 – 88, available at <http://www.cs.kent.ac.uk/people/staff/nsr/arch/vrsig97/vrsig.html>; Franco Niccolucci, 'Virtual Reality in Archaeology: A Useful Tool or a Dreadful Toy?', *Proceedings of the Medi@terra Symposium*, Athens, November (Athens, 1999), pp. 238f.; Glyn Goodrick and Mark Gillings, 'Constructs, Simulations and Hyperreal Worlds: The Role of Virtual Reality (VR) in Archaeological Research', in Gary Lock and Kayt Brown (eds), *On the Theory and Practice of Archaeological Computing* (Oxford, 2000), pp. 41–58; Bernard Frischer, Franco Niccolucci, Nick Ryan and Juan A. Barcelò, 'From CVR to CVRO: The Past, Present, and Future of Cultural Virtual Reality', in Franco Niccolucci (ed.), *Virtual Archaeology* (Oxford, 2002), pp. 7–18; Peter Jablonka, Steffen Kirchner and Jordi Serangeli, 'Troia VR. A Virtual Reality Model of Troy and the Troad', in Martin Doerr and Apostolos Sarris (eds), *The Digital Heritage of Archaeology* (Athens, 2003), pp. 13–20; Maria Roussou and George Drettakis, 'Photorealism and Non-photorealism in Virtual Heritage Representation', in David Arnold, Alan Chalmers and Franco Niccolucci (eds), *Proceedings of VAST2003 Fourth International Symposium on Virtual Reality, Archaeology*

The London Charter website (<http://www.londoncharter.org>), has proven to many readers an essential starting point for understanding both the urgent needs that The London Charter seeks to address and the implications of its principles for those seeking to draw upon them in creating or evaluating computer-based visualizations of cultural heritage. There is a need to reconcile heritage visualization with professional norms of research, particularly the standards of argument and evidence.

Through extensive consultation with expert communities and the ensuing publication of successive drafts, The London Charter has had considerable success in acting as a catalyst for establishing international consensus on the principles that should inform best practice in heritage visualization across disciplines. It is now widely recognized as the de facto benchmark to which heritage visualization processes and outputs should be held accountable. The Charter has been translated into German, Italian, Japanese, Polish and Spanish,[3] and additional translations, including French and Russian, are pending. The Charter has won formal endorsement from national and international bodies including adoption as an official guideline by the Italian Ministry of Culture. It has also been the subject of, and widely cited in, numerous publications and grants have been awarded to study its application. The Charter has also given birth to a new charter, the Seville Charter, which will propose specific London Charter implementation guidelines

---

and Intelligent Cultural Heritage (Aire-La-Ville, 2003), pp. 51–60; Torre Zuk, Sheelagh Carpendale and William D. Glanzaman, 'Visualizing Temporal Uncertainty in 3D Virtual Reconstructions', in Mark Mudge, Nick Ryan, and Roberto Scopigno (eds), *Proceedings of VAST 2005, The 6th International Symposium on Virtual Reality, Archaeology and Cultural Heritage* (Aire-La-Ville, 2003), pp. 99–106; Hugh Denard, ' "At the foot of Pompey's Statue": Reconceiving Rome's *Theatrum Lapideum*', in Alan K. Bowman and Michael Brady (eds), *Images and Artefacts of the Ancient World* (Oxford, 2005), pp.69–76; Sorin Hermon and Franco Niccolucci, 'A Fuzzy Logic Approach to Reliability in Archaeological Virtual Reconstruction', in Franco Niccolucci and Sorin Hermon (eds), *Beyond the Artefact. Digital Interpretation of the Past* (Budapest, 2006), pp. 11–17.

3   *Die Londonder Charta für die Computergestützte Visualizierung von Kulturellem Erbe*, the German-language version of The London Charter (2.1), trans. Susanne Krömker, April 2009; *La Carta Di Londra per la Visualizzazione Digitale dei Beni Culturali*, the Italian-language version of The London Charter (2.1), ed. Enrica Salvatori, November 2009; ロンドン憲章文化遺産の研究とコミュニケーションにおける3次元ビジュア ライゼーション の利用のために, the Japanese-language version of The London Charter, Draft 1.1, trans. Go Sugimoto and Rieko Kadobayashi, November 2007; *Karta Londyńska. Zasady dotyczące komputerowych metod wizualizacji dziedzictwa kulturowego*, the Polish-language version of The London Charter (2.1), ed. and trans. Anna Bentkowska-Kafel, Agnieszka Seidel-Grzesińska and Urszula Wencka, May 2010; *La Carta de Londres para la Visualización Computarizada del Patrimonio Cultural*, the Spanish-language version of The London Charter (2.1), ed. and trans. Alfredo Grande León and Víctor Manuel López-Menchero, November 2009.

for the archaeological community.[4] Both the history of The London Charter and its various translations are freely available online.

The aims of this chapter are: to provide a brief commentary on the current version of The London Charter,[5] which encapsulates the benefits of what has been learned in the few years since the publication of Draft 1.1 of the Charter;[6] to suggest the value of the Charter not only as an indicator of methodological rigour but also as a means of achieving significant efficiencies in teaching and training as well as in the research and communication of cultural heritage; and finally to indicate some of the issues and opportunities that still face the visualization community. What follows is a review of version 2.1 of The London Charter with reference to changes from version 1.1.

Commentary on The London Charter, 2.1

Preamble and Objectives

The Preamble to the Charter notes that 'a set of principles is needed that will ensure that digital heritage visualization is, and is seen to be, at least as intellectually and technically rigorous as longer established cultural heritage research and communication methods'. This notion of demonstrable parity guides much of the thinking underlying the Charter. Previous approaches to this problem were similar in this respect, for example likening the process of archaeological visualization to that of philological textual analysis.[7] The challenge of the scholarly validation of heritage visualization can most simply be illustrated by considering how one evaluates scholarly print publications: authors are expected, as a minimum, to situate their questions and arguments in relation to prior scholarship; to present and assess their sources, duly referenced in footnotes and bibliographies; and to remain within a range of currently acceptable logical and stylistic norms. These criteria draw upon continually evolving conventions that reflect the prevailing assumptions, at any given moment, about (inter alia) the nature and purpose of scholarship as defined by the various disciplines. The inherently linear nature of textual exegesis renders the author's very process of interpretation visible to the

---

4   *The Seville Charter: International Charter for Virtual Archaeology*, revised version, July 2010 published on the International Forum of Virtual Archaeology website, <http://www.arqueologiavirtual.com/forumcronogramaing.php>.

5   The current version 2.1 of The London Charter is available at <http://www.londoncharter.org> and is reproduced in full following this chapter.

6   *The London Charter for the Use of 3D Visualisation in the Research and Communication of Cultural Heritage*, Draft 1.1, June 2006.

7   See, for example, Frischer Bernard, Niccolucci, Franco, Ryan, Nick and Barceló, Juan A., 'From CVR to CVRO: The Past, Present, and Future of Cultural Virtual Reality', in Franco Niccolucci (ed.), *Virtual Archaeology*, Proceedings of the VAST Euroconference, Arezzo, 24–25 November 2000, Bar International Series 1075 (Oxford, 2002), pp. 7–18.

community, which, in turn, allied with the listing of sources, allows the argument to be evaluated.

Consider, by contrast, a visualization. Some subjects, and arguments, do not so readily lend themselves to verbal expression, not only because they may rely on intensive, detailed reference to visual or spatial materials that resist textual description, but because the subject matter and understandings that the author wishes to communicate are inherently non-linear or synthetic – for example, a building or event. If communicating by means of text, the author must force a synchronic perception into a diachronic narrative; that is, must strip the object down into a sequence of layers, to be presented sequentially rather than simultaneously, thereby negating the very cognitive experience that the author ultimately wishes to evoke. In such cases, a visualization – whether static image, real-time model or printed object – might well become the expressive medium of choice, conveying, all at once, the complete, synthetic image of the author's idea.

However, although for certain purposes visualization can exceed text in expressive power, its explanatory value may be less. No matter how thoughtfully a research question is posed in relation to the existing field of knowledge, how painstakingly available sources are researched and interpreted, how discerningly or creatively an argument is elaborated visually, to the viewer, a finished image alone does not reveal the process by which it was created. Even a real-time model, while it allows the user to explore a space in linear time, if it lacks an account of the evaluation of sources or of the process of interpretation, does not, in itself, render the research process visible to the visitor and thus fails to allow the viewer to assess it as part of an argument. Such visualizations, solipsistically adrift in cyberspace, can only slip, unremarked, through the continuum of scholarly discourse. The empirical opacity of the synchronous image, then, is the crisis that threatens to isolate visualizations from meaningful disciplinary dialogue. For a heritage visualization to match the rigour of conventional research, its rigour must be visible. That is why, at the heart of The London Charter is the principle that heritage visualizations: 'should accurately convey to users the status of the knowledge that they represent, such as distinctions between evidence and hypothesis, and between different levels of probability.'

Visibility is also at the centre of the Charter initiative itself: by calling itself a 'Charter' (rather than, say, a co-authored article) the document seeks to draw a certain kind of attention to itself, so that its encapsulation of expert thought on best practice in heritage visualization will be recognized as a common reference point spanning nations and academic and professional contexts. Agreement on an internationally agreed benchmark that insisted on intellectual accountability, it has been realized, could be the single most effective means of enabling heritage visualization methods to become an equal and valued part of communities engaged in the research and communication of human culture. With this in mind, the principles of the Charter are, for the most part, deliberately conservative – no more than a consolidation of existing consensus so that the document might legitimately demand 'wide recognition and an expectation of compliance within relevant subject communities'. Once accepted, its value would be to provide a set of principles that, if adhered to, would virtually guarantee the methodological integrity of a heritage visualization project and act as a common yardstick for professional evaluation – an essential tool enabling the integration of visualization efforts into the process of mainstream peer evaluation and, thereby, scholarly debate.

Indicators of success in establishing the Charter in this role are many and varied. The Charter forms the basis of an EU MINERVA workgroup on standards for the use of 3D technologies in capturing and representing cultural heritage, while Franco Niccolucci, joint chair of The London Charter and Director for Dissemination and Standards of the EU EPOCH Network of Excellence, has written:

> EPOCH considers The London Charter to be one of its most important achievements. The Network believes that this document and the related activity is a much needed milestone as far as the use of 3D visualization in archaeological interpretation, presentation and reconstruction is concerned. After several years of theoretical debate on this issue, the Charter finally proposes robust and authoritative guidelines for this important interdisciplinary subject. Not only has the large EPOCH partnership (90 research, higher education and cultural institutions across Europe) fully accepted and is supporting and implementing the Charter, but also the project reviewers nominated by the European Commission confirmed the validity and usefulness of the policies that the Charter dictates. The Charter has received great attention in EPOCH's Research Agenda Report. Acceptance and support of The London Charter is now spreading beyond the borders of EPOCH.[8]

Between March 2006 and February 2009, *The London Charter for the Use of 3D Visualisation in the Research and Communication of Cultural Heritage* (Draft 1) evolved into *The London Charter for the Computer-based Visualisation of Cultural Heritage* (2.1), reflecting a broadening of scope and ambition. Draft 1's strict focus on '3D visualization' was expanded to encompass 'computer-based visualization' – embracing 2D, 3D, 4D and even hard-copy printouts or computer-generated physical objects such as replicas of museum artefacts. In addition, at a meeting of the Advisory Board in Brighton in November 2007, following much vigorous debate, it was agreed that the Charter should aspire to influence the use of visualizations not only in academic and curatorial contexts, but also in 'those aspects of the entertainment industry involving the reconstruction or evocation of cultural heritage' although omitting 'the use of computer-based visualisation in [..] contemporary art, fashion, or design' (see Preamble). Computer-generated imagery, it was argued, plays an increasingly influential role in shaping public perceptions of the past even when, as so often, it is factually erroneous. Audiences understand that studios are bound to take creative licence. However, such is the persuasive power of visualizations, especially when photorealism is used, that alongside their

---

8   <http://www.londoncharter.org>.

entertainment value, they also often lend an unjustifiable impression of historical accuracy. If we agree – as those with a professional interest in cultural heritage are surely bound to do – that it is a matter of no small importance whether or not a generation's impressions of the past conform to the contours of historical understanding, then it follows that we should take an active role in encouraging and urging the commercial sector to make available, through documentaries and other formats, sufficient information to enable their audiences to distinguish between fact and fiction. An awareness-raising effort of this kind, aiming to raise producers' and audiences' expectations of historical accountability, including an emphasis on the additional frisson that integrity brings to our encounters with the past, would require significant resources and further research. But even in the absence (to date) of a concerted attempt to realize this ambition, this broadening of the scope of the Charter's validity raises numerous questions which are likely to become more, rather than less, publicly and energetically explored in time.

This development also highlights the importance of writing the Charter in a style that is accessible to the widest possible audience, spanning not only a variety of professional and disciplinary contexts, but also all levels of expertise, from the seasoned expert to the general public. This is appropriate given that the Charter addresses issues that affect such diverse stakeholders, from journalists to researchers, and from museum curators to international organizations. This stylistic accessibility is possible because the Charter, rather than making highly specific technical recommendations, addresses methodological issues at quite an abstract level. Having said that, communication across disciplines and languages has presented formidable challenges. A comparative study of the translation issues that The London Charter has encountered, which I shall not attempt here, could deliver fascinating insights into the diversity of cultural approaches that an international Charter relating to cultural heritage must support. Certain key terms such as 'accessibility' and 'sources', for example, mean different things in different academic contexts, and equally crucial concepts, such as 'cultural heritage', 'intellectual transparency' and 'subject communities', have no obvious linguistic or cultural equivalent in different languages. Several of the terminological changes from Draft 1.1 to version 2.1 of the Charter are the result of translators and community members drawing our attention to such issues. Indeed, Principle 3 was renamed 'Research Sources' because of the different connotations the term 'sources' had in humanities disciplines from those in computer science and the other sciences. The effects of this learning process are also registered in Principle 4.9, which draws attention to the importance of making explicit, in an interdisciplinary project, the 'implicit knowledge' that each expert community holds, as well as of 'identifying the different lexica of participating members from diverse subject communities'. The visualization community is deeply indebted to the care and integrity of those who have acted as editors, translators and correspondents in the collaborative search for successful linguistic and cultural analogues for the Charter.

Principle 1: Implementation

In order to retain cross-context relevance, the Charter addresses only fundamental methodological principles that will, by their nature, remain valid even as technologies or technical standards evolve. For this reason, the Charter acknowledges the need for more detailed, discipline- and technology-specific Implementation Guidelines that map out the technical implications of these methodological principles (1.1):

> Each community of practice, whether academic, educational, curatorial or commercial, should develop London Charter Implementation Guidelines that cohere with its own aims, objectives and methods.

One consequence is that one should be able to envisage, in the not too distant future, a definitive text of the Charter. Implementation guidelines, however, will continue to be needed, and revised on an ongoing basis. Daniel Pletinckx's chapter in this volume could be viewed as one guideline of this kind (see Chapter 17). A further example of work on developing implementation guidelines is The Seville Charter, by the International Forum of Virtual Archaeology which, currently at its preliminary draft stage, explicitly aims:

> [...] to increase the conditions of applicability of The London Charter in order to improve its implementation specifically in the field of archaeological heritage, including industrial archaeological heritage, simplifying and organising its bases sequentially, while at the same time offering new recommendations taking into account the specific nature of archaeological heritage in relation to cultural heritage [...][9]

The International Forum of Virtual Archaeology is seeking contributions from international experts working in the field of digital archaeology to ensure that the outcome is a robust, consensus-based document. The Seville Charter initiative is led by Victor Manuel Lopez Menchero Bendicho and Alfredo Grande Leon, with the author and Donald Sanders acting as liaison between the Seville Charter and The London Charter Advisory Boards.

Technologies such as multi-user virtual worlds and the increasing ubiquity of portable devices represent specific challenges to implementation. Addressing these successfully will require a combination of technological and conceptual development. Such work has begun – for example, The London Charter in Second Life (LCSL) project jointly funded by the British Council and the Italian Ministry for Research and Universities which will soon publish a detailed set of guidelines and technical tools for implementing The London Charter in collaborative online

---

9   *The Seville Charter: International Charter for Virtual Archaeology*, revised version, July 2010 published on the International Forum of Virtual Archaeology website <http://www.arqueologiavirtual.com/forumcronogramaing.php>.

environments, and which has also contributed to our understanding of the role that The London Charter can play in education and training.[10]

Having undergone an extensive process of consultation within subject communities, and having achieved significant recognition, The London Charter is well placed to explore formal endorsement by heritage and research funding bodies at a national level, and international organizations including UNESCO and ISO. This will further increase its visibility and influence, and will help to stimulate additional research and the development of implementation guidelines for specific disciplines and methods.

Principle 1.2 of The London Charter states: 'Every computer-based visualisation heritage activity should develop, and monitor the application of, a London Charter Implementation Strategy.' Extensive experience of developing, and helping others to develop Charter implementation plans has unfailingly demonstrated the Charter's value as a coherent conceptual framework that is quickly and easily understandable by people from diverse professional and disciplinary contexts. When used as a set of prompts in the project planning phase, the Charter saves significant amounts of time in designing a robust, structured visualization methodology, and subsequently, during the life of the project, provides a clear and concise agreed reference point for project participants, guaranteeing that the project both is, and is seen to be, methodologically rigorous.

Principle 2: Aims and Methods

The principle that 'a computer-based visualisation method should normally be used only when it is the most appropriate available method for that purpose', while it articulates an enduring and fundamental methodological tenet, can also be seen as the expression of a specific moment of epistemological crisis precipitated by technological change. The London Charter initiative arose as a response to the increasingly widely recognized need to ensure the ever-increasing expressive power of computer graphics become accountable to the rigorous standards of historical research. Those archaeologists, classicists and historians of various denominations who had perceived the enormous potential of digital 3D visualization for fashioning intuitively understandable representations of spatial arguments also, as mentioned above, from the mid 1990s, began to signal, each

---

10   Marco Bani, Francesco Genovesi, Elisa Ciregia, Flavia Piscioneri, Beatrice Rapisarda, Enrica Salvatori and Maria Simi, 'Learning by Creating Historical Buildings', in Judith Molka-Danielsen and Mats Deutschmann (eds*)*, *Learning and Teaching in the Virtual World of Second Life* (Trondheim, 2009); Hugh Denard, Erica Salvatori and Maria Simi, 'Learning by Building in Second Life: Reflections on Interdisciplinary and International Experiences', in Giovanni Vincenti and James Braman (eds*)*, *Multi-User Virtual Environments for the Classroom: Practical Approaches to Teaching in Virtual Worlds* (IGI GLobal, 2011), pp. 134-58; and the King's College London MA Digital Culture and Technology 'Alkedo' project <http://www.cch.kcl.ac.uk/teaching/madct/projects/alkedo/wiki/>.

in their own disciplinary contexts and terms, concern about how this means of representation could so beguilingly elide distinctions between information and speculation.

According to the conventional narrative of the 'evolution' of computer graphics, we were destined to develop increasingly lifelike synthetic simulacra of reality which would, in turn, be experienced in increasingly 'immersive' ways. Indeed, the capacity of 3D computer visualizations to conjoin geometrical information with 'textures' that suggested, or even photographically reproduced, the surface appearance of actual objects, seemed one of the most compelling arguments for the application of computer graphics to the representation of cultural heritage: one day, we dreamed, we might create complete experiences of long-lost places and periods that would be virtually indistinguishable in appearance from actuality. We may at times struggle to distance ourselves from the assumption that methodological advancement is an inevitable sequitur of technological progress, particularly when both our quotidian and our professional lives increasingly rely on and constantly anticipate the emergence of digital technologies. It was a key realization, therefore, that the headlong career towards hyperrealism, photorealism, virtual reality and other such graphical innovations might actually be taking us further away from, not nearer to, accountable knowledge representation. What was needed was a forceful interruption of the flow of teleological assumptions. This realization gave rise to the principle (2.3) that:

> [...] the choice of computer-based visualisation method (e.g. more or less photo-realistic, impressionistic or schematic; representation of hypotheses or of the available evidence; dynamic or static) or the decision to develop a new method, should be based on an evaluation of the likely success of each approach in addressing each aim.

A common misconception is that the Charter prescribes absolute precepts governing which particular method or approach should be used in each given circumstance. Nothing could be further from the truth: the Charter consistently, and insistently, throws the ball back into the court of those about to undertake computer-based heritage visualization, asking them to articulate the particular aims and requirements of each strand of each project, and to make decisions appropriate to each of their specific requirements. Thus, for instance, recognizing that there is a potentially infinite range of valid aims and methods, the Charter asks only that (2.2): 'A systematic, documented evaluation of the suitability of each method to each aim should be carried out, in order to ascertain what, if any, type of computer-based visualisation is likely to prove most appropriate.'

Principle 3: Research Sources

In Principle 3 – which stipulates that, 'in order to ensure the intellectual integrity of computer-based visualisation methods and outcomes, relevant research sources should be identified and evaluated in a structured and documented way' – the comparison with conventional textual scholarship is most in evidence. Visual resources, as Daniel Pletinckx discusses in Chapter 17, pose particular challenges for precisely the same reason that visualizations themselves do: they are inherently non-linear entities that, although they may, as the saying goes, be worth a thousand words, do not tell their own story. Thus (3.3): 'Particular attention should be given to the way in which visual sources may be affected by ideological, historical, social, religious and aesthetic and other such factors.'

Principle 4: Documentation

This principle is a much streamlined form of what, in Draft 1.1, was distributed across three principles ('Transparency Requirements', 'Documentation' and 'Standards'), and its heading-level formulation is in some senses the beating heart of the Charter as a whole, stating: 'Sufficient information should be documented and disseminated to allow computer-based visualisation methods and outcomes to be understood and evaluated in relation to the contexts and purposes for which they are deployed.' The Charter goes on to elucidate the various areas in which documentation should operate in order to (4.2): 'enable rigorous, comparative analysis and evaluation of computer-based visualisations'; (4.4) ensure that audiences can understand what each visualization seeks to represent; (4.5) publish research sources and (4.7) explain the methodological rationale of a visualization. It also makes recommendations on documentation formats and standards (4.11–12).

For the present volume, however, the principle regarding Documentation of Process ('Paradata') is of particular interest (4.6):

> Documentation of the evaluative, analytical, deductive, interpretative and creative decisions made in the course of computer-based visualisation should be disseminated in such a way that the relationship between research sources, implicit knowledge, explicit reasoning, and visualisation-based outcomes can be understood.

Again, this principle necessitates a flexible and relational, rather than rigid and absolute, approach. The Charter emphatically does not provide a checklist of tasks, but rather, in effect, a structured set of prompts that asks us to determine what specific measures are appropriate for each individual project relative to its own particular aims and circumstances. The level of documentation that is appropriate may, for instance, be proportionate to the quality of sources upon which a visualization is based as well as the weight of importance that a visualization has within an argument. Thus, a minimal record may suffice for a speculative visualization based on very limited evidence that aims to do no more than give a sense of the possible approximate size of an artefact, structure or site; whereas a model designed to carry the burden of a detailed reconstruction hypothesis, and which is based on extensive, precise site measurements and a weighty corpus of *comparanda*, will require meticulous documentation of both its sources and interpretative processes if others are to be able to understand and evaluate the quality of the underlying empirical analysis and argument being advanced.

However, documenting 'the evaluative, analytical, deductive, interpretative and creative decisions' is a tall order. As Drew Baker, in Chapter 14 of this volume, shows, no visualization is completely 'objectively' true to fact; despite the aspiration that a 3D model's geometry should be an accurate record of that of the cultural artefact, it is even truer of computer-based visualizations than of photographs that digital surrogates, within the constraints of a particular technology, *represent*, rather than accurately *reproduce*, some aspect of reality. Interpretation is ineluctably involved at every stage: 3D scanning and processing convert the infinitely granular surface of artefacts into point clouds or polygon meshes; digital cameras and video recorders 'capture' analogue waves as binary sequences; while display surfaces – monitors, screens, print illustrations – attempt to convey on two-dimensional planes the impression of three-dimensional space.

Visualization creation involves, and visualization outputs invite, multiple perspectives: technological, optical (including the human eye), cultural, aesthetic (including connoisseurship) and epistemological (within disciplines, but increasingly also within 'intra-disciplines' such as digital humanities or archaeological computing), right down to the real-time model user's choice of path, viewing-point or interaction. In short, visualizations are technical, personal and cultural memory structures, with all the instability that implies, upon which we stage our narratives of the past. Indeed, the whole London Charter is predicated upon the absence of objectivity: tracking the interpretative trail, consensus around methods and representational conventions, are only necessary and meaningful because of the inescapable elusiveness of pure fact.

We are forcibly confronted with this elusiveness when we consider the challenge of documenting dependency relationships. The Charter's glossary defines a dependency relationship as:

> A dependent relationship between the properties of elements within digital models, such that a change in one property will necessitate change in the dependent properties. (For instance, a change in the height of a door will necessitate a corresponding change in the height of the doorframe.)

A visualization is essentially a complex set of dependency relationships, and it is this which makes a visualization at once such a powerful empirical instrument – a means of exploring what the implications of each piece of knowledge might be for each other piece of knowledge – and an entity that is very difficult to render amenable to intellectual accountability. The Charter therefore proposes (4.10):

> Computer-based visualisation outcomes should be disseminated in such a way that the nature and importance of significant, hypothetical dependency

relationships between elements can be clearly identified by users and the reasoning underlying such hypotheses understood.

When this kind of approach is adopted, computer-generated graphics, by enabling us systematically, iteratively and precisely to explore and record the reciprocal interpretative implications of pieces of evidence and hypotheses, remain a uniquely enabling means of constructing knowledge. The spatial specificity that digital visualizations demand, when exploited intelligently and rigorously, far from being a fatal, Siren seduction, becomes a fertile ground of enriched understandings.

The requirement to document process has an impact on working practice that requires consideration, from the lab book's sometimes intrusive interruption of the flow of visual interpretation, to its essential role in providing the detailed record that provides the necessary basis of publication. The Charter proposes that (4.1): 'Documentation strategies should be designed and resourced in such a way that they actively enhance the visualisation activity by encouraging, and helping to structure, thoughtful practice.'

Absorbed by the visualization process, we make an infinite number of moment-by-moment decisions, each shaped by a host of factors, not least the deep, acquired subject and technical knowledge that at any given moment may represent itself to us as little more than 'instinct' – a feeling for what is and what isn't right. As visualizers we need to be as aware as possible of the kinds of decisions that we make on 'instinct' so that we can monitor their validity, but we must also be realistic about what level of detail about the interpretative process it is possible, or even appropriate, to capture. By the same token, as consumers, we must be sophisticated enough to recognize, and accept, the unavoidable role of subjectivity in influencing the style, aesthetics and interpretative choices that we find manifested in heritage visualizations.

A simple reading could view The London Charter as limiting scope for creativity by seeking to tie everything down to the most minute detail. But that would be to forget that heritage visualization is, above all, a hypothesis machine. One may know, for example, that a certain object was part of a greater structure, but lack sufficient information to determine precisely how it fitted into the whole. In such cases, the process of visualization, when documented, gives us in fact greater, not lesser, liberty to try out possibilities, because when a hypothesis is published along with its rationale and evidence base, it acquires a recognizable standard of *methodological* validity. This remains the case even if the visualization output takes the form of an interactive tool rather than a static image or fixed model; one that allows others dynamically to test hypotheses by altering variables within a digital environment. The London Charter encourages manifold interpretative interventions, each being just one of multiple possible stories we might tell about the past. Documentation, while it does not, in itself, legitimize outcomes or conclusions as historical hypotheses, nevertheless allows us to present even highly speculative experiments, and entitles us to expect that they be evaluated on their own terms. Taken further, documented visualization is not only a hypothesis engine, it is an epistemological engine: one that, by licensing ludic intervention as a means of producing knowledge, could ultimately contain the potential to affect our assumptions about the nature, aims and methods of historical research and of the communication of cultural heritage.

Principle 5: Sustainability, and Principle 6: Access

If Principle 4 is the heart of the Charter, then Principles 5 and 6 are its conscience; and if the earlier sections of the Charter represent consensus on achievable best practice, with these two Principles on Sustainability and Access, the Charter steps forward into a space of principled aspiration.

Principle 5, 'Sustainability', draws attention to the fact that computer-based visualizations themselves constitute, in their own right, part of our common 'human intellectual, social, economic and cultural heritage'. Considerable resources, often drawn – directly or indirectly – from the public purse, flow into the creation of heritage visualizations. It therefore behoves the visualization community to behave as good stewards of that investment, both through ensuring that this work is preserved and that it reaches those public audiences to whom it may have genuine value.

Principle 5 therefore stipulates that 'strategies should be planned and implemented to ensure the long-term sustainability of cultural heritage-related computer-based visualisation outcomes and documentation' in order to avoid their loss, and further notes that analogue as well as digital formats should be considered (5.1) depending on which has the best prospects of being successfully sustained.

In a similar vein, Principle 6 advises:

> The creation and dissemination of computer-based visualisation should be planned in such a way as to ensure that maximum possible benefits are achieved for the study, understanding, interpretation, preservation and management of cultural heritage.

These two principles raise all kinds of challenging issues, particularly for the public-funding models that frequently underwrite heritage visualization initiatives. Extensive effort is being made, at present, to develop data models that will enable the integration of 3D content into digital repositories. However, even with such initiatives, the long-term sustainability of digital heritage visualization outputs is far from guaranteed.

Similarly, while national-level public funding bodies tend to concentrate on content creation, and transnational bodies such as the EC invest in the development of new technologies, there remains a critical shortage of funding for promoting the visibility of, access to, and deployment in diverse contexts of visual, digital heritage assets. Principle 6.1 urges stakeholders to consider:

> [...] how such work can enhance access to cultural heritage that is otherwise inaccessible due to health and safety, disability, economic, political, or environmental reasons, or because the object of the visualisation is lost, endangered, dispersed, or has been destroyed, restored or reconstructed.

This gives only a hint of the vast unlocked potential that a well-wrought heritage visualization can have if made available for use in new contexts, including uses beyond those envisaged by its creators. Principle 6.2 further extends the vision, asking us to:

> [...] take cognizance of the types and degrees of access that computer-based visualisation can uniquely provide to cultural heritage stakeholders, including the study of change over time, magnification, modification, manipulation of virtual objects, embedding of datasets, instantaneous global distribution.

There is, partly for this reason, increasing recognition for the need to develop an online index of heritage visualization projects, building for instance on the 3DVisA index by Anna Bentkowska-Kafel (<http://3dvisa.cch.kcl.ac.uk/projectlist.html>), but extending its international coverage in a way that both promotes exemplary London Charter implementation documentation, including through peer review processes, and critically increases the visibility of visualisation projects and their benefits across a range of contexts. Initiatives such as the Virtual Museums Transnational Network (V-MUST), recently funded under the EU 7th Framework Programme, which itself relies on common understandings embodied by The London Charter, are likely to provide vehicles for advancing this kind of work.

As the Charter's methodological principles become increasingly commonly understood and adopted, Sustainability and Access are likely to become increasingly viewed as the central, burning, issues in heritage visualization. Methodological rigour will ensure that heritage visualizations have excellent prospects of being of enduring intrinsic quality; however, it remains for us to take the difficult steps needed to secure their survival and fully to realize their value in a shared future.

Conclusion

This emphasis, at the close of the Charter, on the issue of 'Access' begins to bring us full circle. The London Charter was born out of an anxiety that serious heritage visualization was suffering, in prestige and perceived integrity, by its superficial similarities to computer-generated imagery seen in ahistorical popular games and films. We now find ourselves, however, gravitating towards a, perhaps wiser, recognition of interconnectedness: an observation that computer-based visualizations are valuable in part precisely because they collapse boundaries between the mysteries of rarefied academic research and popular understanding. A visualization may at once embody deep and complex specialist knowledge and at the same time make the contours of that knowledge intuitively accessible to a non-expert audience in a way that a text-based publication never could.

We need collectively to think through the implications of these new parameters, in relation to wider debates about the characteristics and prospects of a 'digital society' and the ways in which the language of 'impact' and 'knowledge transfer' is affecting our professional environments. Our challenge is to shape these exchanges and transactions, and the language we use, in ways that actively enhance the integrity of deep and rigorous scholarly enquiry, including through dialogue with more diverse kinds of stakeholders and audiences than heretofore.

Heritage visualization, as an engine of intensely demanding interdisciplinary research and of lively public engagement, can make a persuasive contribution to the cultivation of popular understanding of the essential role that cultural heritage plays in generating a healthy, changing and self-aware culture. High-integrity, computer-based heritage visualizations can be focal points, equally accessible to all, around which we aggregate debates about what is at stake in the images, experiences and narratives we construct about the past, and by extension the present, of human culture.

Chapter 7

The London Charter for the Computer-based Visualisation of Cultural Heritage (Version 2.1, February 2009)[1]

Preamble

While computer-based visualisation methods are now employed in a wide range of contexts to assist in the research, communication and preservation of cultural heritage, a set of principles is needed that will ensure that digital heritage visualisation is, and is seen to be, at least as intellectually and technically rigorous as longer established cultural heritage research and communication methods. At the same time, such principles must reflect the distinctive properties of computer-based visualisation technologies and methods.

Numerous articles, documents, including the AHDS Guides to Good Practice for CAD (2002) and Virtual Reality (2002) and initiatives, including the Virtual Archaeology Special Interest Group (VASIG) and the Cultural Virtual Reality Organisation (CVRO) and others have underlined the importance of ensuring both that computer-based visualisation methods are applied with scholarly rigour, and that the outcomes of research that include computer-based visualisation should accurately convey to users the status of the knowledge that they represent, such as distinctions between evidence and hypothesis, and between different levels of probability.

The London Charter seeks to capture, and to build, a consensus on these and related issues in a way that demands wide recognition and an expectation of compliance within relevant subject communities. In doing so, the Charter aims to enhance the rigour with which computer-based visualisation methods and outcomes are used and evaluated in heritage contexts, thereby promoting understanding and recognition of such methods and outcomes.

The Charter defines principles for the use of computer-based visualisation methods in relation to intellectual integrity, reliability, documentation, sustainability and access.

---

1 See Chapter 6 here and The London Charter website <http://www.londoncharter. org> for the history of this document, its translations into other languages and further information about this international initiative. The definitions of terms used in The London Charter can be found in the glossary at the end of this volume.

The Charter recognizes that the range of available computer-based visualisation methods is constantly increasing, and that these methods can be applied to address an equally expanding range of research aims. The Charter therefore does not seek to prescribe specific aims or methods, but rather establishes those broad principles for the use, in research and communication of cultural heritage, of computer-based visualisation upon which the intellectual integrity of such methods and outcomes depend.

The Charter is concerned with the research and dissemination of cultural heritage across academic, educational, curatorial and commercial domains. It has relevance, therefore, for those aspects of the entertainment industry involving the reconstruction or evocation of cultural heritage, but not for the use of computer-based visualisation in, for example, contemporary art, fashion, or design. As the aims that motivate the use of visualisation methods vary widely from domain to domain, Principle 1: 'Implementation', signals the importance of devising detailed guidelines appropriate to each community of practice.

Objectives

The London Charter seeks to establish principles for the use of computer-based visualisation methods and outcomes in the research and communication of cultural heritage in order to:

- Provide a benchmark having widespread recognition among stakeholders.
- Promote intellectual and technical rigour in digital heritage visualisation.
- Ensure that computer-based visualisation processes and outcomes can be properly understood and evaluated by users
- Enable computer-based visualisation authoritatively to contribute to the study, interpretation and management of cultural heritage assets.
- Ensure access and sustainability strategies are determined and applied.
- Offer a robust foundation upon which communities of practice can build detailed London Charter Implementation Guidelines.

Principles

PRINCIPLE 1: IMPLEMENTATION

The principles of The London Charter are valid wherever computer-based visualisation is applied to the research or dissemination of cultural heritage.

1.1 Each community of practice, whether academic, educational, curatorial or commercial, should develop London Charter Implementation Guidelines that cohere with its own aims, objectives and methods.

1.2 Every computer-based visualisation heritage activity should develop, and monitor the application of, a London Charter Implementation Strategy.

1.3 In collaborative activities, all participants whose role involves either directly or indirectly contributing to the visualisation process should be made aware of the principles of The London Charter, together with relevant Charter Implementation Guidelines, and to assess their implications for the planning, documentation and dissemination of the project as a whole.

1.4 The costs of implementing such a strategy should be considered in relation to the added intellectual, explanatory and/or economic value of producing outputs that demonstrate a high level of intellectual integrity.

PRINCIPLE 2: AIMS AND METHODS

A computer-based visualisation method should normally be used only when it is the most appropriate available method for that purpose.

2.1 It should not be assumed that computer-based visualisation is the most appropriate means of addressing all cultural heritage research or communication aims.

2.2 A systematic, documented evaluation of the suitability of each method to each aim should be carried out, in order to ascertain what, if any, type of computer-based visualisation is likely to prove most appropriate.

2.3 While it is recognized that, particularly in innovative or complex activities, it may not always be possible to determine, *a priori*, the most appropriate method, the choice of computer-based visualisation method (e.g. more or less photo-realistic, impressionistic or schematic; representation of hypotheses or of the available evidence; dynamic or static) or the decision to develop a new method, should be based on an evaluation of the likely success of each approach in addressing each aim.

Principle 3: Research Sources

In order to ensure the intellectual integrity of computer-based visualisation methods and outcomes, relevant research sources should be identified and evaluated in a structured and documented way.

> 3.1 In the context of the Charter, research sources are defined as all information, digital and non-digital, considered during, or directly influencing, the creation of computer-based visualisation outcomes.
> 3.2 Research sources should be selected, analysed and evaluated with reference to current understandings and best practice within communities of practice.
> 3.3 Particular attention should be given to the way in which visual sources may be affected by ideological, historical, social, religious and aesthetic and other such factors.

Principle 4: Documentation

Sufficient information should be documented and disseminated to allow computer-based visualisation methods and outcomes to be understood and evaluated in relation to the contexts and purposes for which they are deployed.
Enhancing Practice

> 4.1 Documentation strategies should be designed and resourced in such a way that they actively enhance the visualisation activity by encouraging, and helping to structure, thoughtful practice.
> 4.2 Documentation strategies should be designed to enable rigorous, comparative analysis and evaluation of computer-based visualisations, and to facilitate the recognition and addressing of issues that visualisation activities reveal.
> 4.3 Documentation strategies may assist in the management of Intellectual Property Rights or privileged information.

Documentation of Knowledge Claims

> 4.4 It should be made clear to users what a computer-based visualisation seeks to represent, for example the existing state, an evidence-based restoration or an hypothetical reconstruction of a cultural heritage object or site, and the extent and nature of any factual uncertainty.

Documentation of Research Sources

4.5 A complete list of research sources used and their provenance should be disseminated.

Documentation of Process (Paradata)

4.6 Documentation of the evaluative, analytical, deductive, interpretative and creative decisions made in the course of computer-based visualisation should be disseminated in such a way that the relationship between research sources, implicit knowledge, explicit reasoning, and visualisation-based outcomes can be understood.

Documentation of Methods

4.7 The rationale for choosing a computer-based visualisation method, and for rejecting other methods, should be documented and disseminated to allow the activity's methodology to be evaluated and to inform subsequent activities.
4.8 A description of the visualisation methods should be disseminated if these are not likely to be widely understood within relevant communities of practice.
4.9 Where computer-based visualisation methods are used in interdisciplinary contexts that lack a common set of understandings about the nature of research questions, methods and outcomes, project documentation should be undertaken in such a way that it assists in articulating such implicit knowledge and in identifying the different lexica of participating members from diverse subject communities
.

Documentation of Dependency Relationships

4.10 Computer-based visualisation outcomes should be disseminated in such a way that the nature and importance of significant, hypothetical dependency relationships between elements can be clearly identified by users and the reasoning underlying such hypotheses understood.

Documentation Formats and Standards

4.11 Documentation should be disseminated using the most effective available media, including graphical, textual, video, audio, numerical or combinations of the above.
4.12 Documentation should be disseminated sustainably with reference to relevant standards and ontologies according to best practice in relevant communities of practice and in such a way that facilitates its inclusion in relevant citation indexes.

PRINCIPLE 5: SUSTAINABILITY

Strategies should be planned and implemented to ensure the long-term sustainability of cultural heritage-related computer-based visualisation outcomes and documentation, in order to avoid loss of this growing part of human intellectual, social, economic and cultural heritage.

5.1 The most reliable and sustainable available form of archiving computer-based visualisation outcomes, whether analogue or digital, should be identified and implemented.

5.2 Digital preservation strategies should aim to preserve the computer-based visualisation data, rather than the medium on which they were originally stored, and also information sufficient to enable their use in the future, for example through migration to different formats or software emulation.

5.3 Where digital archiving is not the most reliable means of ensuring the long-term survival of a computer-based visualisation outcome, a partial, two-dimensional record of a computer-based visualisation output, evoking as far as possible the scope and properties of the original output, should be preferred to the absence of a record.

5.4 Documentation strategies should be designed to be sustainable in relation to available resources and prevailing working practices.

PRINCIPLE 6: ACCESS

The creation and dissemination of computer-based visualisation should be planned in such a way as to ensure that maximum possible benefits are achieved for the study, understanding, interpretation, preservation and management of cultural heritage.

6.1 The aims, methods and dissemination plans of computer-based visualisation should reflect consideration of how such work can enhance access to cultural heritage that is otherwise inaccessible due to health and safety, disability, economic, political, or environmental reasons, or because the object of the visualisation is lost, endangered, dispersed, or has been destroyed, restored or reconstructed.

6.2 Projects should take cognizance of the types and degrees of access that computer-based visualisation can uniquely provide to cultural heritage stakeholders, including the study of change over time, magnification, modification, manipulation of virtual objects, embedding of datasets, instantaneous global distribution.

PART II
Data Interpretation:
Methods and Tools

Chapter 8
Walking with Dragons: CGIs in Wildlife 'Documentaries'

Mark Carnall

Introduction

Computer-generated imagery (CGI) is now widely used in film, television and in virtual worlds in video games for both entertainment and education purposes. It is pertinent to look at the wider use of CGI before examining the applications of similar techniques for programmes in the specific context of heritage.

Science fiction television shows, such as *Primeval*[1] and *Doctor Who*,[2] regularly use special CGI effects to create believable villains and exciting action sequences. Computer-animated children's television shows such as *Reboot*[3] and *Roughnecks: Starship Troopers Chronicles*[4] mean that there is now a generation who grew up with computer-generated animation. Adult audience dramatizations such as the acclaimed series, *Rome*, use CGI to create a believable living and breathing ancient city.[5] News programmes regularly use digital imagery to illustrate topics, for example by recreating crime scenes, showing the inner workings of weather systems or replicating the sequences of events in war zones.

In film CGI has been widely used for special effects and to create entirely virtual cast members, as in the new *Star Wars* and *Lord of the Rings* trilogies. In addition to using it to support real actors' performances, a number of films are shot entirely in CGI. Box office success of films like *Toy Story*[6], *Final Fantasy VII Advent Children*[7] and *Beowulf*[8] underpin the acceptance of CGI in the public sphere. The increased use of CGI over traditional animation by studios like Disney indicates a shift in audiences' expectation from media and a possible preference for computer-generated images. An increase in familiarity coupled with ever-

---

1   *Primeval*, prod. Cameron McAllister and Tim Haines (2007).

2   *Doctor Who series 4*, prod. Phil Collinson and Susie Liggat (2007).

3   *Reboot*, exec. prod. Jay Firestone (1994).

4   *Roughnecks: Starship Troopers Chronicles*, dir. Andre Clavel (1999).

5   *Rome*, dir. Michael Apted, Allen Coulter, Alan Poul, Steve Shill, Timothy Van Patten, Alan Taylor and John Maybury (2005).

6   *Toy Story*, dir. John Lasseter (1999).

7   *Final Fantasy VII: Advent Children*, dir. Tetsuya Nomura and Takeshi Nozue (2006).

8   *Beowulf*, dir. Robert Zemeckis (2007).

decreasing costs and availability of CGI technology is the reason why traditional animation has all but been replaced in cinematic features.

Video games and virtual worlds are an ever-increasing presence in modern life and, tellingly, a 1995 survey showed that American children could more readily recognize Mario from the *Super Mario Brothers* series of video games than Disney's own Mickey Mouse.[9] In the UK, at least a third of the population aged between sixteen and forty-nine have been exposed to CGI in video games in the form of interactive play and through full motion video (FMV), non-playable cinematic sequences used for character exposition and storytelling.[10] Artists have adopted CGI in video games as a new communicative medium. The increased availability of relatively cheap but effective movie-making tools in virtual worlds has led to the recognition of machinima as its own genre of film.[11] It is now possible to make a CGI feature-length film with a personal computer and video-game software. The product can be made widely and freely available through the internet, bypassing television and cinema outlets altogether. Notable examples include the long-running *Red vs. Blue*[12] series, the feature-length *Borg War*[13] and the early machinima *Diary of a Camper*.[14]

Virtual Natural History

The various media mentioned above help to set the context of this examination of the use of CGI in wildlife 'documentaries' where the subjects of the documentaries are animals and places that have long ceased to exist. These documentaries are presented in a similar format to wildlife documentaries featuring extant animals in their natural environments. Although there is some intersection with fiction-based entertainment, audiences will not be expecting CGIs of a high fidelity and scientific accuracy in films such as *Ice Age*[15] or Disney's *Dinosaur*;[16] both films feature talking anthropomorphised animals interacting anachronistically with each other. There is more overlap with films such as *Jurassic Park*,[17] which draws on scientific information to reconstruct prehistoric creatures. However, the grounding

---

9   Akurosa Henshūshitsu, *Sekai Shōhin no Tsukurikata: Nihon Media ga Sekai o Sesshita hi* (Tokyo, 1995), pp. 41–2.

10   Nielsen Games, *Video Gamers in Europe – 2008* (2008), p. 5.

11   Machinima is a form of making films and other works using in-game engines and some post-processing software.

12   *Red vs. Blue: The Blood Gulch Chronicles*, dir. Burnie Burns and Matt Hullum (2003).

13   *Borg War*, dir. Geoffrey James (2006).

14   *Diary of a Camper*, dir. Matthew Van Sickler (1996).

15   *Ice Age*, dir. Chris Wedge and Carlos Saldanha (2002).

16   *Dinosaur*, dir. Eric Leighton and Ralph Zondag (2000).

17   *Jurassic Park*, dir. Steven Spielberg (1993).

of the film within a fictional story and the interplay between computer models and real actors excludes it from examination here.

CGI is an obvious tool to use when representing and reconstructing extinct organisms. These organisms are no longer around for filming and much of what we know about them comes from fossilized remains, preserved trackways and traces (ichnology), nesting sites and occasionally frozen or mummified hair and flesh. The relative paucity of data for each species and genera of extinct organisms, with few exceptions, means that any reconstruction will be highly interpretive. The use of CGI as a form of representation itself is not under critical examination. Of concern here is the use of CGI to produce a documentary that looks and sounds like a contemporary wildlife documentary and is presented as of educational value.

Before CGI

There is undoubtedly some editing of film sequences when producing traditional wildlife documentaries featuring live animals. Baited traps are often set up so that cameras can capture a particular activity, and in the past animals were captured and set up to show behaviour. In his autobiography *Life on Air*, David Attenborough recounts the ordeal of forcing a flying snake to fly for the cameras in a wildlife documentary.[18] These techniques are employed to show behaviour that has been documented in the scientific literature and some animals require encouraging to perform signature feats. Irrespective of the reliability of what the animals are doing on screen, the animals themselves are real and the environments in which they are filmed are real.

This is in contrast to the BBC series *Walking with Dinosaurs* (*WWD*)[19] and similar documentaries that bring extinct dinosaurs, pterosaurs, mammals and marine reptiles to life using computer-generated graphics. The computer models are superimposed over footage of real environments and complemented with puppetry and animatronics to show details that are hard to replicate digitally and to further the sense of realism. More recent productions, such as National Geographic's *Sea Monsters: A Prehistoric Adventure*,[20] are graphically superior to previous CGI productions, but continue on the palaeontological theme, focusing on resurrecting extinct marine reptiles. These CGI documentaries, of which *WWD* was one of the first, are produced to look like more traditional wildlife documentaries, with a narrator describing the events on screen as if they are unfolding in real time and as if the animals never disappeared from this planet. The state-of-the-art technology is used in such a way as to deliberately create a sense of 'Uncanny Valley' realism. This blurred line of distinction between the real and virtual is intentional. In palaeobiology it is a shift away from documentary programmes that

---

18 David Attenborough, *Life on Air* (2003), pp. 250–52.
19 *Walking with Dinosaurs*, exec. prod. John Lynch (1999).
20 *Sea Monsters: A Prehistoric Adventure*, dir. Sean MacLeod Phillips (2007).

focus on museum skeletons and renowned palaeontologists explaining theories through recent exciting discoveries.

Impact and Reception

With a new take on the traditional palaeobiological documentary, *WWD* and successive CGI documentaries continue to be highly popular. The original *WWD* series won a host of awards including an Emmy award for Outstanding Achievement in Non-Fiction and BAFTA TV awards for Innovation. The series received a number of nominations, notably in documentary or factual programme categories. A book of the series was produced, as was extensive merchandise. Newspapers included special *WWD* supplements and pullout posters. Three following series were made: *Walking with Beasts*,[21] *Walking with Monsters*[22] and *Walking with Cavemen*,[23] as well as a number of television specials and spin-offs, including *The Ballad of Big Al*[24] and *Prehistoric Park*.[25] A live touring theatrical adaptation featuring life-sized animatronic dinosaurs was created in 2007. In the same year, *Walking with Beasts* was made into a touring museum exhibition, of interest in its own right, and appeared at the Horniman Museum in London. The series has been viewed by millions of people and, after the third episode aired in the UK, *WWD* became, for a period, the most watched science programme of all time.[26] The series' sequels and spin-offs also enjoyed similar success but the imagination of the public was truly captured by the first series. Following the success of these series, a number of similar CGI documentaries have been produced by other production companies, including *Sea Monsters: A Prehistoric Adventure*,[27] and many of the techniques and similar computer models were used in *Dinotopia*,[28] *Primeval*[29] and other science-fiction series. CGI has been incorporated into conventional wildlife documentaries alongside real footage, as in the BBC *Life in Cold Blood*,[30] to show the inner workings of reptiles in real time. CGI techniques are now a staple tool in the reality-based wildlife documentary makers' repertoire alongside more accepted techniques, such as thermal imaging and time-lapsed sequences.

---

21 *Walking with Beasts*, dir. Nigel Patterson (2001).
22 *Walking with Monsters*, dir. Tim Haines and Chloe Leland (2005).
23 *Walking with Cavemen*, dir. Richard Dale and Pierre de Lespinois (2003).
24 *The Ballad of Big Al*, writ. Kate Bartlett and Michael Olmert (2001).
25 *Prehistoric Park*, dir. Sid Bennett, Karen Kelly and Matthew Thompson (2006).
26 BBC News, 'Entertainment Ratings Record for Dino Saga', <http://news.bbc.co.uk/1/hi/entertainment/480284.stm> (October 1999).
27 *Sea Monsters: A Prehistoric Adventure*, Philips (2007).
28 *Dinotopia*, dir. Marco Brambilla (2002).
29 *Primeval*, exec. prod. McAllister and Haines (2007).
30 *Life in Cold Blood*, exec. prod. Sara Ford (2008).

Factual Inaccuracies

Despite the clear success of the series, there were also some shortcomings. A number of factual mistakes exist in all of the *Walking with ...* programmes in reconstructing the ancient beasts:

1. Species were seen side by side in the programme yet the remains of these species have been discovered continents apart, and others are separated by millions of years. *Rhinesuchus* and *Scutosaurus* are portrayed as co-geographic although the former is known from South African fossils remains and the latter is known only from Russian fossils
2. Some species were reconstructed in environments in which they have not been found. *Velociraptor* was reconstructed in wooded areas in *WWD* although its discovered remains are mostly from arid and dune palaeoenvironments.
3. Some species were reconstructed correctly at the time of production but subsequently further discoveries have challenged these conceptions. Discoveries in China, for example, show that feathers are more than likely to be a basal characteristic in a large group of dinosaurs, which means that animals like *Tyrannosaurus*, *Velociraptor* and *Troodon*, which appear in a number of the series as scaly, should have been covered in feathers.
4. Some creatures were mysteriously scaled up for the programme. There is certainly an element of doubt when estimating the size of some prehistoric creatures, especially in species known from partial remains, but the scaling in these documentaries was outside the realm of reasonable assumption. Marine reptiles such as *Liopleurodon* and *Tylosaurus* were overestimated by some 40 feet and 20 feet respectively.
5. A number of species were incorrectly placed within phylogenies in the narration. This was, presumably, so that they could be mentioned as ancestors of later groups of animals to keep the narrative of the story flowing more smoothly and coherently.

Some of these errors were later corrected in reworked versions and international releases. However, localization of the series' script incorporated further inaccuracies and errors. The 2000 American release of *WWD* made the unforgivable (and hackneyed) error of using the invalid name *Brontosaurus* instead of *Apatosaurus*. It was claimed that at least three organisms were the largest of their kind/time; this is not supported by current palaeontological consensus.

A number of the mistakes listed above are not outside the realm of possibility, but some are beyond the acceptable limits of probability. It is the very nature of the science that as soon as work is published it becomes outdated with the discovery of new fossil material. A number of the mistakes can be seen to be pragmatic. In the *Walking with ...* programmes, it is necessary to choose a single conclusion out of a number of possible solutions in order to make an engaging television programme that holds together within the narrative style of presentation. The potential for ambiguity is high when calculating the size of extinct creatures. Estimates will vary considerably based on the material available and the analogue species that are used to calculate comparative sizes. This highlights how difficult it can be to make CGI documentaries about extinct organisms, especially when presenting theories where there is no unanimous consensus. Some issues in palaeontology remain contentious until empirically supported by fossil evidence. A paradigm shift may still take a number of years to become accepted. Interpretation of issues where fossil evidence does not exist will be open to debate, and observational subjectivity will necessarily continue to infiltrate the science.

Quantifying and Qualifying Doubt

The issue of intellectual transparency is key when using CGI reconstructions because full transparency cannot be presented without undermining the illusion of 'reality'. An intellectual transparency cannot be achieved without providing audiences with a wealth of information that detracts from the dramatic reconstructions.

In the context of CGI documentaries, it is not within the remit of the documentary makers to provide paradata. Scientific accuracy and educational value are only two factors that contribute to the production of a documentary and these are dependent on other factors such as broad appeal, budgeting constraints and market competition. These programmes might be promoted as 'edutainment', but this does not mean they have to be underpinned by critical review of their content analogously with peer-reviewed scientific publications. Formerly, the scientific accuracy and transparency of palaeobiology programmes was regulated because palaeontologists would appear on screen. They would not wish to undermine their scientific credibility by proposing theories that were not supported by fact. *The Walking with* ... series was produced with advice from a team of established palaeontologists. However, in order to draw the series together, a number of artistic interpretations uninformed by science were made. It is interesting, then, to consider that *WWD* received so many awards and nominations within the category of non-fiction programmes and documentaries.

Providing Transparency

Looking to the future, if CGI techniques are to be embraced within formal education and incorporated into museum displays, it is prudent to look at how paradata can be presented. This is in order to ensure that:

- CGI media can be compared and contrasted with each other;
- the production has value beyond its original context;
- documentary makers can be held accountable for any subjective assertions made.

Without transparency of source information it is not clear if the mistakes listed above are accidental errors, unique interpretations or current scientific thought deliberately misconstrued for dramatic affect. Without data sources clearly stated, what is represented as scientific fact cannot be distinguished from science fiction. As such, there is little evidence that can be used to differentiate *WWD* programmes from programmes such as *The Last Dragon*,[31] a 'documentary' about the palaeontology and history of dragons.

A critical examination of how to present paradata can also be applied outside the realm of CGI documentaries. Many museum displays are partially reconstructed or fabricated altogether. Although dinosaur galleries and animatronic displays remain popular, their grounding in facts is not often fully exposed. Historically, this transparency was paramount. In 1835, a Select Committee of the Houses of Commons was formed to investigate the British Museum for, amongst other charges, questions about the authenticity of some of the public displays of fossil material.[32] A large collection of marine reptiles purchased at great cost featured a number of organisms with skilfully reconstructed limbs, skulls and tails that were not as clearly highlighted as they could have been before the purchase. These specimens are still on display today in the Marine Reptile Gallery of the Natural History Museum London, but with clearer indications of the extent of the nineteenth-century fabrications.

There is also an educational value in communicating the difficulties in making interpretations based on evidence in fields of palaeobiology and archaeology. The Crystal Palace dinosaurs in Sydenham, London are a testament to how palaeontological reconstructions considered accurate at the time can be quite wrong. The Crystal Palace dinosaurs still give today's visitors a lot of information, and demonstrate how science does not always have the correct answers. Some of the earlier CGI documentaries have already become outdated by discoveries in palaeontology. The programmes still have use in recording the scientific thought of their time, but their historical value would be significantly increased if the sources for the interpretations were made apparent.

Illusion Shattering

Existing CGI documentaries do make efforts to remind audiences that what they are seeing may be an artistic interpretation of available data. In the *Walking with*

---

31 *The Last Dragon*, dir. Justin Hardy (2004).
32 Christopher McGowan, *The Dragon Seekers* (2003), pp. 150–53.

... series there are several artistic touches that break the 'fourth wall' and remind the audience that they are not watching real-life events unfold on screen. In *WWD*, a *Tyrannosaurus'* spittle covers the 'camera lens' in one sequence and other organisms appear to sniff, bump or break the camera lens in other parts of the series. This serves to remind the audience that they are not watching life unfold but are watching a supposed recording of prehistoric life. Quite how the camera crew travelled back in time to film events is never explored.

In *Walking with Monsters*,[33] the virtual reality is momentarily shattered during time-lapsed sequences that show the protagonists from one period evolve into another in the space of a few seconds. Unfortunately, many of the factual errors are made during the narration of these sequences, which undermines the effort.

National Geographic's cinematic production *Sea Monsters: A Prehistoric Adventure*[34] is more practical about the artistic licence used and includes a disclaimer during the opening credits, stating that some animals are shown together although they are not thought to have been coeval.

Many CGI documentaries are complemented by 'making of' featurettes. Often these take the format of more traditional scientific programmes featuring scientists discussing the science behind the interpretations. However, the opportunity to source the information used or to highlight contentious reconstructions is often focused on the innovative visualization technologies themselves.

Further Transparency

All of the above techniques are used with some success to remind the audience that what they are watching is a skilfully created programme which draws on scientific data but which is not necessarily bound by them. The following suggestions are three potential ways in which intellectual transparency may be conserved when using CGI technologies and visualization in wildlife documentaries and factual programmes.

Showing Paradata

Although there are a number of other wildlife documentaries that use visualization techniques and computer models, *WWD* will be used as a case study here, as it is the series that was groundbreaking in using the technique and it is probably familiar to readers of this chapter.

---

33   *Walking with Monsters*, dir. Haines and Leland (2005).
34   *Sea Monsters: A Prehistoric Adventure*, Philips (2007).

Alternative Media

In addition to toys and fashion wear, a number of books were released following *WWD*. As a medium, the book allows for a greater exposition of material and a deeper examination of themes, as well as consideration of ideas outside a central narrative. Television programmes are not an interactive medium. Typically, they are structured to be cogently consumed when viewed from beginning to end in order to provide a satisfactory narrative.[35] This linear direction of television programmes requires that few diversions or distractions are made. It also means that a wide range of topics may be covered but not in any great depth. Books, typically reference books, which accompany these series, provide an opportunity to address some of the content and issues that could not be covered in the television series. The more established modes of referencing and showing paradata also allow interested readers to follow up investigations and draw their own conclusions using primary source data. There were two main books produced following the *WWD* series and they present the information in two contrasting ways.

Books Accompanying the Series

Walking with Dinosaurs: A Natural History[36] is an official companion book which firmly places itself within the reality of the series. The book is largely written in the third person, as if describing events as they are happening. For example, the author describes the daily behaviours and interactions of a group of *Utahraptors*.[37] There is little attempt to highlight from where this information is drawn, although the known evidence for each organism is listed.[38] There is no further indication of why particular interpretations are preferred or which material forms the basis of the reconstructions. The book lists only twenty references, many of which are general textbooks and encyclopedias; no specific references are made in the body of the text.

This is in part remedied by another book accompanying the series, *Walking with Dinosaurs: The Evidence*.[39] This publication, written by some of the palaeontologists who worked on the series, shows readers where the information to support reconstructions comes from and – most importantly – the difficulties involved in drawing solid conclusions from evidence that can lead to multi-theory hypotheses. Written in accessible language, it is an intermediary between the intellectually inaccessible primary material and the easily accessible programme itself. It is a good accompaniment to the programme for those wishing to delve

---

35   CD-ROMs, DVD and Blu-ray Disc may be exceptions: see this chapter, pp. 90–91.
36   Tim Haines, *Walking With Dinosaurs: A Natural History* (1999).
37   Ibid., pp. 182–7.
38   Ibid., p. 159.
39   David Martill and Darren Naish, *Walking with Dinosaurs: The Evidence* (2001).

further into the science behind *WWD*. This source is where the paradata for the programme are given. The book does not address each instance in which artistic interpretation is used, but acts as a good guide to further understanding of how design choices were made and to their scientific foundation.

The paradata are partially recorded and anyone wishing critically to examine or use *WWD* in future reconstructions or education can make a good start with the references above. However, the paradata presented in book form is a step removed from the programme. The books and the series are physically separated from each other and the paradata have a financial cost. Ideally, it is desirable to have the paradata intimately linked with the documentary itself for purposes of ease of reference and for data archiving. For television programmes available on commercial release, the best and natural place for paradata to be stored and accessed is on the disc with the documentary.

Digital Versatile Disc (DVD) and Blu-ray Disc Features

DVD and Blu-ray Disc are now the main formats in which many people buy visual media. Many DVDs include extra features that supplement the main programme. Commentaries, featurettes and other common extra features have obvious potential for revealing paradata with the benefit of only being a few remote-control clicks away from the documentary itself. Less commonly used features could be used more to show paradata.

Some DVDs allow audiences to cut away to a featurette or information box when visual anchors appear on screen and are selected using the remote control. This has obvious uses for CGI documentaries as audiences could view information pertaining to the reconstruction they have just seen on screen.

New technologies such as Blu-ray Disc and hypervideo will allow further exploration of these embedding techniques to show paradata as both formats have expanded data storage and transfer capacity beyond that of DVD. Coupled with the wider availability of broadband internet, these formats have a greatly increased potential: Blu-ray Disc works with Java, rather than pre-rendered mpegs used on DVDs. This allows Blu-ray Discs to be updated with information from the internet. This not only allows further information to be kept up to date (an appealing feature in the field of palaeontology, where theories can radically changed depending on new research and discoveries) but it also allows for the documentary to link to other media. Hypervideo is video that contains embedded material that can be viewed by clicking on a visible anchor. In theory, this would enable a viewer of *WWD* to click on a visible anchor to see alternative versions and even source data themselves. Viewers would be able to watch an episode of *WWD*, click on an anchor and go through to the same episode with every artistic representation or contentious point edited out or highlighted in a different colour. Viewers could watch the sequence showing *Tyrannosauruses* with or without feathers. They could watch sequences at any stage of the editing process to show wire-frame models or even storyboards. In the future, videos could even be linked to museum databases and archives to show what material of particular animals has actually been discovered. It would allow viewers themselves to assess whether or not the reconstruction is valid.

These techniques are highly appealing because they allow for seamless integration of paradata with the documentary. Viewers would be able to examine the scientific, artistic and cultural influences of reconstructions as well as the technical data and metadata associated with CGI models themselves. They would have immediate access to interviews and commentaries by documentary makers and the scientific advisers, written media, alternative versions of the documentary and other data sources. In the future, viewers may be able to make these links themselves, creating an all-encompassing web of information held together by the aspects of the documentary.

The technique for using hypervideo has been around since the 1980s and Blu-ray Discs are already commercially available. However, both formats are still in the very early stages of development and have yet to be fully exploited. Hopefully, documentary makers of all kinds will use these hyperlinked, updateable features in order to make paradata readily available to all who wish to access them.

Virtual Worlds

So far it has been seen how paradata can be represented in books and journals, and how paradata may be represented now and in the future with multimedia formats. Perhaps the best way to allow freedom of information and interpretation would be to give people the tools to make their own reconstructions and learn what may or may not be valid through undertaking the modelling process. The ideal format for this technique is to use virtual worlds and virtual editing platforms.

The process of making CGI documentaries is very different from that of making a video game or virtual world but the gap between the quality of visuals generated is closing. Some of today's video games far exceed the quality of the visuals in the original *WWD*. Video games and CGI media share an ancestry and both *WWD* and *Sea Monsters: A Prehistoric Adventure* have been turned into interactive games. *Dinosaur World* is a free downloadable video game where players can investigate and interact with some of the organisms seen in *WWD* and it is still available for download through the BBC website.[40] The video game *Sea Monsters: A Prehistoric Adventure* has been released on the Nintendo DS, Nintendo Wii and PlayStation 2.[41] Players play as the film's star creatures move in a free-form underwater world populated by other marine organisms. The increase in the quality of computer game graphics combined with the ever-increasing connectivity afforded by the

---

40   *Dinosaur World*, <http://www.bbc.co.uk/sn/prehistoric_life/games/dinosaur_world/> (accessed September 2010).

41   *Sea Monsters: A Prehistoric Adventure,* DSI Games (2008).

spread of mobile devices, broadband and wi-fi means that virtual worlds in video games have a great potential to be exploited to enable everyone with an internet connection to contribute to real-world science.

Palaeontological and archaeological 3D modellers already use rudimentary virtual worlds in computer-modelling research techniques. Measured data are entered into a computer and then the results are modelled visually within a virtual environment. The models are relatively simple and the rules of the platform are tailored to the feature that is being explored. For example, palaeontologists wishing to work out how bipedal dinosaurs ran will model the legs, a tail as a counterweight and a horizontal surface. The computer will then run several thousand 'evolutions' until the model satisfactorily completes the task – in this case running without falling over. This model will then be taken as evidence that this is how bipedal dinosaurs ran until further discoveries or research indicates that other factors contribute to the research question. The model is then updated with more rules and models and the model is run again. With an increase in the use, popularity and quality of virtual worlds, these kinds of model and tool are made available to everyone, not just research scientists. By giving everyone the tools to create their own computer models the paradata no longer have to be shown. Ideas like this are not novel. A number of projects and applications that put the interpretive power into the hands of anyone who may be interested already exist. The following list gives examples of some of the available software:

1. *Second Life* is a freely available online 3D open world platform that allows players to create their own objects through 3D tools.[42] Players can interact with other real-world players, but the object creation tool allows players to create their own worlds from objects that can be sold to other players for in-world currency. The objects may include clothing and accessories through to entire buildings or city districts.

2. *Spore* is a video game, which lets players evolve their own organisms from a single-celled organism all the way to space travelling civilizations.[43] Players get to hand-steer their organisms through evolutionary design space and the program automatically works out how the organism will successfully move around, eat and even reproduce. The creation tool in *Spore* allows players an amazing creative freedom. If they so wish they could successfully evolve a civilization of teddy bear-like characters or a civilization of dinosaurs.

3. Hidden beneath the child-friendly surface of the hand-held *Pokémon* series of games, there is a very robust mechanism that allows players selectively to breed their Pokémon for favourable attributes, which give them an edge in online competitions.[44]

---

42   *Second Life*, <http://secondlife.com/> (2003).
43   *Spore Creature Creator*, <http://www.spore.com/ftl> (2008).
44   *Pokémon Diamond/Pearl*, Game Freak (2006).

4. The *Foldit* project is a game that harnesses humans' natural ability for visual manipulation in 3D space in order to help scientists to better understand HIV, Alzheimer's disease and cancer.[45] Thousands of competitive players log into *Foldit* to solve a series of 3D puzzles. The puzzles themselves are models of protein structures and by solving a puzzle people are helping science to look at how proteins fold together. The genetic sequences of proteins are known; however, it is not understood how proteins fold up to perform crucial biological tasks. Computers consistently failed to find solutions for larger proteins even with extensive programming.

5. *Google SketchUp* is freely available software that allows users to create, modify and share 3D models.[46] It is aimed at computer-modelling professionals as well as education sessions in schools and universities. Buildings built with Google SketchUp can be integrated with Google Earth.[47]

Combining aspects of *Second Life*, *Spore*, *Pokémon* and *Foldit* into a single virtual platform for creating and 'evolving' prehistoric creatures would allow people to draw their own conclusions about palaeontological reconstructions as well as contributing to scientific research.

Players could start by choosing a creature or plant to work on. They would be given access to a bare bones model of fragments that have been discovered in the fossil record, each of which are modelled to have realistic weight-bearing and stress properties. Using applications similar to the character creation and object creating sections of *Second Life* and *Spore*, players can then fill in the physical gaps and layer their bare bones with muscle and skin and feathers; the options for individual flair limited only by a combination of evidence from fossil remains and modern organisms. For example, two-headed organisms are technically biologically possible but highly improbable as observed in the fossil record and from animals around today.

Once the organism is created it is moved into a *Spore* and *Pokémon* environment, where it is tested to see how it would conceivably move around in space, modelled with realistic gravity settings and biodynamic information. Players could then alter their creature or automatically 'evolve' their model in a similar way to computer-modelling techniques used in science, until it manages competently to move around without falling over or breaking limbs with every step.

Using further applications similar to the open world and online environments of *Foldit*, *Google Earth* and *Second Life*, the creatures can then be let loose in virtual environments with everybody else's creations. Virtual natural selection would help to identify those creatures which seem the best adapted to survival in

---

45   *Foldit*, <http://fold.it/portal/>.
46   *Google SketchUp*, <http://sketchup.google.com/index.html> (2008).
47   Google Earth, <http://earth.google.com/> (2008).

virtual environments. Online community sites and web fora could allow players to share their creations, design techniques and discuss the validity of reconstructions.

This may sound like an undesirable system, open to exploitation and not founded on 'real science'. However, such an open platform would allow much greater amounts of processing power from large networks of computers directed at solving problems. It would also open up these tools to people who may not be trained palaeontologists but who have a natural keener sense of biological design. This is evident from the *Foldit* project, where teenagers can solve problems on a par with biochemistry professors purely because they are more skilled at manipulating virtual objects. Directly giving people the source data from which to create their model eliminates the need to show paradata in *WWD* reconstructions and other palaeontological CGI documentaries. With so many human minds and networked computer power focused on solving such problems new interpretations and theories will be made. The fictional programme described above is merely a broadening of the computer-modelling work that palaeontologists already undertake in museums and universities using technology that already exists and, in many cases, is free for download.

Conclusion

There is no denying that *WWD* and other CGI documentaries and programmes engage and entertain many people. They also inspire many to research the organisms so magnificently recreated on the small and big screens. With careful implementation of some of the ideas proposed above to preserve the scientific, cultural and artistic knowledge that form the basis of the reconstructions, these documentaries could be accessed and enjoyed by many generations to come.

Chapter 9

Hypothesizing Southampton in 1454: A Three-dimensional Model of the Medieval Town[1]

Matt Jones

This chapter describes a project whose aim was to provide an in-depth account of Southampton for the year 1454. This year was chosen as there is good documentary evidence for the town's structure and commercial activity during this period. The choice of such an exact date is due to the existence of an important document, dated to 1454, known as the *Southampton Terrier*.[2] This document lists and details all the property in the town and from it a town plan has been produced. The goal of this project was to build upon Lawrence A. Burgess's work in the creation of a town plan and to create a computer-generated model of the town in three dimensions (see Plate 1). This model was prepared for public display in the Museum of Archaeology, Southampton. In order to create the model based on evidence it was necessary to interrogate all available sources for information. During this process a number of decisions had to be made. The dataset available is essentially incomplete and to fulfil the project remit it would be possible to recreate elements of the medieval town that are either extant from the archaeological record or in an incomplete state.

This chapter details the types of decisions required during the modelling process and presents a methodology for being open not only about the process but also about the limitations of the finished model.

Combining Data Sources

The first stage in creating a model of the town was to bring together the different data sources to create a plan of the town that was as accurate and reliable as possible. The data sets in question were cartographic data, including archaeological plans

---

1   This chapter is a revised version of an essay which won the 3DVisa Student Award 2007. The award was established by the JISC 3D Visualisation in the Arts Network, UK to promote innovative use of visualization in the Arts and Humanities research. The original essay was published in the *3DVisa Bulletin*, 4 (2008), see <http://3dvisa.cch.kcl.ac.uk/student_award_call.html> (accessed September 2010).
2   Lawrence Arthur Burgess (ed.), *The Southampton Terrier of 1454* (1976).

retrieved during the research phase and the *Terrier*. It was necessary to georeference the *Terrier* based on known points of correlation between the map data and the *Terrier*. This was done successfully with a low RMS error (mean error from where the points should be) of 3.25 based on 30 points. When this was completed the archaeological plans were imported and scaled according to the scale bars of each individual plan. The only exception was the plan produced based on the Friary gate excavation: this was georeferenced in the same manner as the *Terrier* in the absence of a scale bar, and also deemed less accurate than the other plans. The plans were then placed, where possible, based on correlating points on the plan and the map data. Individual reference points have not been recorded as the plans were placed based on all correlating points within the map data for a 'best fit' result. This was not possible for the English Street and Broad Street junction plan. This was placed on the basis of information in the *Terrier* with the points of reference based upon the southernmost property detailed in the archaeological plan on English Street. Having the plans and the *Terrier* scaled, rotated and located according to a contemporary map of the town facilitated the creation of a plan of the medieval town based upon all of these data sources.

The digitization process employed when creating the plan was hierarchical in nature. It made assumptions about the accuracy and utility of the data. Digitization assumed the archaeological plans to be the most reliable, followed by the map data. The *Terrier* was only used in the absence of archaeological data, map or planar. An exception to this came on the stretch of wall at the rear of the Friary: due to the poorer quality of the archaeological plan for this area map data were used. It was inevitable that these data sets were not going to correlate precisely and there would be discrepancies and a need to tie, for example, digitized aspects of the *Terrier* and map information. In addition, other assumptions had to be made: for example, the need to mirror the surviving drum tower of the Watergate to create the non-surviving tower. Layering conventions for this plan were devised to differentiate between sources of data for digitized sections of the medieval town. It is immediately apparent upon viewing the plan how it was put together: dark blue denotes digitized sections based on map data; light blue, archaeological plans; green, the *Terrier*; and yellow; conjectural based on assumption (see Plate 2).

The Decision-making Process

Throughout the modelling process it was necessary to make decisions that have implications for the finished product. The *Terrier* is essentially a 2D version of what the project intended to achieve. Plots were created by Burgess in order to create a model of how the town *could* have been laid out. Indeed the author had to make decisions along the way: for example, what size to make cottage plots and what size to make tenement plots. As this project was focused on using the available archaeology in the creation of a model of the town it was possible to ascertain *actual* plot sizes; these were then used to create generic buildings which could be used throughout the town. This was achieved with data obtained courtesy of Oxford Archaeology from their recent excavations in the French quarter. This was a particularly useful data set as the area south of Polymond Hall showed the layout of both tenements and cottages and was, roughly, coherent with the location of the plots as detailed by the *Terrier*. This was heartening as it both justified the use of the *Terrier* as a tool for defining the town layout and allowed the plan built up by Burgess to be further refined and strengthened.

Using these data, three types of cottage and five types of tenement were built. Excavation plans were used for the ground measurements. Analogy was used through research on medieval houses and evidence from surviving houses in Southampton was used as inspiration and as points of reference.[3] These buildings were then placed throughout the town depending on the tenement type and plot size as suggested by Burgess. The buildings were scaled occasionally to add to the variation. Plots were kept as much as to Burgess's plan as possible, but it was often necessary to adjust plots to fit buildings. A consistent problem was the size granted by Burgess to cottages – this was often very generous compared to the ground plans excavated by Oxford Archaeology. In addition to the eight generic buildings mentioned, it was necessary to create some three-storey buildings such as the Red Lion. Using the Red Lion as inspiration, a three-storey generic building was built up and a number of these were placed on tenement plots in the vicinity of the High Street and the Red Lion. Obviously there are problems with using generic buildings, as they grossly over-simplify the town. However, given the lack of above-ground evidence for most of the town and the time frame involved, it was deemed wholly appropriate to use such buildings for the model.

When it came to model God's House Hospital and the Friary, the large plots allotted to them by Burgess and the lack of archaeological evidence for the greater part of these sites presented a problem. Research shows that it was roughly known what buildings would be present in God's House Hospital. This information was used when creating the model of the complex. Inspiration was then taken from a conjectural sketch of the town and a garden was placed in the centre of the complex. The sketch of the Friary gate and adjacent buildings was used to build up the east of the site. A courtyard was created surrounded by these buildings. This left a large amount of, presumably, enclosed space within the Friary compound. Again a garden was used to fill the area. This approach can be justified in that a model based only on what is known would be limited and thus unsuitable for a museum. Conjecture and creativity were therefore constantly employed in order to create a possible incarnation of the town.

As in the case of the Friary and God's House complex, other buildings required decisions to be made. For example, halls and warehouses needed to be created. Simple structures were constructed, and height data were gauged from similar buildings that survive today. For example, warehouses were sized according to

---

3   Jane Grenville, *Medieval Housing* (Leicester, 1997). Anthony Quiney, *Town Houses of Medieval Britain* (New Haven, 2003).

Wool House, and halls were sized according to the heights of large town houses like 58 French Street. It was necessary to scale down some versions of these buildings as Burgess details some warehouses as much smaller than others. Common sense was therefore employed and such buildings were based on similar structures and then scaled as necessary. Canute's Palace was converted into a warehouse in the thirteenth or fourteenth century; it was thus modelled in this role. The door was placed where excavation showed it to be, and the rear window mirrored and placed on the front.

It was also necessary to make decisions during the modelling process for surviving buildings and those represented in drawings or paintings with regard to additions that would have been made post-1454. Often these were common sense decisions and were made in the belief that due to the role of a building or structure such modification *must* have occurred after 1454. For example: the two smaller doors allowing access to the Bargate at the front; the windows depicted as being presented on the large drum tower making up part of the Watergate; windows and a small building on the top of the Eastgate; the pitched roof on God's House Gate; a window in the Westgate; and the clock on All Saints church. By making these small alterations it was attempted to show more accurately how these structures may have looked. The majority of these changes were made to defensive structures and aspects of these structures that, had they been present in 1454, would have threatened the town's defence.

It was necessary to attempt to recreate the wharfage facilities that were present in the town. For this a plan created and printed in *Excavations in Medieval Southampton, 1953–1969* was used as it detailed, albeit conjecturally, the facilities that would have been present for receiving cargo from ships at the town.[4] These docking areas were given a wood material. The final major problem was how to represent the shape of medieval plots as laid out by Burgess. Excavation had shown that the buildings took up the front of the plot but did not occupy a substantial amount of it. Therefore gardens were created; it is likely there would have been gardens for a large number of the tenements as the *Terrier*-derived plan seems to have accounted for them. It was not known what these gardens may have held structurally, if anything, so low fences were erected to mark out the plots and a grass material placed on the ground. The fences were given a light wood material to fit in with the overall style of the model. To further anchor the fact that these are gardens, trees were added to some of them. These areas were created to ensure clear and simple definition of the medieval plots.

4　　　Colin Platt and Richard Coleman-Smith (eds), *Excavations in Medieval Southampton, 1953–1969* (Leicester, 1975), Fig. 4.

Building the Model

The building of the 3D model was done exclusively in 3ds Max 9 software. The process will not be discussed exhaustively; rather, decisions that were made will be detailed and evaluated, and the merits and problems of particular choices addressed. Once the plan creation process was completed, as mentioned above, it was broken down into different sections. These ranged from an individual tenement to the town walls. These plans were then imported into 3ds Max in order to provide a blueprint for the creation of a representative model of that particular aspect of the town. 3ds Max allows for the creation of complex models from simple geometric primitives. Through the manipulation and building of relationships between objects it was possible to create 3D models of aspects of the town. Once a section of the model had been made, a group was created and named accordingly. For example, primitives making up 58 French Street were placed in a group called '58 French Street'. These individual elements were then externally referenced into a master file to allow them to be joined to create the town – in this manner file sizes were kept much more manageable. The complexity of these models is not excessive and provides a good simple representation of the modelled town element. More complex modelling was not possible due to both time and data-enforced limitations.

For a representation of the medieval town to be presented effectively it was necessary to create a terrain. Due to the lack of any sort of survey for the town in the medieval period and poor resolution data for the area for the modern day it was not possible to create truly accurate terrain. Instead, and in keeping with the simple educational methodology, a terrain was created based on the *Terrier* in order to highlight the defence mechanisms employed within the town; namely the ditches surrounding the walls and similar precautionary measures at the castle. It was also a good way to express the fact that the south and west of the town would have met abruptly with the sea. Due to technological problems with ArcGIS it was necessary to create a digital elevation model (DEM) using digitized data from the *Terrier* with software called Global Mapper. A 1.5 m resolution DEM was created and then imported into 3ds Max. As everything had been created using the same master source data it was not necessary to rescale or move anything as it was already geographically correct. Using a plug-in for 3ds Max called Vue 6 Xstream, it was possible to create an atmosphere in which to place the model. This consisted of a sky, a sun and some clouds, which was done purely for presentational purposes.

As with other aspects of the modelling process, materials were kept simple and designed to allow users to view a good, clear representation of aspects of the town. All materials were made procedurally rather than by draping images over objects. This is more aesthetically pleasing at high levels of zoom and also requires less computation. Furthermore, applying such materials to objects is a far more efficient process than working with image-based materials. Using various filters in 3ds Max it was possible to create procedural materials for black and white paint, stone, wood, fencing, slate, grass, glass, a basic ground material and the terrain.

These are clearly representative of their real-world equivalents even at high levels of magnification.

Three-dimensional Modelling and Archaeology

Three-dimensional modelling is a very useful tool for the discipline of archaeology. Traditional dissemination techniques leave the vast majority of archaeological projects under-appreciated. Archaeological discoveries and excavations rarely find an audience beyond those who read the excavation reports. Although they are not specifically designed to alienate the general public, Hermon and Fabian criticize traditional excavation reports for their linearity, limited use of recovered data and technical focus.[5] The technological advances since the 1990s have facilitated the growth of computational modelling techniques. Driven by a demand for more accessible software, a vast array of desktop programs allow for the creation of such models. The community-driven focus of the internet of the past few years has gone even further to make such software accessible. Open-source software is a cost-free alternative to, often expensive, programs. The community aspect of this form of software development also provides resources for learning and troubleshooting. With such opportunities available, it is inevitable that models representing aspects of the past will become more widespread. It is important that archaeology, as a discipline, engages with this ever-growing community and makes full use of what computational models have to offer.

Of interest to this work is 3D modelling. The proceedings of Computer Applications and Quantitative Methods in Archaeology prove that a section of the archaeological community is validating the use of such models based on archaeological data. Barceló claims that models should be embraced as they offer the means to represent features of a concrete or abstract entity as opposed to the mere illustrations that have been previously relied upon.[6] Indeed, 3D modelling offers a level of control and an ability to reconstruct past built environments in an entirely new fashion. Inexpensive fully 3D environments can be built based upon factual data. The benefits of these models are numerable and range from an educational resource that can be employed by educators and museums alike to complex models designed to address specific questions that, if asked of the archaeological evidence, jeopardize the integrity of the site. For example, stress

---

5   Sorin Hermon and Peter Fabian, 'Virtual Reconstruction of Archaeological Sites: Some Archaeological Scientific Considerations', in Franco Niccolucci (ed.), *Virtual Archaeology*, Proceedings of the VAST Euroconference, Arezzo 24–26 November 2000. British Archaeological Reports International Series 1075 (Oxford, 2002), p. 38.

6   Juan A. Barceló, 'Visualizing What Might Be: An Introduction to Virtual Reality Techniques in Archaeology', in Juan A. Barceló, Maurizio Forte and Donald H. Sanders (eds), *Virtual Reality in Archaeology*, BAR International Series 843 (Oxford, 2000), pp. 9–36.

tests can be applied to ancient bridges and similar structures. Sanders is quick to point out that we should not look back when using these new tools; we should not attempt to mimic traditional representational techniques, namely illustrations. Rather, we should be innovative and find new methods for dissemination.[7] In the case of this project the desire to provide a level of interactivity in three dimensions is deemed far more useful than creating a model and supplying museum visitors with 2D images derived from the model. For this purpose it is necessary to make use of Virtual Reality Modelling Language (VRML) software.

Johnson writes: 'Certainly the past doesn't exist anywhere outside our own head. I have never touched, kicked, or felt the past.'[8] Through virtual reality technologies it is possible to share the past that exists in the head of an archaeologist to a wider audience and, perhaps, get one step close to connecting with the past. Through such models it will be possible to view aspects of the past from an infinite number of angles and provide a context for the models long-since vanished. Another benefit, as anchored by Forte in his compendium *Virtual Archaeology*, is the ability to update models as particular theories or new data is bought to light.[9] Of particular interest in Forte's opening chapter is his use of the term 're-presentation' as opposed to more widely used terms such as 'reconstruction'. His choice of language is wholly appropriate to what we are doing as archaeologists: repackaging and presenting possible aspects of the past based on our knowledge and investigations. It should be accepted that reconstructing past environments is impossible due to the complexity of past cultures but it is possible, through computational methods, to equip the archaeologist with another interpretative tool. Essentially, as Niccolucci proposes, we should treat 'virtual archaeology', as famously coined by Reilly in 1990, as another branch of archaeological investigation much like landscape archaeology, environmental archaeology or even gender archaeology.[10]

The focus of this project was on the creation of a model for display in a museum and this is an issue that will be addressed in more detail. Sanders writes the following of models generated for such contexts: 'Our software becomes a dynamic medium for promoting awareness of past civilizations, understanding of different cultures, and appreciation of different places, people and their cultural heritage.'[11] This is

---

7   Sanders, Donald H., 'Archaeological Publications Using Virtual Reality: Case Studies and Caveats', in Juan A. Barceló, Maurizio Forte and Donald H. Sanders (eds), *Virtual Reality in Archaeology*, BAR International Series 843 (Oxford, 2000), pp. 37–46.

8   Matthew Johnson, *Archaeological Theory: An Introduction* (Oxford, 1999), p. 9.

9   Maurizio Forte and Alberto Siliotti (eds), *Virtual Archaeology: Great Discoveries Brought to Life through Virtual Reality* (London, 1997), p. 12.

10   Franco Niccolucci (ed.), *Virtual Archaeology*, Proceedings of the VAST Euroconference, Arezzo, 24–25 November 2000, Bar International Series 1075 (Oxford, 2002), p. 6.; Paul Reilly, 'Towards a Virtual Archaeology', in K. Lockyear and S. Rahtz (eds), *Computer Applications in Archaeology*, BAR International Series 565 (Oxford, 1990).

11   Donald Sanders, 'Archaeological Publications Using Virtual Reality: Case Studies and Caveats', in Juan A. Barceló, Maurizio Forte and Donald H. Sanders (eds), *Virtual*

an ideal scenario where the modelling process will be an accepted tool for the dissemination of information. For this purpose Kantner promotes simpler models designed specifically for pedagogical use.[12] Such an approach is well suited to this project as it is being created for a learning environment with a definite focus on knowledge transfer. A volumetric representation with limited detail, for example simple textures, is sufficient. This is not to say it was oversimplified to the point of jeopardizing the nature of the collected data. Archaeological excavation data were used, and, where available, ground plans were used to 'extrude' aspects of the built environment of the medieval town. Where structures remain they have been recreated as faithfully as possible within the time provided. Obviously, they do not intend to be photo-realistic representations; rather, they are geometric primitives manipulated to be an adequate representation of reality – it is not the intention of this project to mimic reality. Niccolucci is quick to point out that virtual visualization does not need faithfully to recreate reality to be a successful tool for archaeology.[13] In this case it was sufficient for the purpose at hand and lessened the computation involved – something important, as the museum's resources are limited.

Transparency

As has been discussed, the finished model bought together a number of different data sources and it was necessary to make assumptions and decisions along the way. As such, different elements within the model can be deemed to have different levels of certainty. This needed to be documented in an accessible format. When creating a 3D model it should be easy for the intended audience to access supplementary data that detail where material evidence ends and hypothesizing begins. Different techniques have been employed in the past, for example colour coding aspects of the model. However, such methods were not appropriate for this project. Indeed the museum wanted an exhibit that was presented in a realistic manner, so any overlays or additions to the finished model were not possible. Therefore it was decided that the model would be broken down into its many different parts; these consist of individual buildings including churches and halls, as well as larger structures such as the castle and the town walls. Based on the available data and the level of certainty for each aspect of the town, each structure was given a level of certainty

---

Reality in Archaeology, BAR International Series 843 (Oxford: Archaeopress, 2000), pp. 37–46, p. 37.

12   Kantner, John, 'Realism vs. Reality: Creating Virtual Reconstructions of Prehistoric Architecture', in Juan A. Barceló, Maurizio Forte and Donald H. Sanders (eds), *Virtual Reality in Archaeology*, BAR International Series 843 (Oxford, 2000), also available at <http://www.sarweb.org/kantner/SAA00/index.html> (accessed September 2010).

13   Franco Niccolucci (ed.), *Virtual Archaeology*, Proceedings of the VAST Euroconference, Arezzo, 24–25 November 2000, Bar International Series 1075 (Oxford, 2002), p. 4.

and the rationale behind this explained. This information was presented in a tabular format and was kept as simple as possible to be accessible to all. It is also a very useful quick reference for anyone wishing to know more about how the model was put together (see Table 9.1).

Table 9.1   **Medieval Southampton. Levels of certainty of model parts depending on the available sources of information**

Model Part	Level of Certainty	Source Data	Thumbnail
58 French Street	Very High	The building survives.	
Canute's Palace	Medium	The building survives in ruins in places to roof level allowing the creation of a ground plan and partial elevation. Reports suggest it was a house but later converted into a warehouse pre-1454.	
Duke of Wellington	High	The building survives although it has undergone extensive renovation.	
All Saints Church	Medium	The building does not survive and excavation has not been able to extract a ground plan. However, a sketch of the frontage of the church exists.	
St Laurence Church	Medium	An elevation, a sketch and a ground plan were obtained for this church although excavation has not uncovered such a plan and the building has long since vanished.	

Model Part	Level of Certainty	Source Data	Thumbnail
Bargate	Very High	The structure survives very well and changes over time have been documented.	
Bull/Bugle Hall	Low	A ground plan has been created through excavation but nothing is known of the building's form above ground level.	
Castle	Low	Part of the bailey wall survives but none of the castle keep has survived. Excavation has postulated a basic plan for the site but no definitive ground plan has been created. Representations of the castle exist but are of poor quality.	
Catchcold Tower	Very High	The structure survives today in excellent condition.	
Eastgate	Medium	No ground plan has been uncovered for this site but a drawing made shortly before its demolition shows how it would have looked from the outside of the walls.	
Friary	Low	The Friary church, dorter, gate and reredorter have been uncovered through excavation and ground plans produced. However, nothing is known of the rest of the site and heights and building styles can only be built up conjecturally.	

Model Part	Level of Certainty	Source Data	Thumbnail
God's House Chapel	Very High	The building survives.	
God's House Hospital	Very Low	Only what type of buildings would have been present in the complex are known.	
God's House Tower and Gate	High	Structures survive to this day although the addition of windows and roofs would have come later than 1454.	
Holyrood Church	High	The building survives in ruins after being bombed in the Second World War. Photographs exist of it in its original form and the remains are of good quality.	
St John's Church	Low	Only the ground dimensions of this church are known. Its exact location is unknown as excavation has not been done in this area.	
Medieval Merchants Hall	High	Building survives, despite having been moved. Model derived from more complex model by Heather Papworth.	

Model Part	Level of Certainty	Source Data	Thumbnail
St Michael's Church	Very High	Building survives to this day and changes over time have been documented.	
Polymond Hall	Low	Excavation has uncovered a comprehensive ground plan for the site but nothing is known above ground level.	
Red Lion	High	Undoubtedly having undergone renovation this tenement survives to this day.	
Watergate	Medium	Part of the gate survives in ruins but a painting taken of the gate in the early nineteenth century hints at its original form although obviously this was made a long time after 1454.	
Westgate	Very High	Structure survives in very good condition to this day.	
Wool House	High	Building survives to this day although has undergone renovation.	

Model Part	Level of Certainty	Source Data	Thumbnail
Plots 173–180	Low	Excavation has uncovered the ground plans for these cottages and tenements but nothing is known above ground level.	
Poysage (Weigh) House	Low	Survives in ruins. Ground plan is known but little is known above this level.	
Plots 158–162 and 257	Low	Excavation has uncovered the ground plans for these cottages and tenements but nothing is known above ground level.	
King John's	Low	Building survives in ruins.	
Two houses on Cuckoo Lane	Low	These tenements were not detailed in the *Terrier* or if they were, they were not placed correctly. Ground plans uncovered but nothing known above ground level.	
Towers	Medium	Some survive well such as Arundel Tower, others as ruins, others are completely extant.	

   The creation of elements of the town with little evidence requires leaps of faith and differing levels of assumption. There is often a perceived hypersensitivity towards such leaps of faith by sections of the archaeological community. However, it is important to note that in the creation of such models we are not destroying the data or misleading anybody, assuming the modeller adopts an open approach to their data and assumptions. In essence, we are merely using technology as a means of throwing around ideas. As long as the modeller is honest with the data used and the conclusions drawn, there can be no criticism of the process. Indeed, with the creation of the above table the modeller is able to present their level of certainty and even break down the model into its constituent elements. Furthermore, a report readily available to museum visitors was envisaged to contain the information presented in this chapter. All these supplementary data were provided alongside the model as it was important to present the model faithfully to visitors to the museum. Of course it would be possible merely to portray what is known but that would not be as useful as a resource that attempts to place the archaeological data that remain in its original context. Modelling the data as they now appear would be very restrictive and of far less use. The purpose of models may be identified as to portray information to the human eye that is difficult to perceive or imagine. This project attempted to construct medieval Southampton as it *may* have looked in 1454; uncertainty was inherent, but not fulfilling the project remit due to such uncertainty would be an exercise in futility. As long as processes are recorded in a document such as this and useful supplementary data are provided, such as in the table presented here, a model can be informative and accountable.

Chapter 10

Paradata in Art-historical Research: A Visualization of Piet Mondrian's Studio at 5 rue de Coulmiers[1]

Ryan Egel-Andrews

Introduction

'Three-dimensional' is not a term commonly associated with Piet Mondrian's aesthetic concerns. The abstract works of his mature period which begin to emerge after his return to Paris in 1919 are uncompromisingly flat, volume-less paintings which proclaim as their purpose the destruction of objectivity in favour of abstract line and colour relationships. However, the second Paris period is also characterized by an increasing interest in architectural space, both theoretically and practically, in which Mondrian devoted considerable attention to developing Neo-Plasticism beyond the edge of his canvas. To speak of Mondrian from 1919 onwards as a painter of 2D, abstract canvases is to deny a complete understanding of his artistic ambition.

The seeds of Mondrian's vision of Neo-Plastic architecture were sown in the two studios he occupied in Paris between 1919 and 1921 at 5 rue de Coulmiers and between 1921 and 1936 at 26 rue du Départ. He set about arranging these spaces according to his Neo-Plastic principles through judiciously placed furniture and by the application of painted cardboard to the walls. Seen through the lens of the evolutionary principles to which Mondrian adhered throughout his life, they are intimately connected. Later is not possible without earlier.

Much is already known about both studios but considerably more about the latter, at Départ, thanks to a fascinating set of photographs taken between 1925 and 1930. These photographs form the basis of much scholarly activity, culminating in

---

1   This chapter is based on the author's MA dissertation titled 'Understanding Neo-plastic Space: A 3D Visualization of Piet Mondrian's Studio at 5 Rue de Coulmiers', completed at King's College London, 2009. In 2009, the model of Mondrian's studio at 5 rue Coulmiers was exhibited on the King's College London Digital Humanities region of *Second Life* at 25, 187, 31; a video of the model is available on YouTube at <http://www.youtube.com/watch?v=8YbZYYVviRA>. The documentation wiki is at <http://mondrian.wikispaces.com>.

Frans Postma's precise real-life reconstruction of the studio.[2] No such photographs exist for the Coulmiers studio and there is a tendency in the literature to view Départ as an isolated moment of artistic inspiration. Notable exceptions include the work of Nancy Troy and Carel Blotkamp, but without a suitable means of comparison between the two, insights have remained general rather than specific.[3] This chapter aims therefore to bridge the gap between the two studios, thus setting both in their proper evolutionary context.

Postma's reconstruction of Départ unlocks a great deal of useful information regarding its arrangement – information that would not otherwise be knowable though close examination of the photographs or Mondrian's extensive theoretical writings. Therefore a broadly similar, albeit digital, approach is adopted here in order to release previously undiscovered knowledge regarding Coulmiers and to enable a fuller and more detailed comparison to be made between the two. The idea is not faithfully to reconstruct the studio as Postma has done with Départ (there is not enough data to attempt such a task), but to use visualization as a tool to extract meaning. Leo Feijs's comments regarding his work on programming Mondrian's easel paintings are instructive: 'I do not claim that the computer comes close to real Mondrian compositions; on the contrary, every desired property not formalized well is laid bare immediately. But that is precisely why the computer as a tool stimulates careful observation.'[4]

The collection and dissemination of paradata in this instance is crucial as it offers intellectual transparency, an important factor given the lack of source material. Furthermore, it is argued here that in a visualization such as this, where the final digital object is of diminished significance, it is the accompanying paradata which offer an essential research source. It is also suggested that if visualizations are to be used in the generation of art-historical argument, paradata are as valuable as the digital object itself.

Methodology

The visualization process was carried out in four stages simply described as the collection of source material, the analysis of source material, the construction of the model and finally the analysis of the result. These stages, however, do not represent a linear process, but one of constant re-evaluation in the light of general trends in Mondrian's Neo-Plastic style coupled with what is known about the physical arrangement of the room. The final arguments that are art-historical in

---

2   Frans Postma, *26 Rue du Départ, Mondrian's Studio Paris 1921–1936* (Berlin, 1995).

3   Carel Blotkamp, *Mondrian. The Art of Destruction* (1994), pp. 137–58. Nancy Troy, *The De Stijl Environment* (Cambridge, 1985), pp. 62–71.

4   Leo Feijs, 'Divisions of the Plane by Computer: Another Way of Looking at Mondrian's Nonfigurative Compositions', *Leonardo*, 37, 3 (2004): 220.

nature are not arrived at by drawing conclusions solely from the observation of the digital object. Conclusions are drawn from a combination of source analysis and visual analysis of the model. The word 'model' here does not refer just to digital output, but to the entire process of visualization itself. Insights are taken from all points of the process and additional source material is considered as and when it is necessary.

This process emphasizes the importance of paradata. Because the construction of the model hinges on the subjective and conceptual analysis of source material, the resulting paradata contain knowledge that is of prime importance to the final arguments. For instance, what *wasn't* included by Mondrian in the Coulmiers studio design and hence is not represented in the model is of significance. As mentioned, in this scenario, the significance of the final digital output becomes diminished as it forms only part of the visualization output used to understand the issues at stake in Mondrian's Neo-Plasticism. The dissemination of paradata is therefore crucial for two reasons: first, because it demonstrates transparency in relation to the model; and second, because it informs the art-historical conclusions.

It is suggested here that with art-historical visualization of this nature there are two distinct yet interrelated sets of paradata which can be explained as the varying methodologies used to fill in knowledge gaps in the historical record. It is noted that attempting accurately to model the Coulmiers studio with the current source material is impossible, but that the pursuit of this aim nevertheless produces insights perhaps undiscoverable through traditional inquiry. So while a 3D model might be constructed using the data generated by improvisational techniques, it is the process of extracting the data that is of most interest. Hence paradata allow the high level of subjectivity in the model to be criticized. Paradata are also crucial because they shine a light on the path to argument. The hypotheses presented at the end of this chapter are the result of the visualization process, and the dissemination of the accompanying paradata therefore forms part of the final textual arguments.

Visualizations of structure and space produce much useful metadata, dimensions, colour values, etc. that can be used in future research as a point of departure. However in cases such as this, where the metadata were arrived at using various improvisational methods, the visualization remains subjective and therefore needs to be justified. Techniques including approximating dimensions though measuring photographs and colour matching by eye are far from scientific and should be expressed for reasons of transparency. It is noted that even though the emphasis of this visualization is not on the final digital object, it is still a key output and paradata relating to its physicality should be collected and disseminated. It is an essential record if, for instance, future research involves an accurate reconstruction based on some newly discovered source material.

The metadata and paradata are collected on a wiki (see <http://mondrian. wikispaces.com>), which is a critical part of this investigation. This format has obvious advantages in terms of dissemination and access as it is freely available online. The structure of a wiki differs from its traditional paper counterpart in that it is non-static. It implies continual development and editing and can therefore be amended if new evidence becomes available. A wiki is also a collaborative enterprise. Even though in this case research was carried out alone, provisions are made for any future collaboration that may arise. Material on the wiki is presented in a somewhat haphazard fashion and the metadata is not structured formally or tabulated in the way that might be expected. Neither does it present the totality of the data. A feature of paradata in visualization is the sheer volume of data that is created. While this has obvious advantages, it also presents the lone researcher with a unique set of problems. Time constraints mean certain material must be privileged over others. In the case of this MA research, the focus has remained on the final textual argument at the expense of properly composed metadata.

Art-historical paradata are the information produced by analysing the source material with the intention of filling in the knowledge gap. They are unconcerned with the mechanics of model building and do not produce numerical values from which data objects can be derived, but rather seek to explain more general artistic trends that might be applied to the model. Such a method is intuitive. By analysing both primary and secondary sources, it attempts to collate all information that might be of relevance and use it to produce a visual representation of the studio. This kind of analysis produces indications of the arrangement but no certainty. However, the purpose is not to generate an accurate representation but rather to stimulate debate around Mondrian's approach to Neo-Plastic architecture.

Questions arise as to how adequately to disseminate such material as proscribed in The London Charter. The relationship between paradata and digital output here is not made explicit. A structured narrative is the format which has been adopted for the analysis of sources (see below) while the model of the studio is placed in *Second Life*. *Second Life* as a virtual world offers some ability to embed textual information in the model through the use of 'notecards', but this implies the text exists in segregated, location-specific blocks, which is unsatisfactory for such an analysis. In presenting the analysis of sources as standard text, the primacy of the final arguments – made whilst observing a compromise in the lack of integration between paradata and model – is emphasized.

It is worth noting the relative simplicity and low cost of the digital tools used in this visualization. The *Second Life* 3D engine can be used free of charge and is relatively simple compared to more advanced and expensive software packages. In cases such as this, where source data is lacking and where the technology is used as a means rather than an end, the level of precision available in advanced 3D engines is largely redundant. Here there is no obvious scholarly advantage to using complex technical equipment to realize the model. To a large extent, the model is based on conceptual ideas rather than measurable information and as such a reasonably simple modelling engine can yield effective results.

Such simplistic tools also present a clear benefit to the art historian. They are easily learnt and easily accessed. Provided a clear methodological framework is outlined beforehand, they are a valuable research tool. Their best implementation, it is suggested here, is one in which the process of 3D modelling is used to answer specific research questions and not to replicate past and non-existent spaces.

The limitations of using simplified tools for this visualization are also mentioned here. It is noted that a methodological framework must include an appreciation of these limitations. The major limitation in this case was accurate colour representation in the model. The author had no access, for instance, to advanced technologies used by Postma to extract accurate colour information from the photographs of the Départ studio.[5] Digital images were used, taken without high specification equipment, from the same printed book of the paintings to derive RGB colour values.[6] This lack of accuracy has meant a detailed analysis of colour as a compositional device has been largely omitted. The analysis has therefore focused on the spatial arrangement, and by selecting this as the avenue of inquiry the tools used have been sufficient to draw effective conclusions.

Analysis of Sources

The visualization was carried out with various primary and secondary sources. The sources have been used in two main ways. First, to reconstruct the interior as a 3D model and second, in conjunction with the model itself to form general and specific arguments relating to Mondrian's conception of space. The principal source is the artist's *Natural Reality and Abstract Reality*, known as the *Trialogue*, which contains a written description of an 'abstract real' painter's studio.[7] It is now acknowledged to be a description of Mondrian's own studio interior at Coulmiers.[8] This passage, together with Carel Blotkamp's exploded box plan of the room, his illustration of the south wall based on the *Trialogue* and several pieces of anecdotal evidence found in journalistic accounts and letters between members of De Stijl, form the basic structure of the room. This structure is then refined by interpretive analysis of the later studio at Départ – through Delbo's contemporary photographs and Frans Postma's real-life reconstructed model. Analysis of the colour and composition of Mondrian's easel paintings forms the basis of further refinement. The resulting model is then analysed in the context of Mondrian scholarship, most notably that of Blotkamp, Troy, Postma and Champa, Mondrian's own theoretical writings, his studio at rue du Départ and his only other architectural design, the drawing for the Salon de Ida Bienert, to form the basis of the art-historical arguments.[9]

---

5   Postma, *26 Rue du Départ*, pp. 55–63.

6   Joop M. Joosten and Robert P. Welsh, *Piet Mondrian Catalogue Raisonné,* vol. 2 (Blaricum, 1998).

7   Mondrian, Piet, *Natural Reality and Abstract Reality: An Essay in Trialogue Form,* trans. Martin S. James (New York, 1995), pp. 73–114.

8   Blotkamp, *Mondrian,* p. 140.

9   Ibid., pp. 137–58. Kermit Swiler Champa, *Mondrian Studies* (Chicago, 1985), pp. 69–78. Postma, *26 Rue du Départ*, pp. 9–63; Troy, *The De Stijl Environment*, pp. 63–71.

The building at 5 rue de Coulmiers is still in existence and Blotkamp has outlined the structural dimensions of Mondrian's studio through an exploded box plan.[10] The structure of the 3D model is therefore based on Blotkamp's measurements, which appear to be relatively accurate given that the plan is a simple line drawing. The only unknown is where the staircase and bedroom are located in relation to the corridor underneath the souspend, or balcony, but these are of almost no significance in the context of the final model.

The south wall of studio with the large window was presumably the focus of attention for Mondrian as it is the only element of the room described at length in the *Trialogue*. Blotkamp's interpretation of this passage is as literal as possible and the resulting drawing is, on the whole, a convincing argument. Some doubt exists over the positioning of the curtains and its effect on the entire composition. The *Trialogue* refers to 'those ivory toned curtains now pulled to one side'.[11] Blotkamp's drawing suggests a single curtain on the right side of the window, so presumably it was possible to draw both curtains to one side to produce the effect of a single plane. It is conceivable from the *Trialogue* that the curtains were drawn on both the right and left side of the window but Mondrian's description of the red planes of colour on the wall, one red and one deep red, suggests otherwise. In any case it is probable that Mondrian would have been keen to avoid such an arrangement due to its implicit symmetry.

The colour composition of the south wall is of singular importance but due to the lack of photographs also the most inaccessible. Its importance is highlighted in the *Trialogue* in relation to interior space: '[the colours] must be the *right* red, blue, yellow, grey. Each right in *itself* and *right in mutual relation to the others.*'[12] There is a correlation between the colours described in the *Trialogue* and Mondrian's compositions between 1919 and 1921.[13] The *Trialogue* refers to shades of colour, such as ivory, near-white, red-orange, light red and deep red, which are analogous to his painting style at the time. These compositions, of which *Composition A* (1920, Rome, National Gallery of Modern Art) is a representative example, often contain various shades of grey, blue, red and white on the same canvas.[14] At this stage, at least in terms of colour, Mondrian was treating his canvas and studio wall in broadly the same terms. A comparison between the description in the *Trialogue* and Mondrian's easel paintings is reproduced on the wiki.

The positioning of the colour planes and painted objects is purely hypothetical beyond the general description given in the *Trialogue*. Blotkamp's arrangement of the colour planes recalls work Mondrian was doing in 1917, such as *Composition with Colour Planes 2* (1917, Rotterdam, Boijmans Van Beuningen Museum) where the planes 'float' next to each separated by the underlying white ground plane.

---

10   Blotkamp, Mondrian, p. 143.
11   Mondrian, *Natural Reality and Abstract Reality*, p. 86.
12   Ibid., p. 88.
13   Blotkamp, *Mondrian*, p. 144.
14   All titles of works from Joosten and Welsh.

By 1920, Mondrian was working towards the removal of the impression of colour planes on top of ground plane, the chief advance in this area being the continual implementation of perpendicular black lines which destroy any semblance of a ground–figure relationship. These concerns are evident in the Départ studio although Mondrian appears to have considered black lines inappropriate when working in a spatial environment. The 1926 Delbo photograph of the main wall of the Départ studio shows that Mondrian either placed the colour planes directly next to each other leaving no gap, or chose to overlap them, as can be seen in the two grey planes on the right-hand side.[15] The purpose it seems is to incorporate the colour planes into the wall composition without suggesting the wall as a ground plane.

The extent to which Mondrian had reached this level in the Coulmiers studio is not known, but the stage of development seen in Michael Seuphor's 1930 Départ studio photograph, where the colour planes are smaller and the composition far more complex, seems unlikely.[16] However, the introduction of black perpendicular lines in his easel work was a key moment, which implied a conscious rejection of a singular white ground plane and suggests that as early as 1919 Mondrian would have arranged the colour planes in his studio in accordance with this compositional development. It is fairly certain that no colour planes were overlapping in the Coulmiers studio, as this would surely have been mentioned in the *Trialogue*. The south wall probably contained a more advanced Neo-Plastic arrangement than Blotkamp has indicated.

Similarly, the extent to which the furniture and various objects were arranged Neo-Plastically is of interest. The positioning of the furniture along the south wall can be devised from the *Trialogue* and appears largely correct in Blotkamp's drawing. However, in terms of the relationship between furniture and wall colour planes the drawing is suggestive of the decorative. In the Départ studio Mondrian sought to destroy the fact that the furniture was in front of the wall thereby encouraging the apprehension of flatness. Colour planes do not appear behind objects but rather next to them, plastically articulating each other, where all elements are treated equally as planes of colour and not as hierarchical objects. This is demonstrated in the Delbo image where the red paint box and easel are mediated though a grey colour plane. The grey plane is positioned so its edges run exactly next to the edges of the objects, suppressing any sense of depth. This is a common device and can be witnessed in all the Départ studio photographs. Blotkamp's drawing suggests that in 1919 Mondrian was not at a stage to have considered such a device; in fact, quite the opposite. The black bench, table, chair and paint box are all in an overlapping position with the colour planes, a notion quite alien in the Départ studio.

---

15 Postma, *26 Rue du Départ*, p. 63. The colour reconstruction of the photograph highlights the composition.

16 Blotkamp, *Mondrian*, p. 154.

Clearly in 1919 Mondrian was concerned with the expression of flatness in his studio space. The focus of the *Trialogue* is one of planar expressions, which implies the expression of flatness is appropriate for an interior. In 1922, Mondrian had unequivocally made his thoughts known regarding the subject in *De Stijl*, 'this new vision sees architecture as a multiplicity of planes: again flat'.[17] The genesis of this article occurred in the second half of 1921, when Mondrian was still using Coulmiers as his studio. The studio then must in part be related to his firm pronouncement on the necessity of the flat in architecture, a notion that was increasingly gaining importance in this theory. It is likely therefore that Mondrian was already devoting attention to the problem of integration of wall and furniture into one, flat Neo-Plastic composition during his time at Coulmiers. A key element of this would have been considered alignment of colour plane and furniture.

In the Départ studio, Mondrian made use of smaller objects such as boxes, ashtrays and books to complete the composition. This practice had begun in Coulmiers and the *Trialogue* contains references to two small boxes and two jars. Their exact placement is not known except for the fact that two were placed on the table and two on a shelf on the right-hand side of the south wall. In Blotkamp's formulation, the objects appear roughly symmetrical to each other and to their relative piece of supporting furniture. This organization bears a resemblance to what Mondrian criticized in the *Trialogue* as decorative: 'it is not enough simply to place a red, a blue, a yellow or a gray next to each other'.[18] Indeed, Delbo's photographs of the Départ studio clearly show how Mondrian conceived plastically expressed objects as a means realizing a total composition. The yellow box was placed on the corner of table to remove the sensation of it being a 'thing' on top of a 'thing'. The positioning at the front of table plus its implied proximity to the grey wall plane combines to remove the sense of space between object and wall. The circular ashtray in the foreground expresses a direct link with the yellow box through an asymmetric relationship on the vertical axis of the photograph. This relationship is held in further tension by the asymmetric relationship on the horizontal axis holding them also in strict opposition to each other. In this manner Mondrian was able to plastically articulate the space where objects did not all appear on the same plane.

Clearly this level of sophistication was not yet realized in Coulmiers. Mondrian at this point was placing furniture tight against the walls and evidence suggests the central area of the room was largely empty except for the easel. It is likely, however, that experimentation was being carried out on methods of unifying wall and furniture through the use of smaller objects plastically expressed. When Mondrian mentions in the *Trialogue* that the cylindrical jar 'appears as a rectangular plane' this is not due to any essential properties the jar possesses but is the result of its plastic integration where the planarity is manifest through its relationship to surrounding

---

17   From 'The Realization of Neo-Plasticism in the Distant Future and in Architecture Today', quoted in Blotkamp, *Mondrian*, p. 148.

18   Mondrian, *Natural Reality and Abstract Reality*, p. 88.

planes – in this case wall, shelf and furniture.[19] Therefore the positioning of the various boxes and jars in Coulmiers was likely more asymmetric, and more closely interrelated to both wall and furniture than Blotkamp has suggested, and that they were more integral to the overall composition, not simply existing as planes in front of planes (see Figure 10.1).

Figure 10.1   Visualization of Piet Mondrian's studio at 5 rue de Coulmiers, Paris. Detail of south wall

The organization of the remaining walls is largely unknown except for a few pieces of evidence. Blotkamp has noted that there was a large mirror placed against the north wall and that one of the diamond compositions with lines from 1918–19 hung above the door, a detail mentioned in a 1920 interview.[20] Whether or not Mondrian applied colour planes to the other three walls is arguable. Blotkamp has suggested they were largely untreated due to the lack of any description in the *Trialogue*. This is corroborated in letter Theo Van Doesburg wrote to J.J.P. Oud after he visited Mondrian at Coulmiers in which he describes the studio as 'restricted to one plane (window plane)'.[21]

However, some evidence exists to suggest Mondrian had made more use of the remaining walls. He cuts short his description in the *Trialogue* saying, 'We

19   Ibid., p. 87.
20   Blotkamp, *Mondrian*, p. 144.
21   Quoted in Troy, *The De Stijl Environment*, p. 70.

Figure 10.2   Visualization of Piet Mondrian's studio at 5 rue de Coulmiers, Paris. North wall

could go on in the same way through the entire studio', perhaps indicating he had applied further treatment to the walls. Indeed, a 1920 newspaper article resulting from a visit to the studio seems to suggest as much 'The walls of this room […] are divided spatially by unpainted or primed canvases, so that *each* wall forms a painting of little blocks.'[22] The detail of this treatment is not known. Similarly, there is no evidence regarding what furniture was in the room that is not accounted for in the *Trialogue*. Mondrian certainly had much more furniture by 1926, as can be seen in the Départ photographs, and it could potentially be argued that reasonably advanced spatial compositions existed elsewhere in the studio, particularly on the back wall. These contradictory accounts demonstrate that the Coulmiers arrangement was in a constant state of flux, much as was the case at Départ. In terms of a reconstruction, a more complex arrangement, taking into account the remaining walls, cannot be made due to the lack of evidence. The model therefore is based on Van Doesburg's description in which the south wall remains the focal point (see Figure 10.2).

---

22   Ibid., p. 66. My emphasis.

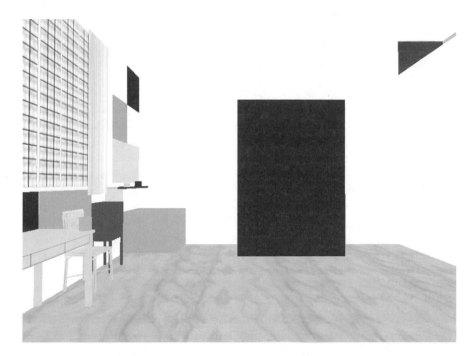

Figure 10.3   Visualization of Piet Mondrian's studio at 5 rue de Coulmiers, Paris. West wall

Analysis of the Model

In terms of evolution, the years 1919 to 1930 were highly productive for Mondrian in his development of Neo-Plasticism in architecture. The peak of his development occurs between 1926 and 1930, the years when he was apparently comfortable enough to have his studio at Départ photographcd extensively. The photographs suggest a confidence that Neo-Plasticism could be realized in the environment and represent the first concrete steps in that direction. The description of the Coulmiers studio in the *Trialogue* by contrast contains little of the confidence implicit in the photographs. Mondrian is hesitant in proclaiming the space as a Neo-Plastic triumph, 'We could continue in this way throughout the entire studio, but one thing I must point out: there is still a lack of unity.'[23] The path taken by Mondrian from hesitant beginnings in 1919 to fully realized self-assurance by 1926 can be explored though this visualization through comparison with the achievements reached in the Départ studio.

Mondrian was unequivocal in the *Trialogue* that '*everything* should contribute' and the realization of Neo-Plasticism in space would require all elements of

23   Mondrian, *Natural Reality and Abstract Reality*, p. 86.

the room – structure, wall treatment and furniture to be equilibrated.[24] In short, unity must be achieved in totality for an interior to be Neo-Plastic. The room at Coulmiers is a start in this direction but the apparent focus on the south wall occurs at the expense of the remaining walls. The south wall appears as it own equilibrated unit where the furniture is placed tight against the wall causing relationships to be expressed only along that plane. The remainder of the room is not plastically expressed in any meaningful way in the organization of the south wall. While the stated goal was to produce the impression of one flat plane, it was simply not enough to place all the focus onto one wall. For example, viewing a corner of the room would produce the effect of disharmony between treated and untreated wall leading to the materiality of objects being maintained. Neo-Plasticism in space thus required a solution that *connected* opposing wall planes through compositional elements (see Figure 10.3).

That Mondrian was aware of this issue is proved by the design of the Départ studio. Delbo's photographs reveal a more spatially complex arrangement in which furniture is placed at varying depths throughout the room so as to articulate each other within the space, not just in relation to the wall. The effect is less 'two-dimensional' than at Coulmiers, a problem Mondrian sought to resolve through the interrelation of wall planes and objects further into the room. Crucially, however, he had now achieved unity between all elements of the room where the north wall was no longer the nucleus. It remained partially the main focus due to the prominence of the easel but the horizontal table and the end of the stove serve to neutralize this effect.

However, the model though reveals a much more general but highly significant issue regarding Mondrian's studio arrangements – one of rectangularity and perpendicular expression (see Plate 3). In painting, the appropriate motif for the expression of modernity was that of universal perpendicular relationships. Neo-Plastic architecture was also to proceed along these lines, as it must retain the spirit of modernity as well prefiguring a cultural shift in which the separate arts were all fused into one.

Postma has shown the method by which Mondrian achieved this at Départ. The studio floor plan is irregular, consisting of five walls, two of which meet on the diagonal. Through placement, also on the diagonal, of the wardrobe, second easel and divan, Mondrian articulated the room by means of two cubes.[25] Also striking from Postma's reconstruction is the lengths to which Mondrian went to underplay the prism formed by the meeting of the east walls of the studio through the two tables, which are expressed in relation to the easel facing them and the wall behind them.[26] In this context, Troy's remarks on the Départ studio are brought into question. She writes:

---

24   Ibid., p. 83.
25   Postma, *26 Rue du Départ*, pp. 39–43.
26   Ibid., p. 46. See image 4 'view from above'.

> Mondrian seems to have gone to considerable lengths to suggest for the purpose
> of individual photographs that his rue du Départ studio was a regular, rectangular
> shape. [...] By the same token, some photographs show oblique angles formed
> by objects and furniture that might appear to have been *repoussoir* elements;
> however, these angles, though exploited to that end, were in fact the result of the
> actual shape and arrangement of the room.[27]

In the Départ studio, Mondrian was not merely suggesting the room was rectangular, but rather explicitly articulating a set of rectangular relationships. The arrangement of the room as two cubes is consistent in all of the photographs, suggesting that it was not simply a photographic device but a concrete structure on which he had decided and which formed the basis for any further experimentation with the room. The implication of Troy's analysis is that the irregularity of the room was a hindrance to Mondrian and that he sought to deny its existence. To some extent this is correct as he was striving to emphasize the rectangular. However, it was precisely because of its irregularity that Mondrian was able forcefully to articulate two cubes, producing a fuller, more profound Neo-Plastic expression. The cubes are articulated through the personal arrangement of objects, rather than relying on the external building structure. Neo-Plastic relationships were determinate and needed to be actively expressed by the artist. The Départ studio provided a space in which he could achieve this, where through irregularity he was able to impose rectangularity. In effect the studio represents the idea of destruction, the subject of Blotkamp's book, in which Mondrian sought 'the cancellation of form in favour of relationships'.[28]

The studio at Coulmiers did not afford Mondrian this destructive opportunity. Whilst he could make forays into Neo-Plastic relationships with colour planes and furniture arrangement, he could not actively articulate the structure of the room beyond what was already built. It is a curious contradiction that the rectangularity of the Coulmiers studio was a negative factor in the expression of rectangular relationships. Mondrian seems at least partially aware of this in 1919 when he writes, 'A room has to be more than an empty space limited by six facing walls. It has to be rather an articulated, *partially filled space with six sub-divided planes opposing one another* [...].'[29] Whilst initially he spoke positively regarding the structure of Coulmiers, in the end the studio *was* a space limited by six facing walls causing its subdivision to be problematic. He mentions that the windows, fireplace and built-in wardrobe provide a sense of subdivision, but this only occurs in relation to their respective wall plane. In Départ he was able to subdivide the space as whole effectively adding three wall planes (see Figure 10.4).

There is little precise information regarding Mondrian's transfer from Coulmiers to Départ. He was forced to leave Coulmiers in November 1921 and

---

27 Troy, *The De Stijl Environment*, p. 141.
28 Blotkamp, *Mondrian*, p. 15.
29 Mondrian, *Natural Reality and Abstract Reality*, p. 82. My emphasis.

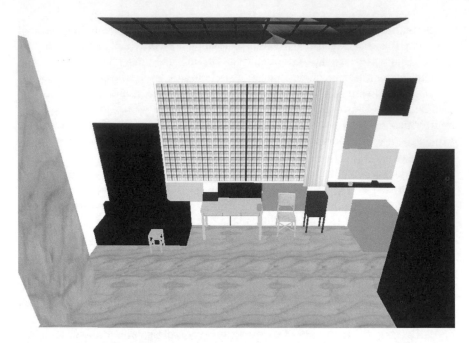

Figure 10.4   Visualization of Piet Mondrian's studio at 5 rue de Coulmiers, Paris. South wall viewed from balcony

returned to the rue du Départ complex where he had previously had his studio, except this time took up occupancy in a different room on the third floor. Why Mondrian ended up in one of only two irregular studios in the entire complex is a matter of some conjecture. It has been suggested, for instance, that the odd shape of the room meant the rent was lower.[30] Certainly on the surface it seems a strange choice given Mondrian's insistence on rectangularity. However, in the context of his experimentation at Coulmiers and the potential problems arising from a rectangular room, it seems possible that Mondrian actively sought out the irregular-shaped room as the next stage in the continual evolution of his ideas on Neo-Plastic architecture.

The problem of a rectangular room for Neo-Plastic expression also seems to have occurred in the only architectural design Mondrian produced during his lifetime. The plan for the room of Ida Bienert in Dresden, the so-called Salon de Mme B (1926, Staatlichen Kunstsammlung, Kupferstich-Kabinett, Dresden), which was rectangular, contained very little furniture with each wall, ceiling and floor covered in colour planes. Blotkamp has noted that the wall surfaces seem to have 'been conceived independently of one another', a problem for true Neo-Plastic expression.[31] Indeed, Michael Seuphor has noted that Mondrian eventually

---

30   Postma, *26 Rue du Départ*, p. 36.
31   Blotkamp, *Mondrian*, p. 155.

deemed it totally inappropriate. 'He showed me the drawing and said "It's a good thing Ida Bienert never carried it out. One should never make such decorative things. That was a mistake of mine.""[32]

The second of Troy's points concerns the oblique angles formed by furniture and objects that can be observed in many of the Départ photographs. Henkels has commented on the 'curious' nature of the introduction of the diagonal. Indeed both critics consider the diagonal an unexpected element and both attempt to explain its appearance as something of an anomaly. Henkels characterizes these as 'old-fashioned *repoussoir*' elements, a description which is hardly suitable given Mondrian's planar attitude to composition. [33] Troy argues that while they function as *respoussoir* elements they were in fact a by-product of the shape and arrangement of the room.[34] It seems self-evident, however, that Mondrian included diagonal elements of his own accord. That he had total control over its arrangement as well as the positioning of Delbo's camera suggests as much.

Mondrian's interest in the diagonal is confirmed by the diamond compositions painted during 1925–6. It functions strictly as a support for the interior composition, which as usual is a set of perpendicular and colour relationships. The success of the 1925 diamond paintings lies in the ever-expanding effect produced where the diagonals of the canvas bisect with the perpendicular lines. Furthermore, the opposition created between diagonal and perpendicular serves to emphasize the interior geometry of the picture plane.

The diamond format occurs at a time Mondrian was particularly concentrating on the issue of Neo-Plasticism in space and he appears to have considered the diamond composition and studio interrelated. In an interview of 1926 with *De Telegraff*, he described one of his diamond compositions as 'an abstract surrogate of the whole [studio]'.[35] The diagonal as a support mechanism is thus at the heart of the success of the Départ studio. Interestingly, Champa has characterized Mondrian's use of the diamond canvas as 'for special occasions or, more specifically, for those times when he needed most to reassure himself of his own artistry and to reassess the terms in which he employed it'.[36] It should come as no surprise that Mondrian returned to the diamond shape when he was formulating his ideas on architecture, which were still highly experimental and potentially extremely problematic. The diamond compositions emphasize, perhaps even over-emphasize, the essential tenets of Mondrian's artistic viewpoint and consequently he used the ideas present in them to re-evaluate his approach to Neo-Plastic architecture after experiencing difficulties with its realization at Coulmiers.

---

32   Postma, *26 Rue du Départ*, p. 16.

33   Herbert Henkels, 'Mondrian in his studio' in *Mondrian. From Figuration to Abstraction* (London, 1988), p. 187.

34   Troy, *The De Stijl Environment*, p. 141.

35   Quoted in Troy, *The De Stijl Environment*, p. 138.

36   Champa, *Mondrian Studies*, p. 10.

Conclusion

My purpose here is to demonstrate that visualization can be used to produce scholarship that develops traditional art-historical debate. The concept of paradata as visualization outcome is crucial for forming these arguments because the process of model building rather than the final digital output is what stimulates inquiry. Dissemination of these paradata is thus needed as it provides transparency for the digital model, but also forms part of the argument itself.

This methodology produces complex paradata which provide transparency for the model and are highly necessary in this case, as source material is limited and many unscientific and improvisational methods were used to devise data from which a model could be made. Strictly, art-historical paradata are generated by assessing general trends in Mondrian's art practice and applying them to the model. While no claims are made regarding the correctness of the final model, it is this process that has allowed the final arguments to made.

Mondrian's theory of Neo-Plastic architecture is one of absolutes. The 'everything must contribute' doctrine proscribed in the *Trialogue*, which underpins its successful application, presents significant challenges to the abstract artist. It is apparent from a comparison of the 3D model of Coulmiers and Postma's reconstruction of Départ where issues regarding Neo-Plastic space arose. Unity through equilibrated relationships did not find proper expression in Coulmiers due to the compositional focus on the south wall and the absence of connecting compositional elements throughout the room. On a larger scale, the rectangularity of the room was also a stumbling block. In the end, for Mondrian, walls that simply faced each other were decorative and contained none of the asymmetry and tension appropriate to Neo-Plasticism – a problem he also experienced with his design for the Salon de Mme B.

Mondrian addresses these issues with characteristic rigour in the Départ studio. He returns to the notion of the oblique line as support for the perpendicular, a motif in which he had confidence, to address the compositional dead ends he had encountered at Coulmiers. The irregular shape of the room allowed him to devise a scheme in which rectangularity could be expressed deterministically without reliance on the existing structure of the room. The resulting design expressed relationships in varying degrees of magnitude from the articulation of two structural cubes down to the placement of tiny compositional objects. The level of clarity seen in the Départ studio was the outcome of experimentation at Coulmiers. Through a re-evaluation of Neo-Plastic architecture, caused by challenges he had encountered in the earlier studio, Mondrian was able to give the 'everything must contribute' maxim full artistic expression.

Chapter 11

Just how Predictable is Predictive Lighting?[1]

Kate Devlin

Introduction

Predictive lighting refers to the use of computer-modelling software to simulate the behaviour of light, resulting in a virtual scene that physically represents the real world in terms of illumination, providing images that appear – and aim to be – 'realistic'. Predictive lighting techniques have been used with great success to simulate illumination in architectural renderings, forensic reconstructions and increasingly in cultural heritage visualizations with the aim of depicting the scene as it would have looked if observed directly.[2] This method uses information about the geometry of an environment, the material properties of the surfaces in that environment and the spectral properties of the light sources to generate a mathematical simulation that one can, to some degree, consider accurate. This enables us to explore new hypotheses and examine the way in which things were viewed and understood in the past by manipulating variables and working with virtual objects in a way that may not be possible with a real site or artefact.

Leaving aside the contentious issues of the content representation, the use of predictive lighting has its own limitations. While one can simulate lighting values and their distribution in a scene, one cannot yet say with complete confidence that one has achieved a match between the perception of the real world and its representation in the form of a computer model. This is due to display restrictions and aspects of the human visual system, such as colour and brightness perception, which affect the interpretation of the output images. Such issues can also influence any images displayed in an electronic manner, as control of the visual output is often reduced or lost after the rendering process is complete. In order to state authoritatively that images used are valid, it is necessary to determine the degree of certainty that one has in the process, and make this evaluation transparent to the user.

---

1   This chapter is a revised and expanded version of the paper presented at the seminar Making 3D Visual Research Outcomes Transparent, co-sponsored by the AHRC ICT Methods Network; EPOCH; PIN, Prato, Italy and King's Visualisation Lab, King's College London, held at the British Academy on 23–25 February 2006.

2   Kate Devlin, Alan Chalmers and Duncan Brown, 'Predictive Lighting and Perception in Archaeological Representations', *UNESCO World Heritage in the Digital Age. 30th Anniversary Digital Congress,* (2003).

Three-dimensional Modelling and Predictive Lighting

Three-dimensional modelling has become a useful, if not indispensable tool for visualizing archaeological information. Although there are a number of ways in which computer modelling can be used, and a variety of outputs that can be achieved, the focus here is on one particular aspect: virtual representations that are intended to be physically accurate in terms of lighting.

The way in which objects are visually understood is governed by their lighting conditions. Today, the steady and clear illumination given by electric light is taken for granted. In the past, however, lighting was either by means of natural daylight or flame. Traces in the archaeological record give an indication of what was used – windows, hearths, lamps – implying circumstances greatly different from the instantaneous and widespread brightness experienced nowadays. At present, the majority of photorealistic, computer-generated images created for archaeological purposes are created, as their name suggests, with the intention of resembling reality in terms of a photograph. They focus on the appearance rather than the accuracy of a scene. Often, that may simply be what is required of them: a visually impressive depiction. As Earl notes, 'a scene might contain 50 lights and atmospheric effects, render times of many hours, and diverse post-production filters'.[3] While such input can generate a visually appealing result, it is more likely that the original environment being modelled would have been lit with perhaps a single or a few light sources. Photorealistic rendering is concerned merely with appearance, often ignoring or using physically impossible lighting values and often giving no consideration to the actual colour of the light source, something which can have a dramatic impact on a scene.

Predictive lighting is a way of using 3D computer modelling to visualize the light levels and appearance of a space given the properties of that space and the properties of the light source. It takes 3D modelling a step further by gathering information about the modelled scene and using it to mimic how light would have behaved in that environment. Predictive lighting has as its basis a technique known as ray tracing. This is a method in which a ray of light is traced backwards through the scene, starting from what the camera (also the viewer) sees. If the ray of light intersects with an object in the scene then its interaction with the object – the reflection, refraction or absorption – is calculated. This is repeated for every pixel in the final image, resulting in an accurate simulation of the path of light. Ray tracing is commonly used in standard 3D modelling software but by adding predictive lighting to the ray-tracing procedure the properties of the source of illumination – namely the intensity and the spectral profile, which dictates the colour of the light – are included in the rendering of the scene.

---

3   Graeme P. Earl, 'At the Edge of the Lens: Photography, Graphical Constructions and Cinematography', in T. Evans and P. Daly (eds), *Digital Archaeology* (2006), pp. 191–209.

Creating a Scene using Predictive Lighting

The following steps give a simplified overview of the process involved in creating a visualization using predictive lighting techniques:

1. Capture/create the scene geometry. This can be done in a number of ways, including making detailed measurements of a real scene, working from plans or using technology such as 3D laser scanning. Once this information has been obtained, a virtual 3D model is built using 3D-modelling software.
2. Assign the appropriate material types and textures. Knowing the surface and other properties of a material in a scene is vital as it will influence how light travels around a scene: for example, some materials will reflect much more light than others. Textures provide a means of displaying surface detail by using images (usually photographs) of that surface within the virtual model.
3. Measure the spectral profile of the light source. This is carried out using an instrument such as a spectroradiometer that can read the emission spectrum of a light source and collect its spectral information. A flame-based light source will have a very different spectral profile from an electrical source and will therefore result in a light that is different in colour. For daylight simulation, information such as the latitude, longitude, date and day is required.
4. Convert these data to an appropriate format. Spectral data are often converted into a colour space such as Red, Green and Blue (RGB). Although the conversion requires some approximation, it makes the electronic display possible and the work easier.
5. Render with a predictive lighting package. Several predictive lighting packages are available. In this research Ward's Radiance was used, an open source lighting visualization tool kit that can generate results in the form of colour images, numerical illumination values and lighting contour plots.

Using the information gathered in steps 1 to 4, Radiance calculates the light directly arriving at a given surface from the light source (the direct component), the light which has been reflected onto that surface (the specular indirect component), and the light transmitted to that surface from other sources (the diffuse indirect component).

Plate 4 shows an example of a virtual scene that has been modelled in 3D then rendered in Radiance. The image on the left shows the scene as it would appear when illuminated under a 50-watt electric light. The image on the right shows the same scene as it would appear when illuminated under the possible original lighting conditions of olive oil lamplight. Changes in the perception of colour within the scene due to changes in illumination colour are evident, and the *trompe l'oeil* paint effects on the walls are thrown into sharper relief due to the change in the spectral component of the light, and due to the shadow effects.

Generating New Hypotheses

Having simulated a scene where one can have relative confidence in its fidelity, the resulting images can be used to generate and test new hypotheses regarding perception of past environments. One's overall impression of the scene – the lights, the colours, the shadows, the features that are visible and not visible – should appear the same today as they would to those who originally occupied that space. One is working with a simulation of their surroundings that can be said to be physically valid. This provides the option of changing and manipulating variables in a manner that is not possible in real life, such as introducing dynamic flame and the effects of smoke or dust,[4] or adding artefacts or furnishings to interiors. This can be done with a good degree of confidence because one has had control over the input to the process.

From Rendering to Display: What you Create is Not What You Get

Aside from the usual problems with the nature of the content of the representations and the contentious issues over how and what can be portrayed, can one really state that using a mathematical, physically based approach one can show how things would have looked to people in the past? It is tempting to say that if, despite the necessary approximations, the process is accurate then one meets the criteria: the light has been accurately simulated therefore the scene should be a faithful reproduction of how it would have appeared. However, Goodman, speaking of representational fidelity in his *Languages of Art*, remarks:

> Even where both the light rays and the momentary external conditions are the same, the preceding train of visual experience, together with the information gathered from all sources, can make a vast difference in what is seen. If not even the former conditions are the same, duplication of light rays is no more likely to result in identical perception than is duplication of the conditions if light rays differ.[5]

This observation also applies in terms of computer-generated images. Even if one has produced a perceptually accurate image, one may not *see* it that way. The processes that occur from the time the image is displayed on screen and before it reaches the retina must be considered. Producing a technically valid image is not necessarily an indicator of the perceived fidelity of that image. Other factors, which occur after the rendering process, adversely influence what one sees. One is at the mercy of the viewing conditions, the display and one's own visual system.

---

4   Diego Gutierrez, Veronic Sundstedt, Fermin Gomez, Alan Chalmers, 'Dust and Light: Predictive Virtual Archaeology', *Journal of Cultural Heritage*, 8/2 (2007): 209–14.

5   Nelson Goodman, *Languages of Art* (Indianapolis, 1976).

This is true for any image, and should be taken into consideration whether one is attempting to create realistic images that simulate a real-world scene or are presenting a surrogate image such as a photograph of a manuscript or artefact intended to record or preserve it.

Perceptual consistency is desirable in cultural heritage applications in the capture and creation of images that can be used as perceptually equivalent representations of an original. Virtual reality and visualization methods can provide highly detailed models of sites and artefacts. Advances in scanning and digital photography have led to the widespread use of this technology to preserve digitally original text and art. For digital archiving to be used as a technique for representation or preservation, the integrity of an image must be affirmed.[6]

Due to the need for image integrity, a number of standards and guidelines have been set in place, including those of the UK's Arts and Humanities Data Service.[7] Reilly and Frey's report to the USA's Library of Congress remarked on the differences between images when viewed on different systems or monitors, stating that Library staff found it problematic 'when discussing the quality of scans with vendors over the telephone, because the two parties did not see the same image'.[8]

Viewing Environment

The lighting in the real world influences the perceptual fidelity of an image. The light already present in a room can cause images to look 'washed out'. For example, a slide projected onto a screen appears faded because the perceived contrast of the image displayed has been reduced by the presence of other light – the ambient illumination – within the room. Often a certain level of ambient illumination in a room is required, for example to enable safe mobility or to facilitate note-taking, so it may not always be desirable to remove the extraneous lighting altogether, but rather to accommodate it in some way.

If one has created an image which one is stating is faithful to the original, this claim may be invalidated when the image is shared and is viewed on a different monitor or in a different location (such as images displayed over a network or on the internet). One loses control over one's own creations once they have been disseminated, so one needs to be aware of any factors that might adversely

---

6   Kate Devlin, Alan Chalmers and E. Reinhard, 'Displaying Digitally Archived Images', in Franziska Frey and R. Buckley (eds), *Proceedings of IS&T Archiving Conference*, Society for Imaging Science and Technology (2004), pp. 157–62.

7   Catherine Grout, Phill Purdy, J. Rymer, K. Youngs, J. Williams, A. Lock and D. Brickley, *Creating Digital Resources for the Visual Arts: Standards and Good Practice* (Oxford, 2000).

8   James Reilly and Franziska Frey, *Recommendations for the Evaluation of Digital Images Produced from Photographic, Microphotographic, and Various Paper Formats*, Report to the Library of Congress (1996).

influence the display medium. By acknowledging – and, better still, correcting – these factors, one retains confidence in one's own creation and assures its quality.

Display Limitations

One goal of realistic computer graphics is that if a virtual scene is viewed under the same conditions as a corresponding real-world scene, the two images should have the same tones. However, due to the limitations of current technology, this is rarely the case. The ratio between the darkest and the lightest values in a scene is known as the dynamic range. The dynamic range in the real world is far greater than the range that can be produced on most electronic displays. The human visual system can accommodate a wide range of luminance in a single view, around 10,000:1 candelas per square metre (cd/m^2). The eye adapts to one's surroundings, extending this range and changing what one sees over time. An image displayed on a standard CRT or LCD screen is greatly restricted in terms of tonality, perhaps achieving at most 150:1 cd/m^2. It is therefore necessary that the image be altered in some way, usually through some form of scaling, to fit a display device that is only capable of outputting a low dynamic range.[9]

Visual Perception

In recent years, knowledge of visual perception in computer graphics has increased, predominately due to the demand for realistic computer-generated images.[10] The aim of perceptually based rendering is to produce imagery that evokes the same responses as an observer would have when viewing a real-world equivalent. To this end, work has been carried out on examining the behaviour of the human visual system. For this information to be measured quantitatively, a branch of psychology known as psychophysics is employed, where quantitative relations between physical stimuli and psychological events can be established.[11] This information can then be used to design systems that are finely attuned to the perceptual attributes of the visual system.

Psychophysical research confirms that there are factors that influence perception in relation to viewing displayed images. One example is colour

---

9   Kate Devlin, Alan Chalmers, Alexander Wilkie and Werner Purgathofer. 'Tone Reproduction and Physically Based Spectral Rendering', in Dieter Fellner and Roberto Scopignio (eds), *State of the Art Reports*, Eurographics (2002).

10   G.W. Meyer, H.E. Rushmeier, M.F. Cohen, D.P. Greenberg and K.E. Torrance, 'An Experimental Evaluation of Computer Graphics Imagery', *ACM Transactions on Graphics*, 5/1 (1986): 30–50. H. Rushmeier, G. Ward, C. Piatko, P. Sanders and B. Rust, 'Comparing Real and Synthetic Images: Some Ideas about metrIcs', in *Proceedings of the Eurographics Rendering Workshop* (1995). J.A. Ferwerda, 'Three Varieties of Realism in Computer Graphics', in *Proceedings of SPIE Human Vision and Electronic Imaging '03* (2003), pp. 290–97.

11   R. Sekuler and R. Blake, *Perception* (New York, 1994).

constancy. This is the ability to judge a surface's reflective properties despite any changes in illumination. Similar to this is lightness constancy, the term used to describe the phenomenon whereby a surface appears to look the same regardless of any differences in the illumination.[12] For example, white paper with black text maintains its appearance when viewed indoors in a dark environment or outdoors in bright sunlight, even if the black ink on a page viewed outdoors reflects more light than the white paper viewed indoors. Chromatic colour constancy extends this to colour: a plant seems as green when it is outside in the sun as it does if it is taken indoors under artificial light.

Other aspects of the human visual system also need to be considered. The visual system adjusts to the stimuli received, resulting in changes in sensitivity known as adaptation. This enables us to respond to large variations in luminance. Visual adaptation from light to dark can take tens of minutes as the photo-receptors in the eye reach their sensitivity gradually. If a scene is simulated with minimal light sources, the original observer within that scene would have adapted to their environment and could well have had a different perceptual response than someone looking at the virtual equivalent on a small monitor. Adaptation also influences contrast sensitivity – when the visual system has adapted to a certain frequency, sensitivity to that, and nearby frequencies, is decreased.[13]

Overcoming the Problems

The problems indicated above do have some solutions and workarounds. As yet, there is no single way to ensure perceptual accuracy once an image is displayed, but a number of steps can be taken to address many of the factors mentioned.

Contrast Correction

Correcting for the 'washed out' appearance caused by reflections off computer monitors can be achieved in one of three ways. First, the display device can be physically altered to reduce reflections, such as fitting an anti-glare screen. Although this changes the amount of light reaching the screen it does not eliminate the problem; it merely changes it in an uncalibrated manner and so is not a principled approach. Second, the environment can be adjusted, thereby controlling the ambient light. Controlled viewing environments are recommended by the International Organization for Standardization (ISO) and by European Commission directives. The conditions they specify are not always feasible, so this is neither a practical nor a simple approach to controlling the ambient light present. Third, the environment can be characterized and the effects of the ambient light can be taken into account when the image is displayed. This involves measuring

---

12   S.E. Palmer, *Vision Science* (Cambridge, MA, 1999).
13   A.S. Glassner, *Principles of Digital Image Synthesis* (San Francisco, 1995).

the amount of reflected light, either through hardware (sensors or cameras) or diagnostic software. Once this information is acquired, algorithmic correction can be applied, for example through the use of colour appearance models[14] or contrast manipulation.

Adjustments such as these are in place in other fields of research, including medical imaging and aviation, where the user must be confident that there is perceptual fidelity between the original image and the image being viewed.[15] Fortunately, it is not an unknown problem within the Arts and Humanities either. The Bodleian Library's online image catalogue at the University of Oxford states:

> Note that the apparent quality of the images as viewed on-screen is in part dependent upon the quality of the monitor used to view them, and the apparent colour-values likewise dependent on whether the monitor has been correctly calibrated, and the ambient lighting conditions of the room.[16]

Tone Mapping

To ensure a true representation of tonal values, some form of scaling or mapping is required to convey the range of a light in a real-world scene on a display with limited capabilities. Although it is tempting to use a straightforward linear scaling, this is not an adequate solution as many details can be lost. Instead, the mapping must be specifically tailored in a non-linear manner, permitting the luminance to be compressed in an appropriate way. Algorithmic solutions, known as tone-mapping operators or tone reproduction operators, have been devised to compress certain features of an image and produce a result with a reduced dynamic range that appears plausible or appealing on a computer monitor.[17] Some of these operators focus on preserving aspects such as detail or brightness, some concentrate on producing a subjectively pleasing image, while others focus on providing a perceptually accurate representation of the real-world equivalent. At present, validation of these operators in still in its infancy and it is a matter of choosing the best tool for the job, although the recent development of high-dynamic-range displays means operators can be compared more accurately.[18] Where required, for the purposes of

---

14   M.D. Fairchild, *Color Appearance Models* (Reading, MA, 1998).

15   National Electrical Manufacturers Association. *Digital Imaging and Communications in Medicine (DICOM) Part 14: Greyscale Standard Display Function* (2003), <http://medical.nema.org/dicom/2004/04_14PU.pdf>.

16   Bodleian Library, University of Oxford, <http://www.bodley.ox.ac.uk/dept/scwmss/wmss/medieval/mss/lat/misc/e/086.htm>.

17   Erk Reinhard, Greg Ward, Sumanta Pattanaik and Paul Debevec, *High Dynamic Range Imaging: Acquisition, Display, and Image-Based Lighting* (San Francisco, 2005).

18   Patrick Ledda, Alan Chalmers, Tom Troscianko, Helge Seetzen, 'Evaluation of Tone Mapping Operators using a High Dynamic Range Display', *ACM Transactions on Graphics*, 24/3 (2005): 640–48.

realistic image generation perceptually accurate operators are, naturally, the best choice.

Perceptually Based Rendering

Work continues in the field of computer science on perceptually based rendering, and interdisciplinary psychophysical research involving extensive user studies is becoming more commonplace. The study of human perception is inseparable from the presentation of images in computer graphics and there is much to be learned from related fields such as vision, psychology and neuroscience, where established knowledge can further developments in computing.

Transparency and the Displayed Image

The attempt, through scientific methods, to make a virtual image as real as possible leads one back to the same problem faced when determining the image content: how does one know what is valid? At first glance, the processes involved in generating an image using predictive lighting techniques seem accountable and quantifiable. It seems that reliability should be achievable because one has carefully calculated and measured each step of the process: the materials, the light sources, their colour and intensity, the geometry. One can certainly account for one's input into the scene and strive to justify one's choices regarding the values that have been used. This can be as simple a matter as documenting in text format the process that one has followed in creating the image. A more robust method would be the inclusion of structured metadata to describe the content in a more thorough manner. This transparency immediately places us ahead of images that have been generated to provide an attractive, compelling, photorealistic impression with less concern for archaeological validity.

The irony of transparency becoming an issue, when one is creating worlds of light, is not lost; how to achieve clarity is not always clear. In attempting to create more realistic images one finds that one needs to introduce more and more variables, and each new variable introduced requires more control. There is no easy solution to this. If one is striving for perceptual realism then one needs to make every effort to justify one's choices and show that one has considered and accounted for the factors that adversely influence what one presents. It is not possible to provide guarantees or give an exact degree of certainty but the decision-making process can be documented and the choices that have been made can be explained, for example by providing sources for information (how lighting values were obtained and what those values are) and reference and citations to supporting material from the archaeological record.

The archaeological evidence used to create images has already come through so many selective stages before it reaches the visualizer – the choice of excavation site, the material that has survived, the way it has been sampled, how it was excavated, how this was interpreted. A definitive explanation is therefore rare in the discipline, and nor can one offer a defining image that says '*this* is real', but in the same way that a more complete understanding can be built from the archaeological evidence, so too can one build towards an image that is valid in certain aspects and allows new insights into the past.

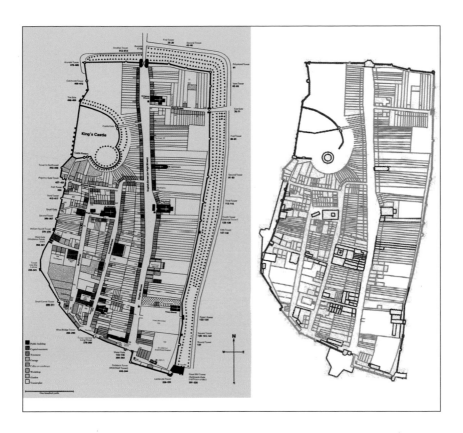

Plate 1   Left: Plan of medieval Southampton based on the Southampton Terrier of 1454. Right: Plan derived from combined sources: 1454 Terrier (green), archaeology (red); cartography (blue) and inferred data (magenta) © Matt Jones, 2008

Plate 2   **Visualization of Southampton as it might have looked in 1454.**
© **Matt Jones, 2008**

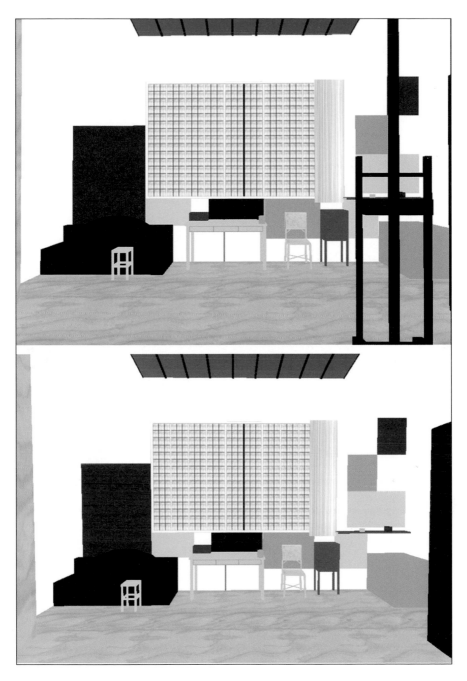

Plate 3   Visualization of Piet Mondrian's studio at 5 rue de Coulmiers, Paris. South wall view with and without easel. © Ryan Egel-Andrews, 2009

Plate 4   Computer simulation of the House of the Vettii, Pompeii, under electric light (left) and as illuminated by olive oil lamp (right) © Kate Devlin

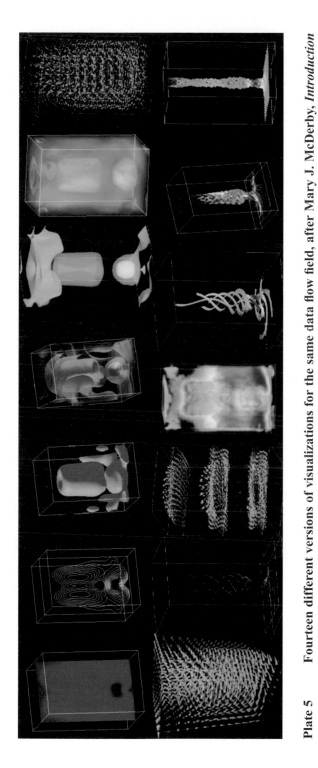

Plate 5 Fourteen different versions of visualizations for the same data flow field, after Mary J. McDerby, *Introduction to Scientific Visualization*, Training notes (Manchester: University of Manchester Research Computing Services, 2007). Reproduced with kind permission

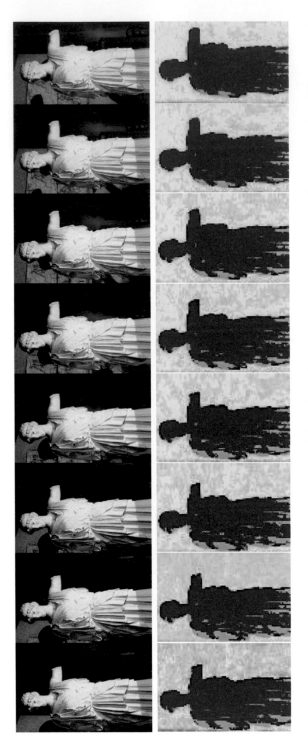

Plate 6 Photogrammetric photo-sequences of the Athena Lemnia statue demonstrating the effectiveness of the random pattern. The sequence consists of 21 photos, the first eight are shown. The second row shows the reconstruction quality from the dense matching: blue indicates that a reliable depth value is available for the respective pixel, yellow means very low quality

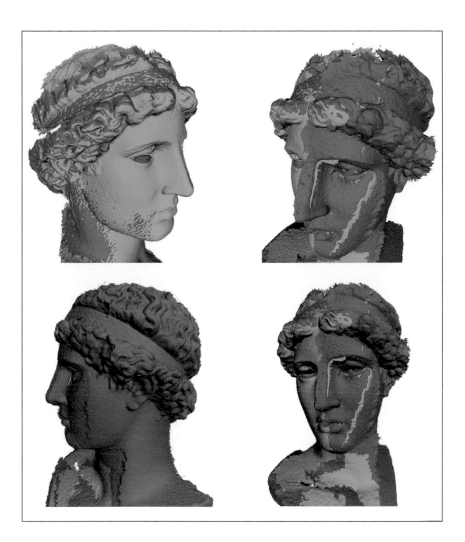

Plate 7 The final step: aligning the resulting meshes from the eight image sequences, then fusing them together. This involves a rough manual alignment, followed by numeric refinement. The ICP algorithm has only a small radius of convergence, so considerable experience is required to perform the alignment and select good feature points

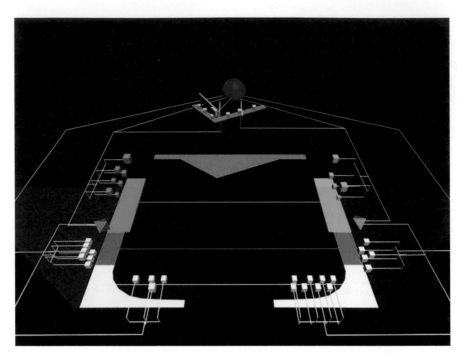

Plate 8   Cybernetic map of the Castiglion Fiorentino Museum by Eva Pietroni. Reproduced courtesy of Eva Pietroni, CNR ITABC

Plate 9   Virtual archaeological reconstruction of the House of Livia
           in Rome where every artefact has affordances such as Space,
           Time, Use, Type and Similarity assigned. Affordances may be
           activated and examined by the users as they interact with the
           model

Plate 10   Virtual reconstruction of the archaeological townscape of Bologna in Roman times (top); archaeological reconstruction of the Certosa area in Bologna in Etruscan times (middle); virtual reconstruction of the archaeological landscape of the Roman *Via Flaminia* and the House of Livia, Rome (bottom)

Plate 11 House of the Centenary Project, Pompeii. Different stages of the real-time navigation and possible interactions. Images courtesy of the Department of Archaeology at the University of Bologna and CINECA

Plate 12   View of Verona from Saint Peter's hill (top). The Roman bridge is visible on the right. Photo © Jacopo Prisco. *Iconogaphia Ratheriana* (bottom) depicting Verona around 1000

Plate 13   Source correlation between two drawings of Ename (top). Proposed 3D visualization of Ename between 1593 and 1596 (bottom)

Plate 14   **Drawing of 1612 showing Wijnendale castle in ruins (top) and a 3D visualization of the castle as it might have looked in 1530 (bottom)**

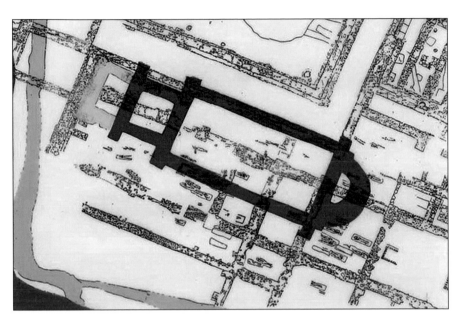

Plate 15   Excavation plan of the church of St Saviour in Ename

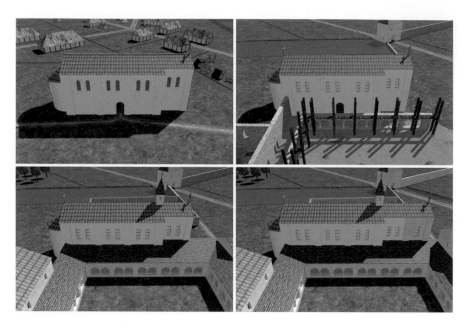

Plate 16   **Different building phases of the church St Saviour Church in Ename: 1020, 1065, 1070 and 1100**

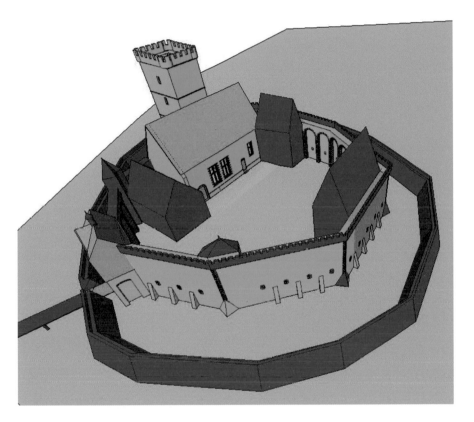

Plate 17 Reliability of the visualization of the sixteenth-century phase of the Horst castle, Belgium: red = low, orange = medium, green = high; after Peter Sterckx

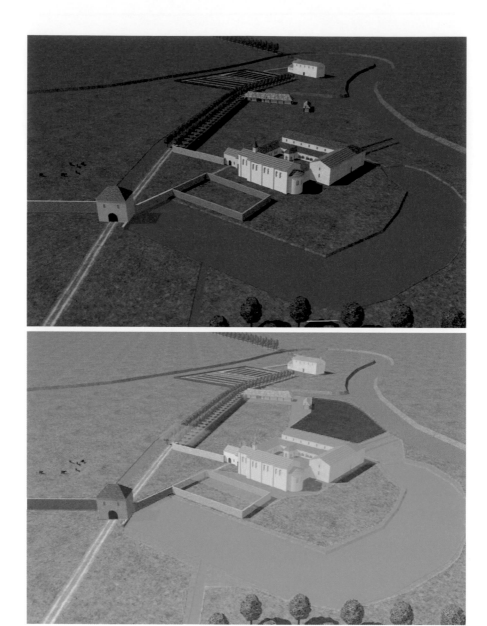

Plate 18   **Scholarly visualization of the Ename abbey around 1070 (top) and its reliability (red = low, green = high) (bottom)**

Plate 19 Visualization of the Ename abbey around 1070 created for public display

Plate 20 Three-dimensional visualization of Roman watchtower in Valkenburg, The Netherlands (bottom). Alternative visualizations with equal probability (top) of which the design on the left is chosen as representative

Plate 21 Panoramic, 360-degree visualization of the Roman landscape of Goudsberg, Valkenburg (top) and a photographic panorama of current landscape (bottom)

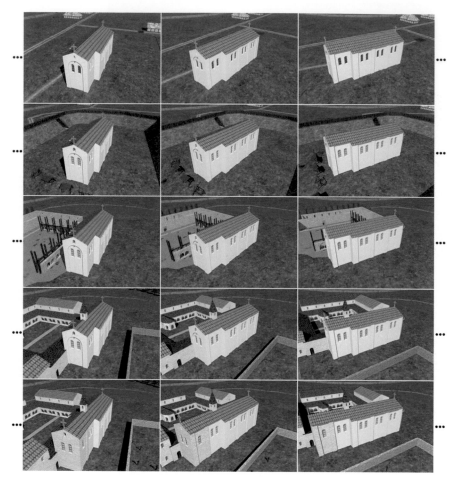

Plate 22   **Part of an interactive, 4D presentation of the St Saviour church in Ename in 1020, 1040, 1065, 1070 and 1100**

Plate 23   Excavations at Ename

Chapter 12

Lies, Damned Lies and Visualizations: Will Metadata and Paradata be a Solution or a Curse?[1]

Martin J. Turner

Introduction

Depending on the reference, approximately one-third of the human brain is involved with the processing of visual input.[2] Therefore, to transmit a large amount of information to the public, visual stimuli can be the most efficient way to increase the required data flow. Will Schroeder et al., in *The Visualisation Toolkit*, summarized this as:

> Informally visualisation is the transformation of data or information into pictures. Visualisation engages the primal human sensory apparatus, vision, as well as the processing power of the human mind. The result is a simple and effective medium for communication complex and/or voluminous information.[3]

The University of Manchester, Research Computing Services, starting with the Computer Graphics Unit, has for over thirty years been considering how efficiently to create and present visual stimuli, and is still learning the best way to integrate and transfer information from computer source to the human user. Even after this extended period of time aiding the visualization needs of various different research communities, there have been discovered no single-step solutions or golden rules that would solve all problems (although there are continual attempts).[4] One of the

---

1   This chapter is a revised and expanded version of the paper presented at the seminar *Making 3D Visual Research Outcomes Transparent*, co-sponsored by the AHRC ICT Methods Network; EPOCH; PIN, Prato, Italy and King's Visualisation Lab, King's College London, held at the British Academy on 23–25 February 2006.

2   Jacqueline Ludel, *Introduction to Sensory Processes* (San Francisco, 1978); Clyde W. Oyster, *The Human Eye: Structure and Function* (Sunderland, MA, 2006).

3   Will Schroeder, Ken Martin and William Lorensen, *The Visualization Toolkit* (New Jersey, 1998), p.1.

4   Martin Dodge, Mary J. McDerby and Martin Turner, *Geographic Visualization: Concepts, Tools and Applications* (Chichester, 2008).

reasons for this is that when analysing data and ideas one forgets to consider the complex fallibilities that exist within the human visual system.

The psychologist James Alcock described human brain as a 'belief engine' – constantly processing information from our senses and then creating and recreating an ever-changing belief system about the world we live in (recently applying belief to all forms of sceptical enquiries).[5] This chapter considers briefly the route a photon of light takes to become a known signal in the human brain, indicating how information is extracted from the visual data that then creates a specific belief. Then the opposite is considered: how erroneous signals can result in this transfer of information from computer to human that may and will mislead. This will imply that there are ways to confuse and obfuscate the human visual system.

Finally, within the field and research of e-science, the author considers the introduction of metadata and paradata as a possible solution to resolve some of these issues.

Photons of Light Turned into Information

Over the last couple of decades neurobiologists have probed ever deeper within animal vision systems to offer a far better understanding of the biological and organizational arrangement of the visual 'belief engine'.[6] The story of how light is interpreted will now be briefly considered, during which one will be mainly concerned with the retina of the eye and the transfer of signals to the brain.

When light enters the eye it is bent by the cornea, including in my case a contact lens. The light then passes through the aqueous humour, the pupil and the main lens of the eye. The pupil varies in size, depending on the contraction of the circular and radial muscles of the iris to regulate the amount of light received. At the lens, the light is finely focused depending upon the intra-ocular muscles to create an image on the retina at the back of the eye. Some of the light is absorbed by the retina and translated into neural information, to become synaptic responses. Synapses occur between (photo-) receptors and neurons as well as among neurons (inter-neurons) and with repeated use increase the ease of further transmission, thus reinforcing the action. Through training this allows faster response to certain stimuli, meaning that as we see, we actually see certain things better, and conversely miss others. Synaptic transmissions may have EPSP (excitatory postsynaptic potential) or IPSP (inhibitory postsynaptic potential), which allow a response to be either positive or negative. These resulting signals are algebraically summed by the postsynaptic

---

5   James A. Alcock, Jean Burns and Anthony Freeman (eds), 'PSI Wars: Getting to Grips with the Paranormal', *Journal of Consciousness Studies*, 6–7 (2003).

6   See amongst others Oyster, *The Human Eye: Structure and Function*; Ludel, *Introduction to Sensory Processes*; and Eric R. Kandel, James H. Schwartz and Thomas M. Jessell (eds), *Principles of Neural Science* (New York, 2000).

neuron, and depending upon their relative strength the axon of that neuron may be 'excited' or 'inhibited'.

Once light is absorbed by the retina it is translated into neural information, to become synaptic responses travelling from one neuron to another towards and throughout the brain. The retina is actually a part of the brain and consists of 110–130 million photoreceptors (consisting of a small number of cones, used for colour vision, and a majority of rods, used for grey-scale vision). The rods are very sensitive to light whereas cones function poorly at low levels, requiring higher levels to respond. For example, at twilight, when cones operate very poorly, one loses all colour information and objects take on a grey value. There is a three-stage process from photon to neural response:

1. Rods contain a single pigment called rhodopsin, which is light-sensitive (a combination of retinal and a variety of the protein opsin). Retinal is a fairly simple molecule, but when a photon hits it, it changes structural shape. *This occurs in a few picoseconds.*
2. This process of metamorphosis continues through a series of intermediary forms until it reaches a form called metarhodopsin II. *This takes a few milliseconds.*
3. Through a substance called transducin, this form activates a messenger system in neurons and alters the ion channels, which close sodium channels.

It is a wonderfully efficient and reasonably fast system, where probabilistically it is possible for a single photon to excite one rhodopsin molecule, causing about 500 molecules of transducin, resulting in the blocking of about one million sodium ions in the rod, resulting in a change of synaptic response. In the right conditions – a dark room and no stimulus for 20 plus minutes – a single photon hitting the retina can be visible. It should be noted that for every photon hitting the retina four to five are likely to be absorbed by the structure of the eye itself, but it does show one of the many ways the evolution of the human visual system is at both the biological and physical limits.

Although there are about 125 million receptors (consisting of 110–120 million rods, and about 6.4 million cones[7]), there are only about one million axons in the optic nerve (1,304,8168 +/– 89,112 in an adult Rhesus monkey[8]) which transmits the information to the brain. There is also a reduced signal rate along the optic nerve that results in a communication bottle-neck requiring a 250:1 compression ratio. Intermediary cells between the retina and the optic nerve achieve this compression ratio by considering differences between large regions so we have the situation of a huge but controlled information loss. The visual pathway in a human

---

7 G. Osterberg, 'Topography of the Layer of Rods and Cones in the Human Retina', *Acta Ophthalmol*, supp. 6 (1935): 1–103.

8 Grant Cull, George A. Cioffi, Jim Dong et al., 'Estimating Normal Optic Nerve Axon Numbers in Non-human Primate Eyes', *Journal of Glaucoma*, 12, 4 (August 2003): 301–306.

splits the right and left sides of the two retinas (information travelling along the optic nerve) to the right and left halves of the brain in an area called the primary visual cortex. This is vitally important for stereoscopic vision in particular as an object focused on the two retinas will be found in two places right next to each other, visible as columns. Within the brain a series of more interactions occur to create more complex signals. This, for example, allows a neuron to detect only a bar of light at any angle and position but of fixed length and width.

As we obviously do not have cells for all types of objects that we may see in our life, it is known that by training and concentration the human brain can become hypersensitive to certain stimuli. This means that due to a lifetime of training, both in the short term and in the long term, everyone sees objects slightly differently depending on age, sex, extra chemical stimulus, living conditions and all previous experiences. When considering details, what you visualize is almost certainly not what I visualize. This signal, which is a fraction of the raw information, along with experience then constitutes our 'belief'. Evolution has created a system at times at the limit of physics, but it is also constrained by the limited size and capacity of the human brain.

Illusions: Creating Too Much Information

This 'belief engine' inside the human visual system means that at times we do not actually believe the correct thing. This can be incredibly convincing, even when logic tells us otherwise. There are hundreds of examples of optical illusion and one of the canniest and simplest is the Kanizsa triangle (see two examples in Figure 12.1). The white triangle is seen despite drastic misalignments of the angles

Figure 12.1   Two Kanizsa triangle illusions

Source: Kaiser, Peter K., *The Joy of Visual Perception: A Web Book*, 2006–2009, <http://www.yorku.ca/eye/thejoy.htm>.

and large separations between the end points. The human visual system is able to interpret a triangle under these extreme cases and the neurological discovery of 'contour' cells is thought to be responsible for joining disconnected edges together. Many other illusions are resolvable now that we have a better understanding of the physiology of our inherited human visual system.

Art has also considered many of these illusions, and discussed them in detail – some a long time before the neurological investigation of the vision system. For example, the movement in Optical Art has been presenting work for many years most notably from the 1950s to the 1970s.[9] Terms used by the Op-Art movement that have neurological explanations include:

- *Assimilation*: our tendency to minimize stimuli and create uniformity. It is a simplifying process, sometimes described as grouping with respect to proximity or similarity.
- *Contrast*: the antithesis of assimilation. This may be described as the accentuation of differences.
- *Negative and positive*: an artist defines the figure as positive space and the ground as negative space. Negative space surrounds positive space and appears to extend continuously behind the figure. Although it is of less importance, it is usually larger in size. Positive space appears more clearly defined. A line – or a contour – is by definition a very positive feature.

As we have said, the human visual system is a wonderful structure built on the efficiency of evolution, but due to limits in information flow there are times when it fails. So this is also a cautionary tale, in that visualizations do not only transmit masses of information but may also in some cases quite naturally create confusion.

How To Say Nothing

In the UK there are a range of taught courses on the use and practice of both information and scientific visualization. In reversing a standard quote, W. Terry Hewitt, at Research Computing Services, has repeatedly stated that 'a picture may be worth a thousand words; but a good scientific visualization requires a thousand words to describe it'.[10] This is due to the limitations of a single visualization image that often does not convey enough of the relevant interpretation and meaning in order to tell the complete story so extra-textural information is required. This is not exactly satisfactory as it appears to indicate that a single visualization is not suitable in itself.

---

9   Rene Parola, *Optical Art: Theory and Practice* (New York, 1996).
10   Introductory comment in lecture on visualization within the Advanced Computer Science MSc course at the University of Manchester.

In 1994, Al Globus and Eric Raible published a seminal paper on how to say nothing with scientific visualizations.[11] Within academic courses these (slightly tongue-in-cheek) rules are taught in order to reduce misinterpretation and avoid simple errors within students' work. We propose that some of the ideas still remain vitally true now, not just for scientific visualizations, but for all forms of computer and non-computer-generated visualization output. The open question here is whether some of these issues can be solved with the introduction of metadata or paradata. The fourteen rules from the paper are listed here. Globus and Raible state that if all the rules are followed, your scientific visualization will look truly great but say very little – possibly nothing.

- Never include a colour legend.
- Avoid annotation.
- Never mention error characteristics.
- When in doubt, smooth.
- Avoid providing performance data.
- Quietly use stop-frame video techniques.
- Never learn anything about the science or data.
- Never compare your results with other visualization techniques.
- Avoid visualization systems.
- Never cite references for your data.
- Claim generality from one dataset.
- Use viewing angle to hide blemishes.
- If viewing angle fails, try specularity or shadowing.
- 'This is easily extended to 3D.'

It is left as an exercise for readers to consider how many of these rules have been met within their own visualization efforts. A lot of these rules are broken by allowing sharing of data and reuse of image-generation systems, and being open to others who can repeat your work and therefore analyse and display the data in a different view or interpretation. These methods and general rules are important things to consider in order to make your data and visualization more effective. With the introduction of metadata, there is the ability extensively to annotate and reference sources, thus improving the options of automatically breaking some of these rules. It is an open question, given the arising definition of paradata, in which choices and other more human-related decisions are included, how many more of these rules can be broken.

A word of warning has to be given at this stage: just breaking all of these rules does not mean that your visualization will be correct or accurate – or even useful.

Not telling the complete truth is not necessarily a bad thing, and is often essential in certain fields. A good example is cartography, where a railway map

---

11   Al Globus and Eric Raible, '14 Ways to Say Nothing with Scientific Visualization', *IEEE Computer*, 27/7 (1994): 86–8, available at <http://www.arsc.edu/~cskills/14ways.pdf>.

will display vastly different features from a road map, even though both give information about travel speed and distances. If the designers of each were asked to describe their map's key features, they would answer in very similar ways, but from two different points of focus. Although we are being 'lied to', we are often happy with this because the highlighted features are significant and important to what we believe we need to know at that point in time – in some sense we want to be lied to. An aim for the designer is to tell us a story, and we are often willing to believe that story. Later we may want to check the facts in more detail to create a more complex narrative, but initially we do not want to be swamped with superfluous information.

Metadata

As stated, many of the rules can be broken with good use of metadata, something that has been known for a long time. The addition of good metadata, including all forms of annotation and description, is very important, even if it takes time and careful thought. Within the science field there have been three developments that may aid in describing these required features. They include: the development of e-Science – which has created a set of middleware linking computing resources to all users; the new definition of a semantic web,[12] which adds meaning to factual components on the internet; and ideas about creating ontologies – which describe how human terms relate to computer actions.

Paradata

Paradata extend the concept of metadata to consider issues of choice and alternatives as well as subjective decisions. This is not only an interpretive issue facing, for example, archaeologists, but also an issue relevant to scientists and those working in many other fields. Plate 5 shows just fourteen different choices and variations for a simple vortex fluid flow visualization (after McDerby[13]). Often only one or two will be used to illustrate a specific scientific phenomenon, but it is very rarely considered in detail and rarely written down why a particular version has been used.

A couple of solutions to address this problem from e-Science are the introduction of recordable and sharable workflows (for example, myExperiment, <http://myexperiment.org/>, 2008), and the controlled recording of researchers' choices, creating an achievable provenance. In both of these cases, collaborative

---

12   Tim Berners-Lee, James Hendler and Ora Lassila, 'The Semantic Web', *Scientific American*, 284, 5 (2001): 34–43.

13   Mary J. McDerby, *Introduction to Scientific Visualization*, training notes (Manchester, 2007).

environments are under consideration – including emphasis on the web 2.0 generic principles of being able to record and annotate everything. An undecided issue is the question of who should do this annotation and who is responsible for ensuring its accuracy and usefulness: the original source gatherers, the main author, a list of peer reviewers, the expert community it is aimed at, or the general public.

Ways Forward and Possible Infrastructures

Many new constructs may be used in the creation of paradata and metadata, but one of the costs is the learning and integration times for users. Early solutions are being considered in relation to the building and definition of VREs (Virtual Research Environments, 2006). These are in a similar vein to VLE (Virtual Learning Environments) and have the aim of creating a central electronic portal that collates and collects all the knowledge required for a research single project, group or complete sector. This programme (sponsored by the Joint Information Systems Committee, JISC), started in 2005, consists of a series of diverse middleware tools from electronic storage systems to collaborative environments. Within the University of Manchester a new centralized server is being built to aid meeting recordings, allowing all interactions and choices to be reviewed, annotated and discussed live or at a later time. This is being tied together with a system for casual logging based on the popular web-like services. It has been considered that all interested parties should be able to annotate as long as the annotations are searchable (CREW, <http://www.crew-vre.net/?page_id=8>, 2008). MyExperiment (<http://www.myexperiment.org/>) considers creating electronic workflows allowing a range of scientists to share the work process as well as data sets and research conclusions. A related project from the University of Utah deals with the province recording of scientific visualization systems and has just released software (VisTrails, http://www.vistrails.org/, 2007).

Connected to this venture is another JISC initiative, the Visualization Support Network (vizNET, <http://www.viznet.ac.uk>), which guides visualization activities and aims to establish a Visualization Support Network spanning the UK academic research community with the objective of consolidating the strengths of major visualization centres and groups, sharing knowledge, communicating best practice between application domains, as well as providing training and support to researchers in visualization. At present, these are just technological solutions allowing a method for storing and connecting with the extra data/information that will be required. A true solution to these issues requires an understanding of the complete system, including the human visual system, the researchers' wishes and interpretation, as well as the users' wishes.

It has been left as an ongoing exercise to show how these 'ways of saying nothing' are universal to any visualization, but with new tools the rules may have to be rewritten. Work not considered here is what extensions and omissions should be added for universal visualization scenarios ranging from the social sciences to the arts and humanities. There is also a final word of caution: the true complexity, as it is human based, of accurately describing metadata or paradata for all purposes is an extremely hard problem.

Chapter 13

Intricacies and Potentials of Gathering Paradata in the 3D Modelling Workflow

Sven Havemann

Introduction

In the context of cultural heritage, the term '3D modelling' very often refers to the process of creating a digital replica of a real object of cultural value. This might be a bone, a coin, a sherd or a whole amphora, a rotten shipwreck or ruins of ancient buildings. In fact, the term '3D modelling' refers to two very different objects. As the result of this process, the digital 3D artefact may derive from two different sources:

- *Acquired artefact*: the dataset was produced, through a number of processing steps, from original raw data. Data were acquired using technical measuring devices, typically photo-cameras or laser range scanners (acquisition technology). More precisely, this is a data-processing task (image processing, shape processing).
- *Synthetic artefact*: the basis of the data set is only very sparse physical evidence. Based on 'educated guessing', certain conclusions can be drawn that allow the creation of 3D objects that represent hypotheses of the past. In the Digital Content Creation (DCC) industry this task is called '3D modelling', and is carried out using tools such as 3ds Max (Kinetix), Maya (Kinetix, formerly Alias) or Blender (Blender Foundation, Open Source).

This distinction between acquired and synthetically created digital historic artefacts seems quite reasonable. It appears strict, but actually it is not. This, in fact, is part of a more fundamental problem. It should be noted that the job of an archaeologist consists of two very different sorts of activities, namely:

- *Digital recording*: an engineering discipline (measuring), where data accuracy, resolution, signal-to-noise ratio, metrology theory and so on are relevant. The difference between measured and true data (the physical artefact) can be evaluated using quality measures (for example, pixel error or Hausdorff distance between mesh and 3D object).
- *Historical interpretation*: requires a background in human sciences. This is a holistic task where the ground truth, if one wants to call it that, is implicit rather than explicit. Through long education and expertise in their

respective areas, archaeologists and historians have acquired more or less precise ideas of the properties and conditions prevalent in the past.

The Shape Description Problem

A new direction in visual computing research, which alludes to the convergence of computer graphics and computer vision, is called 'capturing reality'. In this emerging field, the questions of how to capture, process, store and query shapes are considered in a somewhat broader context, and of course from a computer science point of view. This research evolves around a central – not always explicitly articulated – question: what is the right way to describe the shape of a 3D object? The question of how to represent shape in a digital computer seemed to have been solved by using a textured triangle mesh. While triangle meshes are still predominant, the deficiencies of textured meshes are becoming more and more apparent, and alternatives are being sought. Some of the deficiencies of triangle meshes are concerned with their points and masses of irrelevant data. An individual point or triangle is ignorant of its relative position: whether it belongs to the ground, to a wall or to a statue. It does not contain any quality assessment or reference to the process by which it was produced. The laser scan of a perfectly flat surface will typically yield millions of (noisy) points. The number of triangles is a very imprecise measure of shape complexity, as many triangles of slightly curved surfaces are approximate. It is difficult to estimate how many triangles are needed to approximate a sphere. It depends on many factors. Many questions remain unanswered. There is a blatant mismatch between the questions that users, in particular cultural heritage researchers, would like to pose and those that the mesh can answer. Distances can be measured point to point, but questions about shape features are problematic because the features are not explicitly represented: planes (wall, ground), radii (columns, arches), angles and more general feature parameters (window width, door height) cannot be queried unless – through some sort of fitting process – a feature template is instantiated. The shape description problem has been treated in considerable more detail elsewhere.[1]

   Progress in shape descriptions is technology driven. To some extent, this is due to the advent of new generations of graphics boards with a more flexible display-processing pipeline. They permit the rendering of much more complex surfaces at interactive rates, both in terms of geometry and material properties. Traditionally, a point on the surface has only a single colour, which is the colour of the texture (bitmap) at that point. Modern graphics boards allow us to store and render *for each point* a much more accurate approximation of the 6D surface reflection function (BRDF) at that point. Technically, the coefficients are stored in multiple textures that are used simultaneously, evaluated by a surface-shading program that is executed in parallel by the display hardware.

---

   1   Sven Havemann, *Generative Mesh Modeling*, PhD thesis, Institute of Computer Graphics, Faculty of Computer Science, Technische Universität Braunschweig, Germany, November 2005. See chapter 1.

Shape Descriptions for Cultural Heritage Objects

The shape description problem has also been discussed from a cultural heritage point of view in the context of the EPOCH project.[2] This discussion addressed a simple question: does a round arch exist in reality? This seems like a philosophical question, but it has wide-ranging, practical consequences. The discussion touched on the issue of choosing the right technology for storing, processing and querying 3D data in a digital computer. The two positions were as follows:

1. Luc van Gool: *No real arch can be perfectly round, so it is critical to scan the physical evidence well.* In principle, digital information is protected from degradation. From a theoretical information point of view, documenting cultural heritage means conveying as much information as possible from the physical world into a digital representation. Premature interpretation is harmful because it leads to selective documentation. If possible, every scratch on the surface should be preserved because it potentially carries a meaning that only becomes apparent much later, on the basis of the results of subsequent research (*just in case* or *anticipatory* scanning policy).

2. Sven Havemann: *The only interesting thing about a pile of rubble is that it once formed a round arch.* What is our interest in an artefact which was once a beautiful object of cultural value but has degraded over the centuries? In the object in its original state, or in the details of the degradation? Is it important faithfully to document and preserve the shape of a fracture or any damage? Are we not producing masses of garbage data through anticipatory scanning? Should we rather attempt – physically or digitally – to reassemble and restore historic artefacts in their original shape – and ignore the shape of the fracture? Should we try to determine all parameters of the round arch (midpoint, radius and so on) as faithfully as possible, and then use them virtually to reconstruct the original appearance of the arch?

After lengthy discussion, it was agreed that neither of the two positions was superior; and that in any case, both answer all possible user queries. Both the low-level measurements and high-level parametric shapes are needed.

---

2   For information about EPOCH Network of Excellence, see <http://www.epoch-net.org> and <http://www.epoch.eu/>.

The Seven Open Problems of Semantic 3D

The issues discussed so far are described in a more systematic way by Havemann and Fellner.[3] The authors highlight some issues related to gathering 3D paradata that are particularly relevant to cultural heritage, as outlined in the following:

1. *Classification of all shape representations in computer graphics*: over the last thirty years or so, libraries of numerous digital shape representations were developed in computer graphics. An exhaustive classification could reveal general principles that would eventually lead to less limited 3D technology, file formats and 3D software.
2. *Sustainable 3D file format*: the lack of a common file format is possibly the most frustrating obstacle in further uptake of 3D technology. Most sophisticated shape representations can simply not be stored due to this problem. The format degradation makes sustainable 3D no more than an illusion.
3. *Generic, stable and detailed 3D markup*: to distinguish parts of a shape is essential for all tasks from shape annotation to automatic shape segmentation. The markup has to be generic in the sense that it is independent of any shape representation. Different sorts of markup of 0D points, 1D curves, 2D surfaces and 3D volumes must be possible.
4. *Generic 3D query operations*: evaluation of the markup should be possible irrespective of the markup method and shape representation applied. This means, for example, being able to enumerate triangles or to cut some part of a parametric surface that carries the markup. The issue here is to ensure that the markup survives shape processing and surface editing operations.
5. *Paradata. Processing history or provenance*: only when the first four problems are solved is a technical prerequisite provided for storing detailed paradata with 3D objects. The desired situation is that it is technically possible to track every datum in a complex reconstructed scene, through all processing steps, back to its origin.
6. *Closing the semantic gap: the meaning of shape*: being able to extract higher-level information (for example, the number of columns in a temple, or the number and average shape of bricks in a wall) is vital for all interpretative tasks. Developing methods for the detection of user-definable shape features, and of similarities and symmetries, is a great challenge.
7. *Consistent evolution of the meaning of shape*: interpretations should be stored reliably. Even conflicting hypotheses should be maintained simultaneously. This can only be achieved when 3D is integrated within semantic networks in a bi-directional way: when a CIDOC-CRM database can refer to a digital 3D object (or its part), and a 3D object (or its part) can refer to CIDOC-CRM facts.

---

3   Sven Havemann and Dieter Fellner, 'Seven Research Challenges of Generalized 3D Documents', *IEEE Computer Graphics and Application*, special issue on 3D documents, 27, 3 (2007): 70–76.

The Potential of Shape Description for Maintaining Paradata

The considerations so far demonstrate the limitations of 3D technology, and in particular two areas that are indispensable in cultural heritage applications:

1. *Technology for 3D documentation*: a low-level shape representation that is nevertheless capable of integrating all information captured in the acquisition process in a standardized way. It must be richer than textured triangle meshes, especially in terms of the material properties (BRDF). It should minimize information loss in the acquisition pipeline and serve as ground truth for subsequent interpretation. Ideally, it should allow back-tracking of the acquisition pipeline in order to assess the authenticity of each datum that comes out as the end result of the process.*Paradata*: assessing provenance and processing history of each and every datum.
2. *Technology for 3D interpretation*: it should include three methods: first, a method that allows users to define parametric templates for shape features, i.e. geometric configurations, with a certain degree of freedom; second, a method for detecting user-defined features in an acquired artefact (or scanned data set) by instantiating the template parameters; third, a sustainable and reliable method of storing, maintaining and querying the interpretation. *Paradata*: maintaining intellectual transparency of the interpretation.

When both these problems are addressed, the vision of *informed raw data* will become a reality, as shown in the form of generative surface reconstruction in Figure 13.1. So far, however, it is not that clear how this might be achieved.

Figure 13.1 **Generative surface reconstruction. A parametric shape template (right) is adapted to given raw data (left). The shape template is fully informed; each point on the generated surface contains a link back to the parametric function that has created it. By exploiting geometric proximity, every measured data point can be assigned a meaning: arch, sub-arch, rosette, profile and so on**

Figure 13.2 Shape acquisition in a plaster museum. A coloured random pattern is projected onto the plaster statues. Photos are always shot from the same distance, keeping almost the same surface point in the centre. Typically, 12–17 photos are shot by moving the tripod on a circle arc of ~ 90°. The result is a photo sequence

Practice may provide the experience that is needed to develop ideas on how best to proceed and which types of paradata should be collected.

Case Study: The Plaster Museum

The technologies to be developed need to be useful, in particular in large-scale scanning activities. The issue here is *scalability*: techniques that work for a few dozen objects can fail when applied to hundreds or thousands of objects. In that sense, a quantitative increase can turn into a new quality.

A large acquisition project was therefore carried out at the Institute of Archaeology plaster cast collection of the Karl Franzens University at Graz (KFU, see <http://www.gipsmuseum.uni-graz.at>). The museum houses some 150 casts of classical statues, mostly Greek, but also some copies of Assyrian and Roman statues. The great value of the KFU plaster collection rests in the fact that some casts are unique because the originals have not survived (see Figure 13.2).

The first step was to develop an acquisition strategy. Different exhibits require different photo sequences. The first classification, shown in Figure 13.3, yielded five classes of statues. We have found that many semantic relations exist between the statues. For instance, the Athena statue existed both as a bust and a full-length statue (see Figure 13.4). Some famous statues, including that of Athena, have been an archetype and inspiration for other artists. In other cases, the bust is a mere copy of the full-length statue. We have chosen the Athena statue as our example in the following.

> *Paradata*: the museum records provide information about the original statue, as well as the copy (who made it under what circumstances). In some cases no reliable information is available on one or the other. This contributes to complex metadata and paradata.

The acquisition method we chose was photogrammetric reconstruction. The basis of this method is a sequence of ten to twenty photographs that are taken in a systematic way, as shown in Figure 13.2. All photos have the same point of a statue in focus and are taken, from the same distance and at the same height, by moving a tripod in steps of 5–10 degrees along a circular arc (maintained simply by a rope). The photos were taken by two student apprentices over a period of three weeks. Each photo sequence was sent to the Arc 3D web service of the Katolieke Universiteit Leuven in Belgium (see <http://www.arc3d.be>). The web service computed a depth map for each of the photos. It thus provided each pixel in each photo with a depth value, as described in more detail elsewhere.[4] These dense depth maps may then be imported into the Meshlab software from the VCG group,

---

4   Maarten Vergauwen and Luc van Gool, 'Web-based 3D Reconstruction Service', *Machine Vision and Applications*, 17, 6 (2006): 411–26.

Figure 13.3 **Shape classes in a plaster museum. From top to bottom: busts, heads, full-length figures, active poses and miscellaneous statues. A scanning campaign requires thorough planning. Each class has a typical scanning order. It is a good idea to define the typical scanning patterns beforehand in order to obtain reasonable, repeatable results**

Plaster cast of the Athena Palagi
from the Museo Civico Archeologico, Bologna
Roman copy of a Greek bronze original
mid-fifth century BC

Plaster cast of the Athena Lemnia
from the Albertinum, Dresden
Roman copy of a Greek bronze original
attributed to Phidias, c. 450-40 BC

Figure 13.4 **Plaster casts of the statue of Athena and their metadata. Both casts are believed to derive from the same original. Automatic methods for determining such dependencies through, for instance, similarities between shapes recorded in one or several databases, could benefit cultural heritage research**

led by Roberto Scopigno and Paolo Cignoni of the CNR in Pisa, Italy. Meshlab is Open Source and can be obtained from <http://www.meshlab.sourceforge.net>.

Paradata: the choice of the right acquisition method is a complex issue. Photogrammetric methods work through image comparison, so images features suitable for comparison are required. Consequently, these methods work best for old objects with an interesting surface, and for objects with many edges. Laser scanners work best with uniform mat and light surfaces, and fail with dark, shiny surfaces. Many more trade offs exist, so a provenance record should include some indications of the pros and cons, and why a particular acquisition method was chosen.

Photogrammetric reconstruction does not require expensive devices such as laser range scanners, which in 2008 cost typically 20,000–50,000 Euros. Only a digital camera is needed and this is a great advantage. A NextEngine scanner is approximate 2,500 Euros but is limited to a scanning range of 45 cm. Our plaster statues were larger. Plaster is problematic for photogrammetric reconstruction. We have therefore projected a random colour pattern onto the surface. The image resolution was 1440 x 1050, which is about a fourth of the 6 megapixel camera resolution (2000 × 3000). The projected pixel covered at least 2 × 2 image pixels and yielded optimal reconstruction results (see Figure 13.2).

In the first round of acquisition, we have developed a standard procedure for full-size statues like Athena (see Figure 13.5). Eight reconstruction sequences seemed enough initially, but we later found that the resolution was not high enough to cover the surface at satisfactory detail (see detail images).

It should be noted that in addition to the camera position, an additional degree of freedom was provided by the projector position. Sometimes it makes sense to let the projector shine slightly from below or above camera height.

Figure 13.5 Eight photographic sequences are typically required for a statue such as the Athena Lemnia. They are taken for both the upper and lower parts, from four directions. Due to space constraints in a museum environment it is not always possible to acquire the sequences at the optimal intervals of 90°

Paradata: the camera position can be calculated from the images photogrammetrically (via *bundle adjustment*), so there is no need to document it. In principle, the projector position could also be inferred from the images, although this would require special software. The information about which photos were taken can subsequently be used to assess the authenticity of a surface point if functionality is available to map the point back onto the photos and to determine the back-projection error.

Plate 6 shows the beginning of one of the eight photo sequences of Athena, as well as the quality values of the calculated depth maps. The entire photo sequence, with depth maps and quality values, can then be imported into Meshlab. Here the human is again part of the loop and needs to decide which photos (typically four to six, but sometimes up to ten) should be selected from the sequence in order to generate mesh layers. This is an important and complex decision. On the one hand, only depth maps of high quality should be chosen; on the other, the beginning and end should be present as well – some occluded parts might be present only in very few photos in the sequence. Some experience is therefore required to choose the right photos, and the right reconstruction parameters (see Figure 13.6).

Figure 13.6   **The processing pipeline of a single sequence. (1) Four to six images from sequences are selected. Each image is converted into a mesh, resulting in a multi-layered shape in regions where the image meshes overlap. (2) The meshes are cleaned, unused points and outliers are removed. (3) A Poisson reconstruction converts the multi-layer into a single-layer mesh. (4) Extraneous triangles are cut away manually. (5) Mesh simplification. (6) Providing the mesh with vertex colours**

Paradata: we take notes by hand to record which photos were chosen for reconstruction. This is often a decision about what should be *ignored*. Much data simply have to be discarded in order to keep the data set manageable, and to avoid memory overflow in the processing chain.

The result of the reconstruction is a multi-layered mesh: each selected photo constitutes a single layer. In each layer, the mesh is made from the pixels with a reliable depth value, so it has a very regular rectangular structure (quad grid with quads made of two triangles: see Figure 13.7). With this mesh we create a five-stage processing pipeline which is depicted in Figure 13.6: the multi-layer mesh is cleared (1), Poisson-reconstructed (2), extraneous parts are removed (3), simplified (4) and vertex-coloured (5).

Paradata: we store all the intermediate results of each stage. The reason is that on each stage the human is in the loop, parameters must be set and functions executed. There are so many points of decision that we need the intermediate results to be able to track problems we detect back to their source. If better methods are developed for some of the stages, we will have to re-process the data from a certain point on. In some of the stages, we had to use methods that will certainly be enhanced in the future.

Figure 13.7 **Detailed surface inspection. The multi-layer mesh (left) is regular, but contains much noise (columns 2 and 3). The Poisson reconstruction (right) does a great job at removing this noise, creating a closed surface. It consists of a single layer. It both eliminates (multi-layer) information and 'invents' information (for gaps)**

For instance, we have discovered that we obtain significantly better results with the web service if we correct the lens distortion beforehand. Loosely speaking, this means that the straight edges of the object appear straight, rather than bent, in the image. This was significant, because due to the limited space in the museum, we had to use a wide-angle zoom lens (18 mm) which suffered from significant distortion. The downside of this observation is that we have had to reconstruct and process a number of sequences again. Similar improvements may also become possible at later stages, in which case it is important that we have kept the intermediate results.

It should be noted that the Poisson reconstruction greatly impairs the traceability of the end result. It is a re-sampling step that 'blows up a balloon' constrained by the data points. Three resulting problems are illustrated in Figure 13.7. The resulting shape is guaranteed to be closed, even in regions where data are missing (see Figure 13.6 and, for a close-up, Figure 13.8). So the method 'invents' data. The 'balloon' is a smooth surface which averages the multi-layer information. This involves smoothing, which removes noise, but in fact also destroys information. The resulting mesh looks 'washed out', without any highly curved creases in the surface. The resolution of the output mesh is decoupled from the resolution of the input mesh layers; there is no direct correspondence between input and output triangles.

> *Paradata*: this process is difficult to document. The input images are about 50 MB. A zip file produced by Arc3D for each sequence is approx. 200MB, the meshes of each stage are typically in .ply format something like 90 (0), 70 (i), 17 (ii), 15 (iii), 11 (iv) and 20 MB (v).

One needs to keep in mind that the end result of these processing stages is only reconstructed from one of eight sequences. So in practice eight models result, which then have to be merged again. This involves an alignment step, in which the user has to define a rough correspondence between pairs of models by providing feature points. For instance, a mark is put on the tip of the nose in all models for reference. This initial pose is then refined by means of a numeric procedure, the *iterative closest point* (ICP) method. ICP has only a small radius of convergence, so in case the overlap between models is small, the manually set feature points have to be very good. Otherwise ICP diverges, i.e. stops with a badly aligned model. One typical result and its inherent problems are shown in Plate 7. Apparently the Poisson reconstruction was not cleared well enough, because the boundaries of the parts fold up and stick out of the model. This is an indication later in the pipeline that an earlier operation needs to be re-done.

If the alignment is successful, it is followed by another Poisson reconstruction, with all the implications that its procedures such as smoothing and resampling have for the results.

Paradata: the relation between output model and input data is a little vague and difficult to describe. So much smoothing is applied throughout the process that it is surprising that the results are useful. The output model contains many triangles (arbitrarily many, in fact), but obviously it does not contain as much information as was present in the input data.

Discussion and Conclusion

The case study of scanning the statues in the plaster museum has revealed a number of problems with current technology, but also with the concept of paradata itself. Paradata are data needed for the interpretation of cultural artefacts. In the case of 3D data, this entails recording the relation between the input and output of a complex processing pipeline. At some point, the effort that is needed becomes questionable, all the more so when the paradata become so complex that their usefulness is open to debate.

Naive 3D Paradata

Let us assume for a moment that the 3D paradata problem has been solved, and for every triangle of the resulting mesh there is full information about its provenance, as well as a report about the full processing history. All parameters of all software tools could be recorded, so that all photos with camera and projector positions, all manual editing commands, all smoothing, merging and alignment parameters would be preserved.

With full information, the paradata would eventually have the *redo property*, which means that the result could be verified: all processing could be exactly repeated at any time. In fact, the intellectual transparency requirement can, ultimately, be understood as making 'a redo property' mandatory. If, and only if, all information is available to reproduce a given cultural 3D model, then the model can be said to be intellectually transparent.

The flaws of this strict approach are so obvious that alternatives must be sought. It is completely unrealistic to assume that all versions of the software used would be preserved, along with all intermediate scripts and other software tools; that all thousands of interactive processing and cleaning steps would be recorded and software would exist to play back all manual edits; that any kind of standard would ever exist reliably to record and store processing history logs across different software tools. This will never happen.

A Reasonable Concept for 3D Paradata

The goal must be to store only meaningful paradata that allow users to query and assess the *authenticity of cultural data*, rather than trace back each datum through hundreds of processing steps.

One idea of how this could look is depicted in Figure 13.8. It shows a portion of the mesh of particular interest, namely the head of the Medusa and the knot of the toga. In this case the user can query the paradata database to find out which source images were used and what *all* depth images looked like for a particular area on the surface. This would work best if the depth layer were produced on the fly from the archived webservice results.

The absence of a complete replay property would mean that it would not be possible to obtain *all* the intermediate results that were produced in the processing history. In principle, it should be possible to store any intermediate data, but the obligation to do so is unrealistic. Realizing this less strict concept of 3D paradata, which we have developed in our group, is technically quite demanding. It requires nothing less than to create the possibility of *co-registering* many datasets. Each surface point carries an ID, which is attached to surface patches that contain several hundreds of triangles (*parametrizable* regions). This surface ID is connected, via a lookup table, to photographs. The photograph paradata include the position of the camera and the link to the depth image (once calculated by the web page). With that information, a piece of software is triggered that reproduces a single mesh layer for a particular photo. The user might then wish to retrieve several such

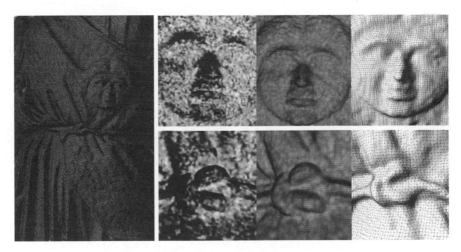

Figure 13.8 **Comparison of input data and resulting shapes. Left: parts of the model of particular interest that invite further investigation. Right: the user queries input data available for these areas (images and depth maps) and compares them with the mesh**

depth maps and compare them with the final model of the statue in a 3D viewer to find out which portions of input data were used.

This would imply a paradigm change away from abundant collections of uninteresting intermediate processing data towards a toolkit of diagnostic software with which objects can be queried and meaningful quality measures computed. The aim here is to assess the *authenticity of the data* which – we believe – is the most valuable asset of IT in cultural heritage.

PART III
Data Management and Communication

Chapter 14

Defining Paradata in Heritage Visualization[1]

Drew Baker

Introduction

Computer-generated images (CGIs) of historical sites and buildings have become ubiquitous in the media over the past decade (2000–2010). Viewers are becoming ever more familiar with the use of CGIs within a historical context. The scholar is presented with the possibility of using CGIs to explain or illustrate history while attempting ethical presentation of hypothetical possibilities to avoid the deception. There is now much greater potential for any individual who has an understanding of 3D modelling to create their 'version' of any historical site or building and publish it at relatively little cost. This is due to the ever-greater accessibility of pervasive CGIs and software for image manipulation and 3D content-creation, as well as lower hardware costs. These factors and acceptance of CGI representation by the general public, as an enhancement to 'edutainment' products, caution the academic community in their view of scholarly publications utilizing CGI for research and illustration purposes.

Researchers who have presented CGI-based work frequently have their research questioned either because detailed, realistic-looking models are associated too closely with entertainment, or because they contain elements based on fragmentary historical information and cannot be proven. Occasionally, one encounters an even more general dismissal.

Reconstruction or Visualization?

The apprehension of academia with regard to CGIs and 3D modelling as a research tool, it is suggested, comes from: the popularization of CGI in extra-academic contexts; poor scholarly methods (images of 3D models are frequently

---

1   This chapter is a revised and expanded version of the paper, 'Towards Transparency in Visualization Based Research', proceedings of the seminar From Abstract Data Mapping to 3D Photorealism: Understanding Emerging Intersections in Visualisation Practices and Techniques, organized by the AHRC ICT Methods Network and Visualization Research Unit, Birmingham Institute of Art and Design, 19 June 2007, available online at <http://www.methodsnetwork.ac.uk/redist/pdf/paradata008-1.pdf>. The same paper has also been published by VizNet at <http://www.viznet.ac.uk/documents>.

presented as illustrations supporting a point without explaining the process of discovery and level of probability); and the desire to 'make it look good' which, while undoubtedly making the CGI more persuasive, also often obscures or dilutes the worth of the research it is intended to communicate.

King's Visualisation Lab (KVL) has addressed the problem of apprehension towards 3D CGI within the Arts and Humanities though a number of projects that aim to demonstrate the academic credibility of such tools. Fundamental to achieving this aim is a move away from the idea of 'reconstruction' – trying to recreate a site or building based on the evidence – in favour of a move towards a process of 'visualization'. This is a subtle but important distinction for both creators and audiences of CGIs. For historians, the ultimate goal of visualization is not the creation of a 'faithful' or 'accurate' presentation of an object; rather, accepting both the inevitability of evidential lacunae and the inescapability of human interpretation in the process of historical analysis, the historian uses visualization to develop and present visual arguments based on a number of carefully researched hypotheses.

Visualization (as opposed to 'reconstruction') of historic architecture does not pretend to show the 'real thing' because what constitutes the 'real thing' is open to far too much speculation, even within fairly recent buildings. For instance, if the viewer is presented with a reconstruction of an existing building, what is actually being shown? The building as designed by the architect, or the structure constructed by the builder? The current or a previous state (or states)? If the viewer does not have access to the research underpinning the CGI representation, then discrepancies between the visible reality of the site and its virtual representation are likely to raise questions about the validity of the model.

The conceptual shift from attempting to create a reconstruction to presenting a visualization is not without its own problems. If the visualization is to be useful as a research object in its own right, it must provide mechanisms to offer the reader access to the evidence and process of reasoning through which it came into being. When this is done, visualization can work as the visual narrative to research, and may be seen to be rivalling, in complexity, subtlety and substance, any linear narrative in traditional print form.

Paradata and the Visualization Process

During the processes of visualization, the creator will make a number of choices. Most of these will be based on research and reasoning. There will also be a significant amount of personal intellectual capital and understanding invested in the modelling process on a conscious or subconscious level. By providing a record of these decisions and thoughts the visualization process becomes transparent to the viewers. They are better positioned to offer critique and refine contested points within the cognitive process of creating visual hypotheses.

A simple experiment was devised and used with multiple participants to test the role of cognitive assumptions made in the course of a visualization process. Using pen and paper, subjects were asked to reconstruct a house described as follows: 'The house has four windows; there is a tree to the side of it; there is a cat in the top window; smoke is coming out of the chimney; there is a garden path leading to it.' Most people undertaking this simple task complete it in a short space of time, producing a frontal view of a house with many similar attributes (see Figure 14.1).

Figure 14.1   Possible outcome of a task testing cognitive assumptions made in the course of a visualization process

This picture, however, is based on certain assumptions, preconceptions, decisions and priorities, which the subject has made consciously or unconsciously. The experiment illustrates that the concept of a house is highly subjective and will be governed by the artist's experience, cultural background and preferences, as well as reasoning from other areas of prior knowledge. If a 'reconstruction' of a house was based on this information alone, the number of different, ostensibly 'accurate', representations would be so vast as to render the value of reconstruction as a means of producing knowledge highly questionable. In fact, one would be very hard pressed to find a building that actually looked like the drawing, although it is clearly a house. If, however, the picture was presented as a 'visualization' – that is, as a visual narrative with the decisions, rationale and context included – then it would become an illustration of the creator's cognitive process, supporting the arguments made. This additional documentary information is essential to understanding visualizations as research artefacts, i.e. as tools through which further research may be conducted, rather than just as pretty pictures. It has been proposed that, in the field of heritage visualization, such documentation should be called 'paradata', which the title of the present volume reflects.

If, instead of reconstruction, one were to use visualization to approach the information given about the house, an investigator could build an argument through paradata as follows: because no additional information regarding the house is available, the assumption is made that the building is in the UK. The primary housing types in the UK are terraced, detached, semi-detached and apartment or flat. Based on these housing types, a checklist of building types may be devised against the information given (see Table 14.1).

Table 14.1 Explicit and inferred information about primary housing types in the UK

	Has Windows	Can have Tree to Side?	Can have a Top Window?	Can have a Chimney?	Can have a Garden and Path?
Terrace	Yes	Possibly [1]	Yes	Yes	Yes [6]
Semi-detached	Yes	Yes [2]	Yes	Yes	Yes [7]
Detached	Yes	Yes	Yes	Yes	Yes
Apartment	Yes	No [3]	No [4]	Unlikely [5]	Unlikely [8]

Notes:

[1] Unless the house was at the end of a terrace (therefore technically a semi-detached property) the position of the tree would be either in front or behind the building to one side.
[2] Depending on which side the conjoining property was, this would be either to the left or right side.
[3] Unless the apartment was on the ground floor and one assumes that the tree's position is not below the property.
[4] Apartments are generally on a single level therefore the existence of a top window is unlikely (unless the description is of a maisonette, which is excluded from this list).
[5] From the implication that the chimney is attached to the building, an apartment is unlikely to have a chimney directly linked to it unless it is on the upper floor.
[6] As with point 1.
[7] As with point 2.
[8] As with point 3.

One can heuristically infer that the house has a door and that the chimney is attached to the house. It is also usual for a chimney to be higher than the roof of a house in order to remove smoke efficiently. As modern buildings in the UK tend to rely on central heating rather than open fires, one can further infer that the house is of a certain age. Looking at Figure 14.1, one can see that there are other elements that have been derived from the description, but with less certainty. Although, using the decision Table 14.1, the apartment type has been ruled out, one of the other three types on which the drawing is based could have been selected. From the description given, one would have been equally justified in drawing a detached bungalow or a town house. In reality, only 21 per cent of the entire housing stock in the UK is detached, with 31 per cent semi-detached, 28 per cent terraced, 16 per cent apartment and 4 per cent 'other'.[2] Why, then, do the overwhelming majority of subjects choose to draw a detached house? Perhaps because it is an aspiration and romantic desire of the suburban British to live in a detached house where space is at a premium or, indeed, because it is the type of house in which the subject was brought up. The choice is therefore based not on hard evidence about the house but on the subjective experience of what ideally constitutes a home.

More likely, perhaps, is the fact that the described elements happen to coincide with those of the archetypal child's drawing of a house. Such a culturally and aesthetically identifiable 'type', awakened in the drawer's mind by the description, elicits a corresponding stylistic response. The creator of a visualization may find their own, unspoken cultural and aesthetic assumptions among the most difficult to identify.

The form of the house, with windows arranged in a two-up two-down configuration, with a supposed door between them in the lower middle, is also iconic rather than realistic; this symmetrical arrangement is uncommon in the real world. Figure 14.1 shows the windows of equal size and crossed; a personal interpolation without any foundation in the textual description. The cat sitting in the right-hand window is black – there is no reason for its location, colour or attitude other than that it evidently appeals to the subject's sense of humour to have it looking towards the tree in the vain hope of spotting a bird – and is congruent with the archetypical style and composition of the drawing. The example of the cat again illustrates the extent to which assumptions, interpretations and inventions all routinely play their part in the process of visualization.

Such decisions and inferences – whether conscious or unconscious – may or may not in fact be appropriate for a particular building. When the paradata are captured and associated with the drawing, the visualization of the building becomes intellectually transparent. Its creator can explain and defend his or her work and

---

2   These figures are based on the 2001 census, see Survey of English Housing, Office of the Deputy Prime Minister; General Household Survey, Office for National Statistics; Continuous Household Survey, Northern Ireland Statistics and Research Agency available at <http://www.statistics.gov.uk/STATBASE/ssdataset.asp?vlnk=7714>.

the viewer will find it easier to understand the rationale for its construction and where the boundaries between fact and interpretation lie.

The experiment discussed above involved a very simple drawing and paradata discovery process, much of which is shaped by unconscious assumptions. If one now considers a more scholarly subject – such as the Mausoleum at Halicarnassus as described by both Pliny the Elder in his *Natural History* and Vitruvius in his *Ten Books on Architecture* – the problem becomes more complex. Pliny writes:

> The circumference of this building is, in all, four hundred and forty feet, and the breadth from north to south sixty-three, the two fronts being not so wide in extent. It is twenty-five cubits in height, and is surrounded with six-and-thirty columns, the outer circumference being known as the 'Pteron'.[3]

Vitruvius offers additional details:

> above the Pteron there is a pyramid erected, equal in height to the building below, and formed of four and twenty steps, which gradually taper upwards towards the summit; a platform, crowned with a representation of a four-horse chariot by Pythis. This addition makes the total height of the work one hundred and forty feet.[4]

While these accounts, with their discussion of concrete measurements and proportions, may at first glance seem reasonably precise, our experiment in drawing a simple house alerts us to the vast volume of information that they omit. For example, Pliny's description uses two different measuring systems: feet and cubits. Are 'feet' imperial, Roman or Greek? How is a standardized measurement to be interpreted? What kind of column was used, and what type could fit into the spaces described using the classical rules governing intercolumniation? Does the mathematics of the building work? What are the building materials used, their colour, ancillary decoration? One could continue more or less ad infinitum.

While interpreting such ambiguous source material, the need to record the decision processes is vital if the final visualization is to have any significant weight and stability when placed under academic scrutiny. Through the recording and publishing of paradata, the intellectual capital generated by visualization processes becomes more widely available with the result that others can debate and develop both the research sources and their interpretation. Whereas a visualization published without paradata risks being discredited by criticism of the validity of the least of its conjectural elements, a properly documented visualization enables reviewers to adopt a more nuanced approach, both identifying and assessing the provenance

---

3   Pliny the Elder, *The Natural History*, trans. J. Bostock and H. Riley (1857), 36:4 (4).

4   Vitruvius, *The Ten Books on Architecture*, trans. M. Hickey Morgan (New York, 1960), 2:8.12.

and reasoning behind each individual element and considering the alternative pathways that the visualization could have taken at any given point in the research process. This transforms the role of the reader/viewer from passive receiver of manipulated data to that of active participant in the evolution of the argument. This principle of inclusion leads us back to the essential shift that is required from 'reconstruction' to 'visualization'. A representation of historical subject matter, if it has no visibly associated paradata, is dead to scholarly discourse. Once these elements are included, however, such representations become transparent research tools in their own right, complementing and supporting the rationale for historical visualization and promoting its discussion.

Defining Paradata

Because of the formal, structured way in which the task of documentation should be approached, metadata play a vital role in the management and understanding of data objects (material objects, perceptible by one or more of the senses, about which data are held).[5] The Dublin Core Metadata Element Set, for example, offers fifteen fundamental properties (or 'elements') that may be attributed to a data object: contributor, coverage, creator, date, description, format, identifier, language, publisher, type, relation, rights, source, subject and title.[6] In a description of a data object, each of these fields may be repeated or omitted as required, and several elements have subsidiary properties. The 'type' element, for instance, has twelve recommended additional terms: collection, dataset, event, image, interactive resource, service, software, sound, text, physical object, still image, moving image. Data recorded and attributed to a data object can be termed a 'data artefact'.

Typically, when implementing a metadata scheme, controlled vocabularies are used to ensure standardization. For example, many organizations responsible for cataloguing cultural heritage assets use the Getty Thesaurus of Geographic Names (TGN) and Art and Architecture Thesaurus (AAT) to ensure common terms and spellings are used from record to record and collection to collection. The 'description' element, common to many metadata schemes, is often used to record 'contextual metadata', which typically constitutes a textual account of some properties which the cataloguer deems important to the understanding or management of the data object, but which do not obviously fit within any of the other element fields.

Whereas metadata, including contextual metadata, describe the properties of data objects in order to facilitate the management and dissemination of collections, paradata, as the term is used here, describe the processes of interpreting and

---

5   Belkis W. Leong-Hong and Bernard K. Plagman, *Data Dictionary/Directory Systems: Administration, Implementation and Usage* (New York, 1974).

6   Dublin Core resources are available at <http://www.dublincore.org>.

creating data objects in order to enable understanding and evaluation. Metadata also tend to describe more or less static properties of data objects, while paradata describe ephemeral processes: physical and measurable properties of data objects tend to be fixed (for example, the height, weight, location), rendering them ideal for description within a conventional metadata schema. By contrast, the properties of the discussions and decisions that are entailed in the visualization of an object are more fluid and difficult to define (see Figure 14.2).

DATA OBJECT

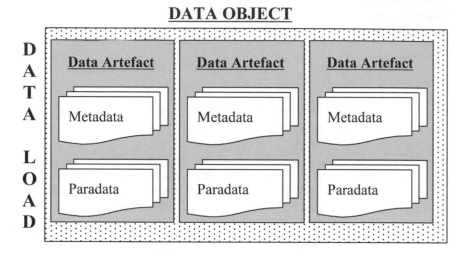

Figure 14.2 Overview of a data object

Paradata relating to heritage visualization, when identified, captured and published, are potentially of immense value to all who seek to access, extend or communicate understandings of human culture, from researchers and curators to educators, media organizations and the general public.

Data Metamorphosis

The phrase 'data metamorphosis' refers to the processes of combination and association through which data become transformed into useful information.

When data (for example, '9.10') and metadata (for example, 'height in cm') are combined, some property of something is described (for example, 'height in cm = 9.10'). When sets of metadata are combined, even more meaningful information is produced: for example, 'name = vase; identifier = 7014b; height in cm = 9.10'. A combination of such descriptions produces a record or data artefact about an object. It should be noted that the data themselves do not change, but rather their significance changes as they are combined with other data and metadata.

The term 'data load' refers to the quantity and extent of information that a record, or data artefact, contains. Thus, a 'low' data load signifies that little is recorded about a data object, while a 'high' data load indicates that a large number of data artefacts is associated with a data object.

One of the popular models of data metamorphosis is the Data, Information, Knowledge, Wisdom (DIKW) hierarchy proposed by Cleveland, Zeleny, Ackoff and others.[7] Used by both the disciplines of Information Science and Knowledge Management, this model attempts to create a hierarchy of data 'worth' as a data artefact moves though stages of transformation.

An individual datum is manipulated and combined with other data to form 'information'. To form 'knowledge', information is combined with yet further data and information, and processed to allow further connections to be made that are understood (or reproducible). 'Knowledge' is combined and interconnected through experience and replication. Thus further insights are produced which enable forecasting or predicting possible outcomes of a cause of action; in the DIKW model, this additional understanding is termed 'wisdom'.

The dilemma of the DIKW model's description of the metamorphosis of data is that the further data are abstracted from their original source, the more likely it is that errors will enter the metamorphic chain. Each context, assumption and decision made in relation to data and their products, each new interconnection that is created between data elements (see Figure 14.3) while potentially increasing the understanding of the data also makes them potentially 'contaminated'.

The DIKW model implies that the further up the hierarchy a data artefact goes, the more data it accrues. This highlights a major challenge to be faced in the heritage visualization context. If, for example, a fragmentary piece of architecture is used to recreate a temple (using, for instance, Vitruvius' principles), is the temple a data artefact in its own right, or extended metadata for the original data object? Conversely, is the visualization of the fragment a data artefact of the visualized temple which is itself a data object?

Further complexities arise when additional data artefacts are brought to bear on the metamorphic process. Where do these new data artefacts fit in? What are the relationships between different data artefacts? What are the processes that govern the decisions made during the visualization process?

It is not the author's purpose, here, to criticize an established data model but rather to demonstrate what it might suggest for the better understanding of visualization research and its presentation. The DIKW model, while it draws one's attention to the importance of understanding what happens to 'evidence' as

---

7   Russel L. Ackoff, 'From Data to Wisdom', *Journal of Applied Systems Analysis*, 16 (1989): 3–9. Harlan Cleveland, 'Information as a Resource', *The Futurist*, 12 (1982): 34–9. Milan Zeleny, 'Management Support Systems: Towards Integrated Knowledge Management', *Human Systems Management*, 7, 1 (1987): 59–70. Milan Zeleny, 'Human Systems Management: Integrating Knowledge, Management and Systems', *World Scientific*, 9 (2005): 15–16.

it is subjected to the process of visualization, would require further elucidation and development in order to yield more substantial gains for our theoretical understanding of heritage visualization.

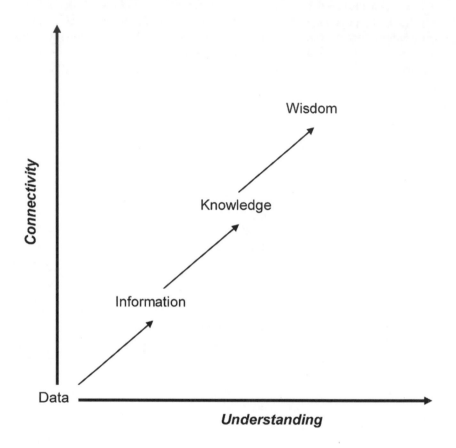

Figure 14.3   View of the Data, Information, Knowledge, Wisdom (DIKW) model

Source: Cleveland, 'Information as a Resource'; Zeleny, 'Management Support Systems; Ackoff, 'From Data to Wisdom'.

Paradata

Paradata are chronologically and ontologically dependent upon data but do not constitute a type of 'hyper-' or 'superdata' pertaining to data artefacts; rather they pertain to the critical process. The prefix 'para-' describes a parallel stream of data that exists each time data are transformed. Paradata can capture the decisions, selection processes, and reasoning behind the interaction and combination of different data artefacts. Paradata captures the processes through which data artefacts are created, recombined, detached and discarded from their parent data objects as they are transformed. These paradata records, documenting observations, decision and reasoning processes, selection and rejection criteria, and so forth, become an extension of the data load, sitting alongside metadata records (see Figure 14.4).

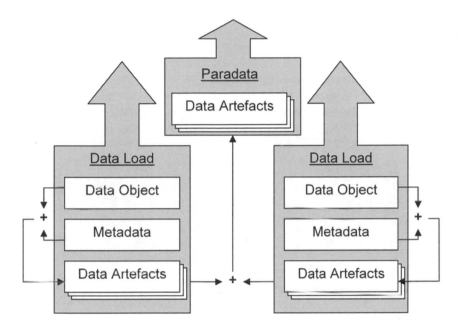

Figure 14.4   Paradata relationship between data loads

In heritage visualization, the metadata of an object is ideally kept as objective as possible, while the subjective process of combining data to transform them into something more useful is held in the paradata documentation. Paradata captures the selection, evaluation and exploration of ideas, as well as entropy and cultural assumptions, research and technical decisions, inference and implied possibilities and probabilities. By recording these ephemeral data it becomes possible to track the reasoning and construction of the visual hypotheses presented in a historical visualization. The output of the visualization process becomes more than simply a pretty picture derived from research. Rather it becomes a vital component of the research narrative, giving others the ability to see how the argument has been constructed. Instead of the teleological narrative that 'reconstructions' typically engender, paradata allow the scholar to document the journey of the visualization process, with all its inevitable uncertainties visible and intact.

In this approach, the degradation of 'purity', implied by the DIKW model, as one progresses from 'data' to 'wisdom', holds less true. The process of reasoning through which different data are connected together or discarded is made explicit, becoming, in effect, a further set of data. The process of producing a hypothesis can be more varied than it might otherwise have been, because the decisions and rationales employed by the researcher in developing the visualization are recorded and made visible.

The exercise of capturing paradata reminds us that, contrary to the positivist instincts of 'reconstruction', in 'visualization', the journey is often more important than the destination (see Figure 14.5).

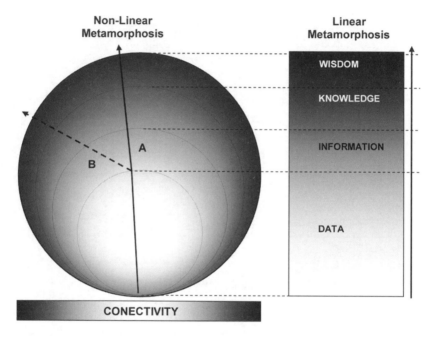

Figure 14.5   Non-linear versus linear data metamorphosis

Limitations

While in theory the acquisition of paradata to capture the intellectual capital behind a visualization is clearly valuable to research, the practical implementation of documenting paradata is not without its challenges and limitations.

One important issue is the quantity and level of detail ('granularity') of the paradata that should be recorded. Clearly there are some major data items that must be recorded such as the evidence that informed the creator, the reasoning and decision made on that evidence and how it was implemented within the visualization. However, there are limits to the value, and sustainability, of documentation. When a column is modelled, for example, should the reasoning behind a column be recorded as a single paradata record, or must the reasoning behind each of the column's potential scores of components and sub-components be given? The finer the detail in which such information is recorded, the more time-consuming the documentation process will be. The value of the record in providing intellectual accountability must be weighed against the cost of producing the record, including the potentially disruptive effect of high-granularity documentation to the interpretative process itself.

When considering granularity and quantity of paradata recorded, their quality must also be taken into consideration. How much weight can be attributed to a specific data artefact within a hypothesis? How reliable are external paradata that may be anecdotal, biased, not directly relevant or 'tainted' in some form, but still potentially valuable to the research project as a whole?

These are just some of the many questions that need to be investigated in order to reach a successful compromise that will enable paradata to be used effectively without suffocating the research objectives.

Conclusion

In conclusion, documentation and publication of paradata enable audiences to acquire fuller and more nuanced understandings of the processes, especially interpretative decisions, involved in producing historical visualizations. A number of further studies must yet be conducted before one can claim to have solved the problem of implementing paradata within scholarly research in the humanities. It is important to learn how to identify the types of data that should be retained to suit a variety of different contexts. New methods and tools must be created to enable researchers to capture and publish paradata efficiently.

However, as the association of paradata records with heritage visualizations becomes the norm, it will become increasingly easy to see and to explain the vital role that visualization can play in exploring hypotheses and constructing arguments – a situation far preferable to that in which visualization outputs appear, belatedly, as mute, unverifiable 'illustrations' of supposedly prior knowledge. By understanding and marking the journey taken by the researcher – the evidence that is used and discarded, the paths that are taken and where they lead in the construction of an argument – the visualization is allowed to function as a research artefact in its own right. Paradata documentation thus enables visualizations to provide the stimulus for debate and to become one part of a living and growing corpus of richly understood data.

Chapter 15

Transparency for Empirical Data

Mark Mudge

Introduction

Transparency is a necessary element for the use of digital representations in scholarly and scientific discourse. Digital-based scholarship, distributed collaboration and future reuse of today's investment in digitization require the means to evaluate a digital representation's quality and reliability. Reuse and repurposing are a fundamental test for digital information. If digital information is sufficiently transparent to allow evaluation of its trustworthiness by contemporary and future scholars, it has passed this test. If not, its value is doubtful.

Understanding that transparency is necessary has little value unless it is possible to realize it using the tools and practices of cultural heritage professionals and their associates in the natural sciences. If there is to be widespread adoption of digital practices, cultural heritage specialists must be able to generate transparent, trustworthy digital representations as a normal part of their practice without significant disruption to their working cultures.[1] Whether this happens or not will determine the digital future, or lack of it, in these domains.[2]

Art, Visualization and Digital Surrogates

Humanity's legacy can be unlocked and shared between people through digital representations. Digital representations can communicate knowledge in a variety of ways. For clarity, we can define three different types of use for such representations: art and entertainment, visualization and digital surrogates of the world we experience.

---

1   Adam Rabinowitz, Carla Schroer and Mark Mudge, 'Grass-roots Imaging: A Case-study in Sustainable Heritage Documentation at Chersonesos, Ukraine', Proceedings of the CAA Conference March 22–26, 2009 Williamsburg Virginia (Oxford, 2010), pp. 320–28; Mark Mudge, Tom Malzbender, Carla Schroer and Marlin Lum, 'New Reflection Transformation Imaging Methods for Rock Art and Multiple-viewpoint Display', in *VAST2006 The e-Volution of Information Communication Technology in Cultural Heritage* (Budapest, 2006).

2   Mark Mudge, Michael Ashley and Carla Schroer, 'A Digital Future for Cultural Heritage', in A. Georgopoulos and N. Agriantonis (eds), *Anticipating the Future of the Cultural Past XXI CIPA International Symposium* (Athens, 2007), pp. 521–6.

Digital representations can be fine art in their own right, and they can entertain. They may also be used to visualize concepts, and illustrate hypotheses. In this case, we use the term 'visualization' in its broadest sense to include sight and hearing; in the future this may be extended to smell, taste and touch. For example, a computer animation of a large asteroid striking the Yucatan Peninsula 65 million years ago aids in the visualization of the theoretical cause for the worldwide extinction of the dinosaurs. These images are useful not because they give a faithful representation of the shape and colour of the actual asteroid moments before impact, but because they communicate an idea effectively. Visualizations may be speculative in nature to varying degrees in a continuum from the totally speculative to nearly complete grounding in empirical data. A central goal of The London Charter is to bring transparency to visualizations. Other authors in this volume are exploring ways to describe the extent and nature of this speculative content explicitly.

The third type of digital representation, digital surrogates, sometimes referred to as 'virtual surrogates', serve a different purpose. Their goal is to represent reliably the acquirable attributes of real observational content in a digital form. Their purpose is to enable scientific study and personal enjoyment without the need for direct physical experience of the object or place. Their essentially scientific nature distinguishes them from speculative digital representations.

Two essential elements of scientific practice are found in all digital surrogate acquisition and generation and also in many visualizations. First, the attributes of the studied material must be observed by two or more people. In other words, the experience must be inter-subjectively verifiable. Second, any subsequent operations performed upon this raw information must be recorded for later review by others. A transparent digital surrogate, or visualization, ensures access to the original raw observations and provides a complete record of all subsequent operations in the equivalent of a 'lab notebook'. In science, the term 'provenance' has traditionally been used to refer to these records. Scientific information cannot be understood in absence of the meaning of the data and the history of its generation. The term 'metadata' as data about data is frequently used interchangeably in scholarly discourse with the term 'provenance'.[3]

The experience of those engaged in distributed, internet-based scientific inquiry confirms the necessity of documenting how digitally represented information is generated. These collaborations, frequently found in the biological sciences, rely heavily on accounts of the process of digital data creation to assess the quality of information contributed by the cooperating partners, and make their own work

---

3   Mark Mudge, Tom Malzbender, Alan Chalmers et al., 'Image-based Empirical Information Acquisition, Scientific Reliability, and Long-Term Digital Preservation for the Natural Sciences and Cultural Heritage', *Eurographics 2008: Tutorial Notes* (2008), <http://homepages.inf.ed.ac.uk/rbf/CVonline/LOCAL_COPIES/MUDGE/EG-mudge-tutorial-notes-final.pdf>.

valuable to others.[4] A similar need for lab notebook metadata process accounts for reliable digital representations of cultural heritage materials was presented and discussed during a panel on *Computers and Cultural Heritage*, chaired by Holly Rushmeier of Yale University, at the SIGGRAPH 2004 conference.[5]

In the previous chapter, Drew Baker defined the term and domain of 'metadata' though analysis of its usage patterns as applied to the Dublin Core metadata structure. The philosophy of language often bases definitions of linguistic elements upon empirically identifiable use patterns found in language.[6] Limiting the scope of usage analysis of the term 'metadata' to its use in relation to Dublin Core is too restrictive. This limitation is not supported by empirical evidence from existing language usage patterns of 'metadata' and its role as applied to the generation and preservation of provenance within scholarship, science and digital representations.

The Dublin Core structure is one among a wide selection of metadata architectures. It is non-recursive (flat), lacks representation of events, actions and complex semantic relationships such as long running interpretative discussions, and offers one of the most restrictive characterizations of acceptable metadata entries. Were the use of 'metadata' in language limited to its role in Dublin Core, Drew Baker's analysis of its limited ability to describe process history would appear reasonable. However, Dublin Core is not a de facto worldwide standard, lacking adoption by the US Library of Congress, the University of California, and other leading worldwide museums, libraries and archives. Dublin Core is functionally limited compared to far more robust international ISO standards of metadata architecture.

One such example is ISO 21712, the UNESCO chartered International Council of Museums' Documentary Committee's (CIDOC) Conceptual Reference Model (CRM).[7] Within ISO 21712 the term 'metadata' can encompass discussion, commentary, conditional understanding, disagreeing opinions and much more. ISO 21712 can link this information between and among archives using dissimilar metadata architectures.[8] With the recent development of CRM Digital,[9] and capture technology explicitly designed by Cultural Heritage Imaging and their

---

4   Jun Zhao, Carole Goble, Mark Greenwood et al., 'Annotating, Linking and Browsing Provenance Logs for e-Science', in *Proceedings of Second International Semantic Web Conference (ISWC 2003) Workshop on Retrieval of Scientific Data*, Florida, October 2003, pp. 158–76.

5   Mark Mudge, 'Cultural Heritage and Computer Graphics Panel', in *SIGGRAPH 2004 Conference Presentations, Web Graphics/Special Sessions/Panels*, 2004.

6   Ludwig Wittgenstein, *The Blue and Brown Books* (New York, 1965). Willard Van Orman Quine, *Word & Object* (Cambridge, MA, 1964).

7   *CIDOC Conceptual Reference Model*, <http://cidoc.ics.forth.gr>.

8   Martin Doerr, 'The CIDOC Conceptual Reference Module: An Ontological Approach to Semantic Interoperability of Metadata', *AI Magazine*, 24, 3 (2003): 75–92.

9   Maria Theodoridou, Yannis Tzitzikas, Martin Doerr et al., 'Modeling and Querying Provenance by Extending CIDOC CRM', *Distributed and Parallel Databases*, 27, 2 (2010): 169–210.

collaborators to use it,[10] one can track empirical acquisition events recorded in a digital lab notebook's step by step (processes history) in a machine-readable form and enable advanced, semantically organized querying of the information stored within.

The linguistic use patterns of the term 'metadata', applied within the functional scope of a robust architecture, such as ISO 21712, combined with the extensive usage history predating The London Charter discussed above posses, at minimum, the same descriptive and relational attribute set as the term 'paradata'. The term 'paradata' compared to the term 'metadata' now represents a distinction without a significant difference. Below, we will examine further undesirable conceptual conflations flowing from the use of the term 'paradata'.

Given that scholarly discussion has been ongoing, widely engaged in by the museum, library, archive, computer graphics and scientific communities, and considering the substantial costs associated with the introduction of new vocabulary into an existing discussion using widely understood concepts, any new vocabulary needs to demonstrate strong comparative advantages to justify adoption. The latest version of The London Charter, presented by Hugh Denard in Chapter 7, is clear, self-evident, and comprehensible within the existing vocabularies of current scholarly discourse, with one exception, section 4.6. The lack of clarity in this section is due to the introduction and sole use of the term 'paradata', which does not have a widely understood usage history. Were 'paradata' to be replaced by a 'lab notebook of the means and circumstances of the visualization's generation', section 4.6 would be immediately comprehensible to all. Since 'paradata' is unnecessary for successful ongoing scholarly discourse, one can suggest the term 'paradata' be retired.

Nonetheless, much credit is due to all The London Charter collaborators. Charters like the Venice, London and emerging Seville charters focus attention on necessary improvements of practice. They are especially important to promote change in the cultural heritage establishments of some countries and regions. The London Charter has underscored the central importance of process history and lab notebook accounts to the adoption, reliability and future reuse of digital representations. The London Charter and the invention of the term 'paradata' are sincere manifestations of the acute need for and the practical willingness to do something about transparency in digital representations.

It would also be useful to sharpen some of the distinctions between the various uses of the term 'provenance'. The different characteristics of visualizations and virtual surrogates aid this analysis.

One traditional use of the term 'provenance' refers to attributes of the original, 'realworld' material. Here 'provenance' may refer to where it came from, ownership history, identifications, interpretations of the material and other useful

---

10   Jassim Happa, Mark Mudge, Kurt Debattista et al., 'Illuminating the Past: State of the Art', Virtual Reality, 14, 3, (2010): 155–82, <http://www.springerlink.com/content/d04 72051303777n0/?p=38c05227cf864b7ca15c87e10c147cae&pi>.

domain-specific features. Much of the metadata contained in archive catalogue records is of this type. For clarity in this discussion, but not proposed as a long-lasting term, this will be referred to as 'world provenance'.

A second and distinct form of provenance is the process history of the empirical data collection and subsequent operations that generate a digital representation. This records the journey of original, unaltered empirical evidence from its initial data capture all the way through the process pipeline to its final form as a digital surrogate. Just as 'realworld' cultural material requires a provenance identifying what it is, establishing its ownership history and proving its authenticity, this type of provenance documents the digital practices employed. It describes the circumstances of the digital representation's generation, not the 'realworld' subject of the representation. For clarity, though it is not proposed as a long-lasting term, this form of provenance will be referred to as 'lab notebook provenance'. It will be discussed at length in the following pages. The domain described by the term 'paradata' is subsumed under the combined domains of world provenance and lab notebook provenance.

The provenance and semantic management requirements of visualizations and virtual surrogates are significantly different. As the term 'paradata' draws no distinction between these two provenance types, there is a danger of confusion and missed opportunities if the attributes that define the distinctive natures of these two provenance domains are conflated.

The utility of these concepts becomes clear when we apply them to the distinctions between visualizations and digital surrogates. Visualizations will usually include world provenance, particularly in respect to the interpretations and concepts associated with it. If we go back to the example of the visualized asteroid that ended the age of dinosaurs, there are relationships to mathematics, scientific ideas and material evidence pointing to the geographic and geologic condition of the world 65 million years ago. It may be possible to use this information to estimate uncertainty and track relevant interpretive discourse using semantic knowledge management tools.

It is also possible to combine empirical digital surrogate information with visualizations. A hypothetical reconstruction of a building sitting on a digital surrogate documenting an extant foundation is a common example. In these situations, a clear identification of the different content types may aid scholarly evaluation.

In cases where visualizations do not incorporate digitally captured empirical data and contain no expert judgements based on the expert's experience, no provenance account of the empirical data acquisition process or subsequent operations performed on it are required. For example, the asteroid-dinosaur visualization makes no claims about the actual colour of the specific asteroid that landed 65 million years ago. If the asteroid was created using the imagination of a digital artist using modelling/animation software, it makes no claim to be a digital surrogate and its provenance does not need to be demonstrated.

On the other hand, a digital surrogate requires a complete account of the process history of the empirical data collection and subsequent operations employed to create it. For digital surrogates to find widespread use in science and cultural heritage scholarship, easy-to-use transparent qualitative evaluation of their authenticity and reliability by others is essential. Widespread adoption of digital surrogates by science in all fields, including the multi-disciplinary study of our cultural heritage, requires confidence that the data they represent are reliable. For a scholar to use a digital surrogate built by someone else in their own work, they need to know that what is represented in the surrogate is what is observed on the physical original. If archaeologists are relying on virtual 3D models to study Palaeolithic stone tools, they must be able to judge the likelihood that a feature on the model will also be on the original and vice versa. If they cannot trust that it is an authentic representation, they will not use the digital surrogate in their work.

Digital surrogates of our 'real world' can robustly communicate the empirically recordable features of cultural heritage materials. When digital surrogates are built transparently, according to established scientific principles, authentic, reliable scientific representations can result. These representations allow repurposing of previously collected information and enable collaborative distributed scholarship. Information about the digital surrogates stored in a semantically rich 'common language', accessible to and from locally determined archiving architectures, permits concatenation of information across many collections. It also demystifies complex semantic query of vast amounts of information to find relevant material efficiently. Digital surrogate archives can remove physical barriers to scholarship by allowing public access. They contribute to fostering widespread knowledge and enjoyment of nature and our ancestors' achievements.

The advantages presented by the adoption of digital surrogates are significant, but can only be attained if well-recognized obstacles are overcome. The need to do this is driving the ongoing development of new tools, methods and standards.

Lab Notebooks for Digital Representations

A digital representation's lab notebook is for digital surrogates the equivalent of what a traditional lab notebook is for non-digital representations. Digital representation lab notebooks are the extension of classic scientific method into the digital documentary practices used to build digital surrogates. They provide a basis for quality evaluation of empirically based elements of visualizations.

The attributes of a lab notebook's information for a given digital surrogate are dependent on the tools and methods employed to build it. For a digital photograph, the lab notebook information would include data such as the camera make and model, firmware version, shutter speed and aperture, as well as parameters used to convert the raw sensor data into an image, such as colour temperature; and all editing operations performed in Photoshop or similar software, such as cropping, resizing, distortion correction and sharpening. These editing operations can have a profound impact on image reliability and are examined in greater detail below.

For a 3D geometric model displaying photorealistic surface texture and reflective material properties, the lab notebook is complex. Complete process history accounts are required for the alignment of shape data acquired from different viewpoints, the registration of textural image data to geometry, the correction of geometric acquisition errors such as voids, smoothing in low-signal-to-noise-ratio situations, the effects of compressive data reduction, and other issues raised by the selected imaging method.

In each case, whether digital photo or 3D model, the attributes including quantity of records and the ease, difficulty or even possibility of empirical provenance collection result from the practices used to build the digital surrogate.

Many tools employed today in cultural heritage and natural science pursuits require such a high level and number of subjective judgements and hand-editing actions to be made that tracking these operations becomes impractical. The use of these tools must be restricted to entertainment and significantly speculative visualization applications. The users of these tools cannot be expected to know which parts of a scientific lab notebook are relevant to their contemporary colleagues and to generations of colleagues who have not yet been born. If comprehensive lab notebook generation cannot be achieved with a given tool, a next generation tool designed to record this information in a simple fashion is needed. Transparency requires the absence of arbitrary, ad hoc, random, self-serving, absent-minded, well-meaning, conventionally determined and sometimes simply omitted gaps in the record of the means and circumstances of a digital surrogate's or visualization's generation.

Only practices able to provide complete lab notebook provenance can be used to construct reliable digital surrogates. If they cannot do so they cannot create reliable digital surrogates able to be subjected to rigorous qualitative evaluation. Similarly, many past empirical data digitization projects that never recorded or have lost their lab notebook information have little to no value as digital surrogates. They may serve as visualization content and uncertainties may be estimated to some degree in relation to the provenance information about realworld materials, but the digital representation's opportunity for rigorous quality evaluation, and assessment for reuse of the data in new scholarship or scientific inquiry is essentially lost.

The requirement for lab notebook information has bearing on the development of digital technology and its adoption. Many tools and methods used to build digital surrogates feature simplification and trivially configured automation of empirical, post-processing data (including lab notebook provenance generation). Such tools and methods present significant benefits over those that call for a great deal of subjective judgment by a skilled operator, since every operator action that transforms empirical content must be documented in a digital log for future scientific evaluation.

The importance of automation in the construction of reliable digital surrogates is highlighted by a major study from Rochester Institute of Technology. This study, published in 2005, examined the digital imaging practices in leading US museums and libraries. The final report from the study states,

> Most museums included some visual editing and other forms of image processing in their workflows. […] When investigated closely, it was found that visual editing decreased colour accuracy in all cases. [..] In addition to visual editing, many images also incurred retouching and sharpening steps. The fact that many of the participants sharpened the images either at capture or before the digital master was saved raised the question of whether the implications of the choices made were well understood. Most of the image processing carried out was not automated; automation represents a possibility for improvement in setting up consistent, reproducible workflow.'[11]

While an artist's touch can increase the sales of a print in a museum gift shop or create a stunning cinematic effect, it has little direct role in the scientific construction of digital surrogates. The development of many of today's digital imaging tools was driven by the entertainment industry's desire to create special effects for movies and television, computer animations, video games and multimedia products. Unlike the entertainment business where a good-looking image is the goal, scientific documentation requires that the material be represented reliably. If the lab notebook, enabling assessment of reliability, is lacking, the digital representation may be enjoyed for visualization or entertainment purposes but not used as a digital surrogate.

As well as reliability, the synergistic combination of lab notebook provenance and automated digital processing, requiring trivial operator configuration, offers advantages for the organization, communication and preservation of digitally generated knowledge.

Once the process used to construct a digital surrogate is largely automated, a lab notebook log, describing this process, can be automatically produced. Knowledge management tools such as ISO 21712 can then map a history of actions performed in the course of this process to semantically robust information architectures.

Semantic Knowledge Management

The empirical content from which the architecture of ISO 21712 was designed came from museum and archive catalogues, recorded metadata in numerous domains and various interpretations of materials, including inconsistent interpretations. Consequently, applications for the CRM were centred around the mapping of existing metadata systems to the CRM, inter-operability among those mapped systems and communicating this knowledge to the broader world.

---

11   Roy S. Berns and Franziska S. Frey et al., *Direct Digital* Capture *of Cultural Heritage: Benchmarking American Museum Practices and Defining Future Needs* (Rochester, NY, 2005), p. 57. Available at <http://msc.mellon.org/research-reports/Direct%20Digital%20Capture%20of%20Cultural%20Heritage.pdf/view>.

As robust construction of digital surrogates, including 3D content, was in its infancy during this formative period, concepts specifically dealing with lab notebook provenance were not included in the CRM. As attempts to build scientifically useful digital surrogates increased and the analysis of the issues evolved, including the need to archive lab notebook provenance, it became clear that the CRM needed to address these issues.

Cultural Heritage Imaging (CHI) is an institutional member of ICOM, and the author of this chapter serves on the CIDOC/CRM Special Interest Group. CHI has worked with the group, particularly with the help of Steve Stead and Martin Doerr, to craft extensions to the ISO 21127 standard. The extensions added two new types, 'Digital Object' and 'Digitization Process'. These extensions were specifically designed to enable the representation of the information described by lab notebook provenance and generated during the creation of digital surrogates. These extensions are now part of ISO 21127. The CRM Digital work mentioned above is an example of this ongoing development.

The use of the CRM can now be extended to engineer digital surrogate capture and generation methodologies. The design of empirical data acquisition tools and subsequent processing operations can emphasize automation and seek to reduce operator involvement to trivial levels. If an acquisition method can use tools and methods that generate a log of activities, this log can be mapped to the CRM. Once this mapping process has been completed, digital processing can automatically record the information about lab notebook provenance into these semantic architectures as the digital surrogates are 'born archival'.

Reflectance Transformation Imaging (RTI) is an example of an empirical data acquisition tool specifically designed to permit complete lab notebook recording and semantic knowledge management through the CRM. RTI is an example of computational extraction of 3D information from a sequence of digital photographs to capture the colour and 3D shape of 'realworld' objects. RTI is an image-based technology where the operator's post-processing can be reduced to trivial levels. The RTI process has been used as a model to explore the development of empirical provenance and semantic knowledge management tools. CHI designed the RTI processing pipeline explicitly to enable the possibility of automatically capturing and mapping empirical provenance information to ISO 21712. These tools create a machine-readable log file of all operations performed during RTI processing. Combined with information stored in .XMP files generated during original RAW digital image conversion, all empirical provenance for the RTIs can be recorded. With the assistance of Steve Stead and Martin Doerr and funding from the US Government's Institute of Museum and Library Services (IMLS) National Leadership Grant Program, CHI has successfully mapped the entire empirical capture process of single-view Reflectance Transformation Imaging using the CRM extensions. During the 2008 Eurographics Conference tutorial,[12] Martin

---

12   See Martin Doerr's section in Zhao et al., 'Annotating, Linking and Browsing Provenance Logs for e-Science'.

Doerr reported that he and his team at ICS-FORTH in Crete had determined that a tool could in fact be constructed to map automatically the empirical provenance of RTIs to the CRM with only trivial involvement of the operator.

This was the first application of CRM semantic knowledge management concepts to image-based empirical acquisition processes and associated empirical provenance information. Prior to this work, CRM applications focused on uses within and among museums, libraries and archives. Martin Doerr presented these findings to the Conceptual Modeling Conference on 5 November 2007.

This work laid the foundation for the development of new, semantic knowledge management tools that promise to increase digital technology's ease of use for cultural heritage professionals, to enhance digital surrogate reliability and to lower barriers to digital technology adoption. The ability to map lab notebook information into a semantic knowledge management structure like the CRM creates many potential advantages that can be attractive to cultural heritage professionals, policy makers, funders and the public.

Long-term Preservation of Digital Information

One advantage of semantically knowledge-managed information contained in a lab notebook is found in the archival preservation of digital information. The need for long-term preservation of digital information is both clear and urgent. There are a number of curatorial advantages to semantic knowledge management generally and archived lab notebook information specifically. The more a digital curator knows about the files and the methods used to generate them the better they can perform preservation activities. If a file and the Open Source software that created it are available to the curator in the future, the file will more likely be preserved to new media standards than a file produced by proprietary, copyright-protected software that is no longer published or maintained.[13]

This topic is large and beyond our scope. In this limited document we will suggest only one major preservation opportunity stemming from the archival use of semantically managed lab notebook knowledge.

There is an important curatorial need to determine what needs to be preserved and what can be thrown away. Semantically managed lab notebook knowledge can generate dependency information that helps solve this problem. An investigation of these dependency relationships was conducted by CHI and the University of California Berkeley (UCB). The UCB has recently established a semantic knowledge managed archive called the Media Vault Program (MVP) designed to store the University's digital collection assets. A collaboration between CHI, the University of California Museum of Paleontology (UCMP) and the MVP

---

13   See Michael Ashley's section in Zhao et al., 'Annotating, Linking and Browsing Provenance Logs for e-Science'.

demonstrated the value a digital surrogate's lab notebook information can have in archival conservation.

Among the single-view RTIs CHI captured in the UCMP collection was a 220-million-year-old dinosaur trackway of species *Coltoni* in the genus *Cheirotherium*. RTIs were produced in four resolutions from full resolution, 5000 pixels along the image's long aspect, to a dimension of 500 pixels in length. Lab notebook information from the RTI generation process permitted the analysis of data dependencies created during processing. This dependency analysis enabled determination of which files were essential to the scientific record and which files could be regenerated from the originally acquired empirical data along with the lab notebook information. Files that could easily be regenerated were discarded. CHI, in cooperation with the Media Vault's architect, Michael Ashley, analysed the data dependencies and reduced the number of files requiring archival storage from 516 to 63, a significant advantage in a preservation context. The investigation reviewed this result with Martin Doerr, and his ICS-FORTH team concluded that it would be possible to create a semantic knowledge management tool automatically to determine file dependencies from the empirical provenance records of CRM-designed and mapped processes like single-view RTI.[14]

Democratization of Technology

The central theme of this discussion is that for the promise of transparent, trustworthy digital scholarship to become part of our world, new tools and methods of digital scholarship must be adopted. For widespread cultural heritage adoption of digital surrogates to occur, the cultural heritage workers who build and use digital surrogates must be able to employ these new tools themselves. The means by which robust digital information is captured and synthesized into digital surrogates requires great simplification, cost reduction, increased ease of use and improved compatibility with existing working cultures. As we have seen, new tools permitting automatic lab notebook capture and semantic knowledge management offer a means to this end. From a research and development perspective, if our goal is to get practical, usable tools in the hands of cultural heritage professionals as quickly as possible, image-based tools using digital photography are particularly promising.

Research into the development of capture methods that are based on digital photography will accelerate the near-term adoption of digital scholarship because digital photography skills are already widespread. Employing digital photography to provide the empirical data for digital surrogates also lowers financial barriers to digital technology adoption. Rich 2D and 3D information can be captured with the equipment commonly found in a modern photographer's kit. Recent research and commercial product development have shown that computational

---

14   See the author's and Martin Doerr's sections in Zhao et al., 'Annotating, Linking and Browsing Provenance Logs for e-Science'.

extraction of information from digital photographs can create digital surrogates that reliably describe the 2D and 3D shape, location, material and reflection properties of our world. This family of robust digital documentary tools, with the potential to offer automatic post-acquisition processing, overcomes an important barrier to the adoption of digital workflow. As was discussed above, automation requiring trivial configuration offers enhanced reliability and greatly reduces the computer technology expertise necessary to manage a digital workflow. Research can leverage new capture methodologies and intelligent semantic knowledge management to enable cultural heritage professionals to build digital surrogates with a minimum of additional training. In turn, this automation frees cultural heritage workers to concentrate on the cultural heritage tasks before them.

The ability of cultural heritage professionals simply to do the work they love, paying little attention to the digital tools they use, will mark our success.

Chapter 16

Behaviours, Interactions and Affordance in Virtual Archaeology[1]

Maurizio Forte and Sofia Pescarin

Introduction: Behaviours, Affordance and the Interpretative Process

Interpretation and communication are dynamic processes. Reconstructions in the field of virtual archaeology are the result of a process of research and interpretation. They commonly use both top-down and bottom-up rules, integrating multiple methodologies. The bottom-up rule starts with modelling data captured during fieldwork. Spatial connections, represented by the extrusion of plans and front elevations are used to create a final virtual *anastylosis* of the archaeological structures. The *anastylosis* is achieved by connecting all points and traces found on the ground and by reproducing shapes of any artefacts. Top-down rules use the mental faculty of making reference patterns, or 'mental maps', to interpret and reconstruct the past. These rules can be better used when integrated within a virtual reality (VR) environment, where dynamic interactions are basic behaviours.

In our cybernetic approach, learning involves the experience of the difference between us and the surrounding ecosystem.[2] This difference becomes evident throughout interaction and the user's feedback. The multi-modal accessibility is processed by virtual behaviours.

We often think of communication as part of the very final archaeological process and related to content dissemination. We believe that scientific knowledge and communication should be integrated into a single process. In fact, the 3D research outcome is not only visual but it is the result of a multi-modal and multi-sensory dynamic interaction. A model does indeed represent a complexity of relationships

---

1 This chapter is a revised and expanded version of the paper presented at the seminar *Making 3D Visual Research Outcomes Transparent*, co-sponsored by the AHRC ICT Methods Network; EPOCH; PIN, Prato, Italy and King's Visualisation Lab, King's College London, held at the British Academy on 23–25 February 2006, see <http://www.vhlab. itabc.cnr.it/openheritage/resources/Transparency_OS_AdvMethod06.pdf>.

2 Gregory Bateson, *Mind and Nature: A Necessary Unit* (New York, 1979); Luigi Calori, Carlo Camporesi, Maurizio Forte and Sofia Pescarin, 'Interactive Landscapes Reconstruction: A Web 2D and 3D Open Source Solution', in Mark Mudge, Nick Ryan and Roberto Scopigno (eds), *VAST 2005. The Sixth International Symposium on Virtual Reality, Archaeology and Cultural Heritage. Short Presentations* (2005), available at <http://public-repository.epoch-net.org/publications/../short2003.pdf >.

termed 'affordance'. This term was coined by the perceptual psychologist J.J. Gibson (1977 and 1979) to refer to actionable properties between the world and an actor. According to Gibson, affordances are environmental relationships. In everyday practice we experience a continuous, complex and spatial passage from one digital ontology (fieldwork and data acquisition) to another (communication), in order to perceive and communicate knowledge.[3]

Initially and in terms of its relation with the environment, an archaeological object, or site, is 'auto-poetic' because it is able to communicate its meaning by itself.[4] In this case, the context of the very culture which has produced the object and its territory constitutes 'a map' for a possible interpretation of relationships and meanings. The context changes with the passing of time. Due to the transformation of an ancient archaeological context, its self-communication may be difficult and partial; this is because the original relations are removed and the interpretation depends on the capacity to reconstruct them. In such a case, the archaeological map is not the ancient map. Maps are fundamental in the interpretation–reconstruction process but are not the territory.[5] They offer the code or an alphabet essential to interpret information, while the context represents a communication system. Is a museum a map or a territory according to this scenario? The museum is a non-encoded territory because it removes artefacts from their original setting and decontextualizes them. However, the museum is also a map because it creates a new context (alphabet) within the topology (ontology) of the display. While the original context is auto-poetic and self-organized, the museum object is devoid from its earlier meaning and acquires a new significance in cultural communication (see Plate 8).

Transparency in Virtual Reality Systems

In the humanities, transparency implies communication and reliability. It is a metaphorical extension of the meaning used in physical sciences: a transparent object is the one that can be seen through. In the digital domain transparency can be enabled through two concepts, namely interactivity and openness.

---

3   James J. Gibson, 'How Perception Really Develops: A View from Outside the Network', in Davide L. LaBerge and S. Jay Samuels (eds), *Basic Processes in Reading: Perception and Comprehension* (Hillsdale, NJ and London, 1977), pp. 155–73. James J. Gibson, *The Ecological Approach to Visual Perception* (Boston, MA: Houghton Mifflin, 1979).

4   See Humberto Maturana and Francisco Varela, 'Autopoiesis and Cognition: The Realization of the Living', in Robert S. Cohen and Marx W. Wartofsky (eds), *Boston Studies in the Philosophy of Science*, vol. 42 (Dordecht, 1980).

5   Alfred Korzybski, *Science and Sanity: An Introduction to Non-Aristotelian Systems and General Semantics* (Lakeville, CT, 1950); Gergory Bateson, *Steps to an Ecology of Mind* (San Francisco, 1972).

We believe that real-time VR systems are a medium suitable for managing archaeological landscapes. Intended as ecosystems, they are interactive and visual, and rely on relationships. External visualizations are likely to augment internal visualizations 'by providing information or insights that are additional to those that can be inferred from internal visualizations. In this case there is continuity between what can be internally visualized and what can be learned from an external visualization [...]'.[6] The design of effective external visualizations could be based on 'an understanding of internal visualization abilities'. In particular, dynamic navigation through an artificial environment has the property of suggesting mental paths through internal visualizations.

In a virtual environment, we experience a complete integration of data and information: all the data are in the same spatial domain; they are comparable and dynamic, interactive and interrelated. The user of the virtual world is therefore surrounded by spatial information that may be linked to metadata. The potential capability of connecting data and metadata relates to the concept of affordance. As explained above, affordance is any possible relation between users, avatars and digital ecosystems. Affordance represents potential interactions and behaviours. In this sense, in a VR environment an affordance is the possible interaction with an object (see Plate 9).

Another kind of interaction that contributes to the transparency of reconstruction is the exchange of information. Knowledge develops owing to a continuous alternation between the real and the virtual, through spatial context of information as well as its redundancy; users move along informative itineraries and progress to new learning levels. In the alternation and exchange between the real and the virtual in a cognitive *anakyklosis*, every step makes a difference (see Figure 16.1).

Why should data be made transparent? The experience of TV programmes, where no access is available to 'behind the scenes', demonstrates that one depends on the information as presented. Anyone who represents information also has the power to make it believable. This may not be wrong, but it should be noted that the less understanding of the representation one has the more vulnerable one is to misinformation. This is particularly true with storytelling and visual representation: both are powerful means to activate cognitive process of understanding and *learning*. Such a process should be activated even when one remains only a passive recipient.[7]

---

6   Mary Hegarty, 'Diagrams in the Mind and in the World: Relations between Internal and External Visualizations', in Alan F. Blackwell, Kim Mariott and Atsushi Shimojima (eds), *Diagrammatic Representation and Inference. Lecture Notes in Artificial Intelligence*, vol. 2980 (Berlin, 2004), pp. 1–13.

7   Eric S. Raymond, *The Cathedral and the Bazaar: Musings on Linux and Open Source by an Accidental Revolutionary* (rev edn, Beijing, 2001). Barry N. Hague and Brian D. Loader (eds), *Digital Democracy: Discourse and Decision Making in the Information Age* (Cambridge, UK and New York, 1999).

years how one can be inspired by the Open Source movement, particularly by the model offered to the programmers. As Douglas Rushkoff stated in his book *Open Source Democracy*, 'The operating principles of networking solutions, as the kind of collaboration required to create them, offered a new cultural narrative based in collective self-determination.'[9]

Among the first to tackle the problem of transparency seriously has been the Open Source community. In the early days of the information technology era, it was quite common for programmers to share their codes freely. The result was rapid development of the sector and improvements for users.[10] Software was distributed with its code and had to be compiled to work. Commercial strategy changed towards the end of the 1980s with the introduction of patents and copyright for software. As the new generation of programming languages developed, software was delivered in the form of binary files. This kept the code and software separate. While many programmers were forced to supply the user with closed binary programs, others proposed an alternative solution. Groups of programmers who liked to collaborate and exchange codes and ideas, and believed in transparent development of software set up a 'free-software' foundation (1984) and then the Open Source movement (1998).[11] The Open Source projects such as Linux, OpenOffice and Apache Server are undoubtedly a success story. The question remains whether this approach could be proposed for areas different from computer science, even if initial motivations are different? We believe that this approach may be extended to cultural heritage.

In our view the Open Source approach involves more than using free software. It extends to cultural projects that use similar method for ensuring transparency of data and information. In the authors' experience, the adoption of such a technological approach meant the reframing of Cultural Heritage reality, creation of new relationships, new tools and new metaphors, and establishing relevant connections.

In Table 16.1 the authors propose a possible application of the Open Source Model, borrowed from computer science, to cultural heritage. Professionals working in this field generally prefer to use simple tools that do not involve programming or advanced computer techniques. A tendency is to adapt readily available software, even if originally created for a different purpose, to data under scrutiny. When operating systems such as Unix and DOS were superseded with user-friendly systems they allowed almost anyone to use computers. One has soon got used to closed tools and opaque computer interfaces. The lack of transparency

---

9   Douglas Rushkoff, *Open Source Democracy* (2003), chapter 2; available at <http://www.gutenberg.org/files/10753/10753.txt>.

10   Joseph Feller and Brian Fitzgerald, *Understanding Open Source Software Development* (Reading, 2002).

11   Richard Stallman, *Free Software, Free Society: Selected Essays of Richard M. Stallman*, ed. J. Gay, intr. Lawrence Lessig (Boston, 2002).

was soon evident even in this process: making computers easier to use, in fact, had also the consequence of preventing users from gaining access to their processes.

Table 16.1   Comparison of the Open Source model between the IT field and possible applications in Cultural Heritage

Open Source Model	Cultural Heritage Projects
Collaborate with programmers within a community	Build collaborative communities of authors and creators of archaeological content
Exchange the code	Exchange data within the community through interactive collaborations using web interfaces
Disseminate work-in-progress versions	Disseminate cultural and other information, including work in progress, new metaphors and interpretations (if documented) over the web
Modify software freely, produce new versions or new tools	Let users analyse the content
Download and distribute free software	Familiarize the user with open formats allowing them to choose a preferred technology
Test software and produce documentation	

How can this model be introduced to archaeology? First, by using and testing Open Source tools. The second step may involve modifying these tools, and devising projects and interdisciplinary teams with interest in those tools. Finally, creating new Open Source tools, programs and applications, and disseminating them through the web. Collaborative work is indeed very important. A wide use of internet and Open Source may provide the basis for collaboration in order to answer participants' needs making greater use of interactivity. The Open Source communities would benefit from the enhanced participation of experts in cultural heritage, such as archaeologists, historians, art historians and educators. This participation would enable them to move away from being 'just' users to the position of evaluators, authors and creators.

Case Studies

The Nuovo Museo Elettronico (NuME) Project was amongst the first in Italy to be concerned with data transparency.[12] This project, jointly conducted by the

---

12   Francesca Bocchi, *Nu.M.E.: Nuovo Museo Elettronico della città di Bologna. La città in quattro dimensioni*, <http://www.storiaeinformatica.it/newdef/italiano/ndefault. html>; Bochi, 'The Long Road of Nu.M.E. (Nuovo Museo Elettronico, Bologna virtuale):

University of Bologna and the CINECA Supercomputing Centre in 1998, has created a real-time interactive system for the city of Bologna. A number of models of the historic city centre, from the Middle Ages to the present, were built. The viewer could switch from one model to another. VRML and Java were applied. The VRML models were connected to HTML pages, which offered an explanation of the sources for the reconstructions.

In the House of the Centenary project, the user could interact with models of the *domus* in Pompeii and switch between different views.[13] Through analysis of the differences, he or she could understand the difference between the appearance of the building today and how it might have looked in Roman times. The visualization aimed to be realistic, didactic and scientific, with the hypothetical parts depicted in grey (see Plate 11).

A more recent project, the Certosa Virtual Museum, also involved a virtual reality environment.[14] It enabled the user to navigate in the reconstructed historical model as if moving within the actual building as preserved today. Information about historic events and people could be called upon online by querying a database connected to the application. Navigation could either respond to movement within the site or be guided by the queries performed on the database (see Figure 16.3).

The River Po Delta project made available a hypothetical reconstruction of a Roman villa as well as models of archaeological excavation (see Figure 16.4).[15] Pictures taken during the digs on the remains found *in situ* were geo-located and are displayed when clicked on.

The main goal of the four-year Via Appia project was the mapping of activities in a large archaeological park in Rome.[16] It resulted in a number of different pilot projects. In particular, a VR application was created for the exhibition, Building Virtual Rome in 2006 and an associated VR application for the web.[17] It provided

---

Criteria and Methods', in *Proceedings of the 6th IEEE-VRIC Virtual Reality International Conference*, 11–16 May 2004, Laval, France.

 13 Daniella Scagliarini Corlàita, Antonella Coralini, Antonella Guidazzoli et al., 'Archeologia virtuale e supporti informatici nella ricostruzione di una domus di Pompei', in *Archeologia e Calcolatori*, 14 (2003): 237–4.

 14 Luigi Calori, Tiziano Diamanti, Mauro Felicori et al., 'Databases and Virtual Environments: A Good Match for Communicating Complex Cultural Sites', in *SIGGRAPH Educators' Program* (New York, 2004), p. 30.

 15 Antonella Guidazzoli, Sophia Pescarin, Maurizio Forte et al., 'From GIS to Landscape Virtual Reality Museums', in Maurizio Forte (ed.), *Archaeological Landscapes through Digital Technologies*, Proceedings of the Second Italy–United States Workshop, Rome, Italy, 3–5 November 2003 and Berkeley, USA, May 2005, BAR S1379 (Oxford, 2005).

 16 Maurizio Forte, Sofia Pescarin and Eva Pietroni, 'The Appia Antica Project', in Maurizio Forte (ed.), *The Reconstruction of Archaeological Landscapes through Digital Technologies*, Proceedings of the Second Italy–United States Workshop, Rome, Italy, 3–5 November 2003 and Berkeley, USA, May 2005, BAR S1379 (Oxford, 2005), pp. 79–95.

 17 'Building Virtual Rome', various events which took place in Rome between September and November 2006; see <http://www.itabc.cnr.it/buildingvirtualrome/stampa.

Figure 16.3   Certosa Virtual Museum Project. Connection between models and data related to events and people, stored in an online database

Figure 16.4   Delta Po Project. Analysis of the archaeological finds and a comparison with the hypothetical virtual reconstruction

the opportunity to test different VR behaviours, benefiting from direct access to fieldwork data, such as topography and architectural surveys. The authors were able to process them in their lab, model the landscape and monuments, study archaeological and historical sources. The project benefited from institutional collaboration and student dissertations. The approach to the VR application was strongly directed towards a narrative register. The aim was to give the user a complete idea of all the work behind the synthetic environment. For instance, 3D menus were used for each archaeological model. The menus could be used to

htm> and <http://www.vhlab.itabc.cnr.it/Img/Events/building_virtual_rome_call.pdf>. Luigi Calori, Carlo Camporesi, Maurizio Forte and Sofia Pescarin, 'Interactive Landscapes Reconstruction: A Web 2D and 3D Open Source Solution', in Mark Mudge, Nick Ryan and Roberto Scopigno (eds), *VAST 2005. The Sixth International Symposium on Virtual Reality, Archaeology and Cultural Heritage. Short Presentations* (2005), available at <http://www. cineca.it/stdoc/VAST2005_PescarinCamporesi.pdf>.

Figure 16.5   Movie shown within the virtual space

activate movies explaining the digital process used to produce a particular model or its interpretation (see Figure 16.5). The user could switch between different views of models as part of the observed landscape or as part of the reconstructed landscape, both within the same geographical space, as for example in the case of the church of Sant'Urbano, which was once the Temple of Ceres and Faustina. Meeting a historical character or a modern avatar was designed to enhance understanding of the landscape (see Figure 16.6).

The goal of VR application was not only to publish models and metadata on the web, making them available to the entire community as well as, in a separate section protected by a password, to the research team, but also to create a web platform, based on Open Source tools, for sharing archaeological data, metadata and interpretations. The same approach and GIS application were adopted for offline use. This was very important for ensuring long-term compatibility and repeatability. Two Open Source libraries were used and modified, namely OpenSceneGraph (see <http://www.openscenegraph.org/projects/osg>) and Virtual Terrain Project (see <http://www.vterrain.org>). GIS data were processed with a terrain generator and the 3D, paged and tiled terrain was built. A low-polygon version of the models was also created and geo-located. Vector geographical information was overlaid over the terrain in order to give more readability to the interpretation of landscape reconstruction. This entire material was subsequently published on the web, using a plug-in created by the CNR ITABC and CINECA

Figure 16.6　Virtual encounter with historical characters inside Sant'Urbano

team for Mozilla Firefox and Internet Explorer browsers (see Figures 16.7 and 16.8). Some interaction was also added using PHP programing to allow a dynamic construction and analysis of the archaeological environment, including loading 3D models, switching between different terrains and vegetation, as well as vector layers and viewpoint registrations (see <http://www.appia.itabc.cnr.it>).

Conclusion

As Maurizio Forte has noted, 'Noticeable gaps are represented by the fact that the models are not "transparent" in respect to the initial information *(what were the initial data?)* and by the use of the peremptory single reconstruction without offering alternatives (*it could have been like this but we can also offer other models* ..).'[18] It was a promising observation but, unfortunately, it seems that little has changed. Very few applications of virtual archaeology include a path of validation and transparency for the data used in the final reconstruction. It should be noted that the processes of analysis and reconstruction are dynamic and involve multiple

---

18　Maurizio Forte, 'About Virtual Archaeology: Disorders, Cognitive Interactions and Virtuality', in Juan A. Barceló, Maurizio Forte and Donald H. Sanders (eds), *Virtual Reality in Archaeology*, BAR International Series 843 (Oxford, 2000), pp. 247–59.

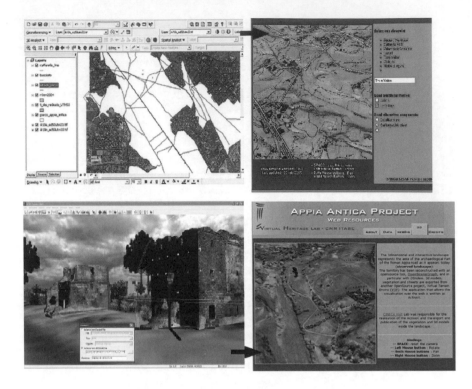

Figure 16.7   Via Appia Project. From GIS to 3D navigation and interaction on the web (top). 3D dynamic offline environment for landscape reconstruction and 3D data published online (bottom)

relations or affordances. The quality of information depends on the interaction between users and digital ecosystems: during the interaction the user creates new information, hence the information evolves according to the affordances present in the ecosystem. The transparency factor therefore supports not only the scientific method of validation, but also constitutes a dynamic process that brings theoretical neutrality to the information and thus takes it to a higher level of knowledge.

The authors identify a cybernetic cycle of interaction-affordances-difference-learning communication and knowledge in the ecology of the virtual and in the virtual archaeology. They believe that transparency needs to be linked to a methodological process that connects knowledge and communication; integrating the bottom-up and top-down approaches within the same digital environment. The key issue for the future is to share this process with a wide community of user-avatars, keeping all the behaviours within a 3D ecosystem.

Several developments concerning the web platform are planned. Editing tools should be developed in order to enable a real, shared working environment. The academic community should consider, as a matter of priority, the guidelines concerning the content to be published while the VR and webGIS communities may use this opportunity to share points of view, different interpretations and diverse perceptions of ancient landscapes.

Further experimentation with simulated virtual environments should be encouraged, particularly the application of complete spatial dimensions to numerical or statistical data. There have already been some experiments in this area that brought together simulation and artificial intelligence (AI), a field with enormous potential for the humanities. For instance, in the installation *A-Life* a community of autonomous agents, equipped with a personal neural network, develops the capacity to recognize and search food in order to survive; they also develop a 'society' of evolving creatures.[19] The integration of AI within the virtual environment may prove beneficial when one wants to describe not only cultural objects, but also their more complex ecological context. These attempts may eventually lead on to create an artificial society living in the archaeological landscape. In fact one of the existing limits for such applications is the desolate character of the virtual landscape, with characters or animals responding to predetermined animations. To achieve more evolved VR systems within an archaeological landscape, one might consider introducing autonomous agents, able to make decisions satisfying their objectives in relation to their knowledge and experience, and able to learn new information strategies for problem solving. In this perspective, pioneered by Craig Reynolds and others, global behaviour depends on the composition of local interactions with the environment.

19   Mauro Annunziato, Matteo Lucchetti, Giuseppe Orsini and Stefano Pizzuti, 'Artificial Life and Online Flows Optimisation in Energy Networks', in *Proceedings of the IEEE Swarm Intelligence Symposium*, Pasadena (CA), USA, June 2005 (Rome, 2005), pp. 412–15.

Chapter 17

How to Make Sustainable Visualizations of the Past: An EPOCH Common Infrastructure Tool for Interpretation Management[1]

Daniel Pletinckx

Rationale

Current technology makes it possible to create 3D models of landscapes and man-made structures ever more easily and to visualize these models in several interactive and non-interactive ways. IBM pioneered the use of this technology in the 1980s for designing and visualizing structures that still had to be built, as well as for visualization of structures that had existed, but disappeared for one reason or another.[2]

Although there is no fundamental *technological* difference between visualizing structures that are yet to be built and structures that have existed, there is a major *conceptual* difference. This is because the knowledge of the past is partial and uncertain. In fact, the past cannot be reconstructed at all. Even for the not too distant past, there is no sufficient information fully to reconstruct structures that have not survived.

One may try to piece together all information there is about a certain structure in a certain historical period, and try to visualize this incomplete and uncertain information in the best possible way. This text explains the methodology for doing this in a structured and reproducible way. In fact, similar methods have been

1   This chapter consists of an edited report originally produced with support from the European Commission under the Community's Sixth Framework Programme, Contract no. 2002–507382. See the author's *Interpretation Management: How to Make Sustainable Visualisations of the Past*, EPOCH Knowhow Booklets, <http://media.digitalheritage. se/2010/07/Interpretation_Managment_TII.pdf>. For more information about the European Research Network of Excellence in Open Cultural Heritage (EPOCH) see <http://www. epoch-net.org/>.

2   A handful of still images from the IBM Cluny project can be found at <http://www. mediaport.net/CP/CyberScience/BDD/fich_054.fr.html>. For an application of the IBM WINSOM modelling software see 'Winchester Minster', in Anna Bentkowska-Kafel (ed.), *3DVisa Index of 3D Projects*, <http://3dvisa.cch.kcl.ac.uk/project12.html>.

used in archaeological and historical research for a long time but, despite some pioneering efforts, they are yet to be implemented in 3D visualization.[3]

This chapter explains and illustrates three methods, namely *source assessment*, *source correlation* and *hypothesis trees*, which help to structure and document the process of transformation of the source material into 3D visualization. Also discussed here are different approaches to 3D visualization in research and public presentations. A tool for the management of the interpretation process is presented. The aim is to propose a methodology and tool for making 3D visualizations of the past sustainable and open to peer review, and to turn them into an instrument that is accepted in both research and public presentation. This Interpretation Management or InMan tool is part of the EPOCH Common Infrastructure that provides concrete tools and solutions for common problems in the cultural heritage domain.

Background

Three-dimensional visualization uses current capabilities to create spatial models of objects, and to show them in different ways and with varying degrees of realism and interactivity. It has been proven that 3D visualization is able to recreate and visualize historical structures (buildings, cities and other man-made structures, landscapes, and so on). It is becoming an ever more acceptable method for presenting interpretation in historical and archaeological research.

Three-dimensional visualization however had and partially still has the connotation of lacking credibility and documentation, something which can result in too optimistic and even false conclusions about the past and about the premises and possibilities of archaeology as a discipline.[4]

Although the term 'interpretation' has other meanings and connotations in other domains, it is used here to indicate the intellectual process of drawing conclusions from sources. In this context, these conclusions focus on all aspects of visualization. In fact, the visualization process is embedded in most cases in the wider interpretation, supporting research and helping with the dissemination of knowledge to a wider audience.

The term 'virtual reconstruction' is not used here, because the main goal is not to reconstruct the past – this is something one simply cannot do – but to

---

3   See, for example, Nuovo Museo Elettronico (NuME), 4D visualization of Bologna at <http://www.storiaeinformatica.it/nume/english/ntitolo_eng.html> and Rome Reborn, <http://www.romereborn.virginia.edu/>.

4   See Nick Ryan, 'Computer-based Visualization of the Past: Technical "Realism" and Historical Credibility', in Peter Main, Tony Higgins and Janet Lang (eds), *Imaging the Past: Electronic Imaging and Computer Graphics in Museums and Archaeology*, British Museum Occasional Papers No. 114 (London, 1996), pp. 95–108. Nick Ryan, 'Documenting and Validating Virtual Archaeology', *Archeologia e Calcolatori*, 12 (November 2001): 245–73.

bring together all available sources of information and visualize this process with 3D technology. Visualization can be very useful in a research context but also for public presentation. This means that photo-realistic, complete models of landscapes or man-made structures are not always necessary. Sometimes a schematic or simplified representation is all that is needed or all that is possible. In such cases, the general term '3D visualization' seems more appropriate.

Most technological issues in this field have reached a sufficient level of solution, and a variety of tools is available for most 3D visualization tasks. The conceptual process of turning available sources into a 3D visualization is, however, far less defined. This interpretation process not only takes most of the time spent on visualization; it is also a complex, non-linear process that can benefit significantly from tools that manage and organize this process. In other words, *interpretation management* is a key element of 3D visualization of historic structures, as it records and manages the process of establishing how the available sources have led to the 3D visualization; it also supports, smoothes and structures the interpretation process.

The Purpose of Interpretation Management

There are several reasons why interpretation management is necessary when visualizing historical structures in 3D models. First, it enables the *recording* of the interpretation process, that is documents how all elements in the visualization have been derived from the available sources. This is a necessary step, as practice shows that some 80–90 per cent of the work in 3D visualization of historic structures goes into the assessment and interpretation of the sources; only 10–20 per cent of the time is spent on building the 3D model. Practice shows that this interpretation process is complex and can extend over a long period; that the amount of source data can be overwhelmingly large; and that in many cases many people work simultaneously on the same project. It is therefore crucial to follow well-defined procedures, supported by a tool that records and manages this interpretation process, in order to safeguard the financial and intellectual investment in visualization in the best possible way.

The second reason for having interpretation management is the ability to *update* 3D visualizations when new information comes to light from new excavations, recently discovered historical sources or new scientific interpretations and insights. Integration of such new data is in most cases far from straightforward. Having a well-defined process for altering the initial interpretation according to these new findings is necessary to manage existing 3D visualizations. In other words, 3D visualizations should be kept 'alive' many years after initial excavations or research efforts have ended.

The third reason is concerned with *scholarly transparency*. When visualizing historical buildings or landscapes, a lot of information is needed to build complete 3D models. In most cases, sources are indirect and insufficient to construct the 3D model. The process of transforming those available sources into a complete 3D model is a difficult process. One has to understand that the uncertainty of elements in a 3D visualization can vary largely across the model. Some elements are well defined while other are unclear. The process of how to compensate for these uncertainties is undefined, and can yield several good solutions. Furthermore, when basic choices are unclear (for example, is the excavated structure a small church or a large house?), results can depend to a large extent on small details or even speculations or assumptions. This means that many 3D visualizations, or at least parts of them, can be uncertain. For public presentations, it is not always useful to expose this uncertainty: a choice is often made between what should be shown and how. For scholarly purposes, a 3D visualization needs to be transparent. The uncertainty and choices made should to be well documented and made available for scholarly critique and research. In other words, interpretation management is a way to disseminate and publish 3D visualization.

The fourth reason is concerned with *data preservation*. Practice shows that most visualization processes yield binders of unstructured documents from which those not directly involved in the project cannot reconstruct the interpretation process. This means that the intellectual efforts of creating a 3D visualization cannot be passed onto the next and later generations. By providing a methodology and tool for recording and managing the interpretation process of a 3D visualization in a structured way, a means may be provided for storing these data in the long term, thus ensuring access to the data and the interpretation process for future use and research.

The final reason is *multi-disciplinary cooperation*. It should be noted that 3D visualization brings together a wide range of skills, from history and archaeology to architecture and structural engineering, from pollen analysis and hydrography to 3D modelling and rendering. No individual can master all the skills needed to interpret all available sources. A tool that brings together all sources and all interpretations is in fact also a *collaboration platform* that allows the subject specialists involved in the project to contribute in an iterative process.

Recording Methodology

The InMan tool supporting the 3D visualization process is intended to be simple and adaptable to a wide range of visualizations, and therefore practical. Not many such tools have been introduced to the 3D visualization community so far. Broad use by a large number of practitioners will show how this tool may be developed further. It is believed that it would be wrong to be too prescriptive, or restrictive, by forcing a rigorous framework. The tool should rather serve as a flexible repository of information that will act as a guide through the interpretation process.

The methodology for interpretation management presented here is based upon many years of experience in 3D visualization. The main features of the methodology are:

- clear references to all sources used, no use of implicit knowledge;
- in-depth source assessment, making the reliability and potential bias of each source clear;
- correlation of all sources used for a 3D visualization in order to detect common ground as well as inconsistencies, outliers or dependencies;
- structural analysis of the object to be visualized, and division of the object into logical sub-units;
- listing all potential hypotheses, never 'hiding' a discarded hypothesis;
- recording the interpretation process by making a clear link between the sources, the reasoning and the resulting hypothesis;
- showing the hypotheses in a tree structure, with sub-hypotheses depending on main hypotheses;
- keeping the recording process separate from the modelling and visualization process, as the former is far from linear.

It is the rigorous implementation of this methodology in general, and the use of correlation techniques for iconographic sources and a hypothesis tree in particular, that makes it well suited for optimizing the process of constructing a virtual 3D model derived from related sources. The methodology proposed here is a multi-step process consisting of:

1. Creating a source database.
2. Source assessment.
3. Source correlation.
4. Creating hypothesis trees with conclusions.
5. Updating.

Issues that need to be addressed include the reliability of the hypotheses, multiple hypotheses of equal probability, ways to express uncertainties and means for visualizing historical development. This chapter explains the goals and approach of The London Charter, and demonstrates how the InMan tool can be used to implement these goals. The methodology presented here, and its implementation, are illustrated with a case study (see the end of this chapter) concerning the visualization of St Saviour's church in Ename, Belgium.

Creating a Source Database

It is good practice to record all sources in a *source database* and refer to them systematically throughout the visualization process. Having a rigorous system of referencing sources – whether iconographic, textual or other – helps avoiding incorrect assumptions and misinterpretation of this material. It is often forgotten that text is one of the most important sources in a 3D visualization process.

There is no standard structure for the source database, as many different types of source can be integrated (from iconography to pollen analysis, from unpublished excavation data to well-known historical sources, from historical analysis of existing buildings to oral history). The guiding principle requires *all sources to be identified uniquely so they can be located easily when needed*. This does not differ from standard practice in archaeological and historical research (where footnotes are used in most cases). The same approach needs to be adopted by technicians making 3D models.

Each source is recorded on a source sheet (see Ename case study for an example) which also contains digital images enlargements of specific features, as well as transcriptions of text where necessary. Having such key information transcribed and included in the interpretation management system is very useful and saves on physical retrieval of documents, some of which may only be available in libraries and archives.

Source Assessment

A key element in the interpretation process is *source assessment*. It normally yields some understanding of the degree of reliability of the source, and more specifically provides clues why certain information is not reliable.

This *assessment* can be a detailed study of the context of the source or the way the source depicts the reality. For example, iconography needs to be examined to offer clues concerning its creator(s), the reason why it was made or how it could be interpreted. In fact, source assessment is an attempt at understanding the process of representing reality in a given source. One also needs to be aware that all sources – whether textual, iconographical or archaeological – were already subjected to interpretation at the time of their creation, hence errors, omissions, incorrect, accidental or deliberate alterations. One needs to understand this contemporary context to gain as correct information about the source as possible. Correlation of sources (see next step) may further reduce the level of errors which is present in every source.

The example of Verona may serve as an illustration of source assessment. This ancient Italian city is situated in a bend of the Adige river and is dominated by St Peter's hill on the other side of the river (see Plate 12). The city's Roman and medieval structures are well preserved and include the Roman coliseum, theatre and bridge.

In the course of research leading to a 3D visualization of Verona around 1000 it is necessary to examine all surviving iconography, also of later periods, as such material is likely to depict earlier features. Two well-known iconographic sources have survived, of which one (see Plate 12, bottom) appears to contain many valid and useful details, while the other (see Figure 17.1) is historically inaccurate. Assessment of both sources should be recorded, so that other researchers may benefit from this assessment.

Figure 17.1   View of the city of Verona by the cartographer Hartmann Schedel (1493)

When analysing the city around 1000 (Plate 12, bottom) the extant buildings are immediately recognizable. The castle or church on St Peter's hill by the river (top middle), the Roman coliseum (bottom left), the archaeologically confirmed double wall (middle bottom), the Roman theatre (top middle) and Roman bridge (middle of the picture) prove the authenticity of the drawing. In Figure 17.1 a castle on a hilltop and a river are noticeable, but the layout of the city is incorrect: the river should be at the foot of the castle and the city should be on the other bank of the river. The lack of landmark buildings, such as the Coliseum, leads to the conclusion that this drawing is more fiction than reality. This drawing must therefore be classified as historically inaccurate. On top of that, two completely different views of Verona by Hartmann Schedel are known, as is the fact that he never visited this city.

Another aspect of source assessment is a detailed study of information about its creator and the original context of the source, as well as the visual language used. The drawing shown in Plate 12, for example, was created in the tenth century at the time of Ratherius, Bishop of Verona and a friend of Emperor Otto I. Many buildings depicted are churches and may relate to the numerous churches built by Ratherius, thus explaining the rationale behind the drawing. Two examples of a source sheet are included in the Ename case study, one for an iconographical source and one for an archaeological source, with an assessment of both.

Source Correlation

The *correlation method* serves comparison of different sources and allows for conclusions to be drawn from correspondences, differences and inconsistencies between the sources. Conclusions can be that a source is totally unreliable, or contains certain deliberate errors or accidental mistakes, or is a correct and detailed representation of the subject it depicts or describes. *Consistency checking* is a basic correlation method for sources that contain the same information. This can happen, for example, between different iconographic sources depicting the same scene, or between an archaeological and iconographic source. It is important to keep the contemporary pictorial conventions in mind: a medieval drawing, for example, cannot be expected to represent geometrical perspective correctly. The character and limitations of the sources (as recorded in the source assessment) also need to be taken into account.

Consistency checking may prove particularly informative when *several versions* of a certain source exist. Through a historical analysis of small differences between the different versions the most reliable (often the oldest) source can usually be identified. The source correlation method can be illustrated with a case study of the village of Ename in Belgium. Four drawings of 1596 provide important information for 3D visualization of the village.

Figures 17.2 and 17.3 show St Laurence church in Ename in 1596. Figure 17.2 is one of two views of Ename depicted in a pilgrim vane; Figure 17.3 is a detail of a drawing that illustrates a legal case document of the same year. Both views are taken from the same point, and surprisingly also display the same error (marked with an arrow). The door in the south aisle wall has not been confirmed by an archaeological survey of the church which has, however, confirmed such a door in the north wall. The artist of the pilgrim vane drawing (which is probably the older of the two) made an error by depicting the door at the wrong side of the church. As the same error appears in both drawings one can assume that Figure 17.3 was modelled on Figure 17.2. This has important implications. These two drawings are the only evidence for the octagonal church tower. If these two drawings were uncorrelated they could have been taken to imply the existence of the octagonal tower, but the fact that these drawings are not independent makes such a conclusion less plausible (see Figure 17.4).

When correlating the pilgrim vane picture (see Plate 13, top left) with a recently discovered map of Ename in 1596 (see Plate 13, top right) similarities (indicated by numbers in green) but also important differences (indicated by numbers in red) can be noted. In the image on the right, there are more houses

Figure 17.2   St Laurence church in Ename in 1596. Detail of a pilgrim vane

Figure 17.3   St Laurence church in Ename in 1596. Illustration in a trial document

Figure 17.4   Ename in 1596. View of the centre of the village in a recently discovered map

depicted on the common (6), and a cross (2), well (4) and a pillory (5) are visible in the common (3). This open square area was a wheat field in the image on the left. The church (1) is depicted in a sketchy way, but seems to have a square tower. This comparison indicates the need for understanding the reasons behind the differences in drawings dated to the same year.

Although an in-depth historical analysis of the map is yet to be undertaken, a preliminary explanation of these differences seems as follows. The church records indicate that St Laurence's was unused from 1578 (after the monks were expelled by the Protestants) until 1592, as confirmed by archaeological research. Monks reclaimed the village as their rightful property and started rebuilding the abbey in 1596 (in the image on the right, one building (10) seems to be operational again). The cross and pillory in the second image clearly show this re-establishment of the governing rule of the abbey. This suggests that the first image is a few years earlier than the second. While the left-hand side picture probably shows the celebrations on the feast of St Laurence (10 August) before 1596 (but not earlier than 1592), the right-hand-side picture probably shows the village in 1596. It is possible that this latter drawing dates from the rebuilding of the abbey, and the tent (11) belonged to the stonemasons. The drawings probably evidence the major changes that the village went through in the last decade of the sixteenth century, recovering from the devastations that took place between 1578 and 1582.

There is a potential, logical and plausible explanation (to be confirmed by further research) for the differences between the iconographic sources of 1596. This is well supported by textual sources, making both relatively reliable. If further research confirms that there is in fact a few years' difference between the older and later sources (possible dates being 1593 and 1596 respectively), the virtual models can be updated accordingly (see Plate 13 bottom) and a new 1596 model created to show the development of the village. Once this later phase has been correlated with the next phase (1640) to show the historical development of the village, a 3D visualization of 1596 can be created of the village and abbey making a new start after the devastations.

Finding multiple iconographic sources depicting the same subject is often difficult. There are normally different types of sources created for different purposes that depict the same environment at different points in time. Correlation in such case involves a *systematic comparison* of all visible elements, recording of common elements and an attempt at understanding why some elements are different or absent. To understand the historical development of a given structure, all available sources need to be correlated (see 'Visualizing historical development' below).

A 3D visualization of the Wijnendale castle in Torhout, Belgium (see Plate 14, bottom) illustrates well the correlation between different sources. This extant eleventh-century castle played a major role in the history of Flanders. It was destroyed and rebuilt several times, and thus consists of several phases. Although no archaeological or structural surveys of the building are available, some useful historical documents have survived. The oldest known drawing of the castle in ruins in 1612 is shown in Plate 14. The structure of the castle could be determined by correlating this drawing with an important inventory of 1530 compiled following the death of the owner. The inventory lists all rooms on each floor, indicating their functions, and itemizes all furnishings, thus giving an idea of the size of the room. The inventory was matched with the 1612 drawing and facilitated the completion of the 3D model of the castle in 1530. The drawing in question was assessed prior to modelling work as being highly reliable: many details matched perfectly with later cadastral maps and other iconographic and textual sources. It was assumed that the inventory, being a juridical document, was also correct.

Several methodologies were considered for formalizing this correlation process. As this is a very non-linear and complex process, it seems that only *description through text* can capture all the necessary nuances and is easy to adopt. A short description of the InMan tool and the Ename case study, below, give a good idea how this can be done.

Making a Hypothesis Tree Showing Conclusions

When visualizing a building, a landscape or a city, one needs to impose a certain top-down analysis of the object, decomposing it into *sub-structures*. These sub-structures do not always follow the normal 'structural' decomposition of the object, but rather the logical decomposition. They are therefore closely linked to the hypothesis that tree will be introduced here.

Nevertheless, the object needs to remain well structured and plausible. Creating too much structure where no information is available is only an additional burden for the person making the visualization. The methodology needs to support the visualization process, not making it more complex. The hypothesis tree is the *formalization of the interpretation process*. It shows in a top-down fashion possible alternatives, analyses each of the alternatives in relation to the available sources and draws *conclusions* about the probability of the alternatives, based upon the available sources.

Each hypothesis is broken down into *sub-hypotheses*, which again are evaluated and from which the most probable one is selected. The reasoning as to how the sources (indicated through hyperlinks) influence the hypothesis is presented in writing. No formal structure can be devised that is both flexible and user-friendly enough to refrain from the normal written word commonly used to express interpretation. It is important to adhere to the method of a branching hypothesis tree to ensure no possibility is overlooked. Although unlikely branches need to be recorded (see 'updating methodology'), it is common sense that unlikely branches do not need to be expanded as this is not useful.

At first sight, a hypothesis tree implies that the analysis progresses in a top-down fashion. At this stage all information needs to be available, relevant excavations and historical studies have to finalized. Archaeologists however prefer working in a bottom-up fashion while they excavate. They can only merge fragments into complete structures when excavations finish. Hence, the tool for documentation of the interpretation process needs to accommodate this workflow effectively. A tree-like structure is certainly suitable for this bottom-up workflow.

Most historical structures show a *development through time*. When interpreting source data and proposing certain hypotheses, one needs to think in fact in four dimensions – that is spatially and chronologically. In other words, every hypothesis needs to be checked for consistency with the data pertinent to the phases before and after a specific 3D visualization. Arriving at a consistent development is a major part of the interpretation, and a major validation step when building or updating virtual models. Therefore, it is important to entangle the different *phases* of a historic structure so that the interpretation covers the entire history of a building, landscape or site. In case of a discontinued development (for example, when a site is demolished and rebuilt in a totally different manner), the interpretation can be divided and each phase treated separately.

Ename between the tenth to twelfth centuries provides another case study. The excavation plan (see Plate 15) of St Saviour's there can be interpreted as a church consisting of a nave, east apse and tower, or alternatively as a nave with a west and east apse. Its ground plan is also very similar to a tenth-century palace, or *palatium*. It shows two phases, the initial phase in red and an extension in yellow.

The structure of the building invites three hypotheses:

1. A church consisting of a nave, east apse and tower.
2. A church consisting of a nave and west and east apses.
3. A palace building.

These hypotheses are documented on a single page (see Ename case study). Each hypothesis is argued for and against and linked (through hyperlinks) to the appropriate sources. At the beginning of the page, a conclusion is drawn as to which hypothesis is most probable. There is no need to quantify this probability, but it is certainly useful to express its level of preference as a hypothesis.

Figure 17.5 shows different visualizations that have been made on the basis of excavation of St Saviour's between 1987 and 1998 (more recent visualizations are shown in Plate 16). Visualizations are shown in chronological order from left to right and from top to bottom:

- church with west apse (the east apse had not yet been excavated at the time of the publication in *Archaeologica Belgica*, III, 1987, p. 216);
- church consisting of a nave, east apse and two-storey tower with a later extension which is interpreted as a portal (artist impression, 1994);
- church consisting of a nave, east apse and three-storey tower (TimeScope application on the Ename archaeological site, 1997);
- church consisting of a nave, east apse and reoriented three-storey tower, modelled on German examples. The later extension is interpreted as a portal (TimeLine application version 1, Archaeological Museum Ename, 1998).

Following extensive source assessment and correlation, since 1999, a church with east and west apses and a later extension to include the west apse and a

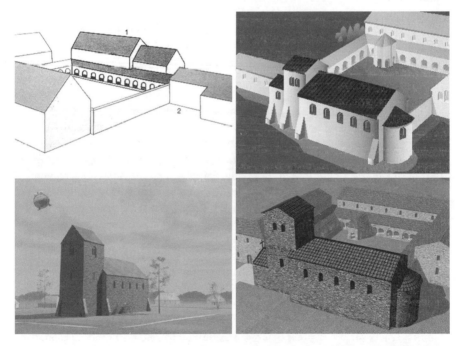

Figure 17.5   Different visualizations, created between 1987 and 1998, of the church of St Saviour in Ename

small bell tower, seems most probable (see Plate 16). Each hypothesis shows the different structural elements that reside under that hypothesis. In hypothesis 2, for example, the double apse church consists of such structural elements as the roof, nave, doorway and windows. There are sub-hypotheses for each of these structural elements. For example, the main roof can be the sub-hypothesis 2.1 – that is a single level (see Plate 16) – or sub-hypothesis 2.2 – two levels (see Figure 17.5, top left). A single level roof turns out to be most probable.

Through the interpretation of the sources, a certain hypothesis will be put forward as most probable for each of the structural elements. These conclusions are again put at the top of each sub-hypothesis page. Different structural elements are described on a single page, rather then separate sheets, to better show the dependencies between the different structural elements.

In the St Saviour's case, there are three main phases that have little continuity and can be treated separately: a wooden building, probably a church (950?–1005); a double apse church (1005–1139, see the historical development in Plate 16) and an aisled abbey church (1139–1795). Each of these phases can be considered in a separate hypothesis tree, as long as the links to the previous and/or next phase are made clear.

Updating

One of the most important reasons for undertaking interpretation management is keeping the visualization up to date. As new sources of information appear and new insights or correlations are found during the study of sources, one needs to be able to record how this new material influences the existing 3D visualization. There are four different kinds of updating.

First of all, when a *new source* becomes available it needs to be added to the database, compared and correlated with other sources. The new source may impact on the assessment of other sources, the reliability of the visualization or even the hypotheses made (see below). Another update action is a *new assessment of an existing source* when new insights, new sources or new studies (all of which need to be added to the source list) render the earlier assessment invalid. This new assessment can alter the existing hypotheses section and reliability of the visualization.

New sources, changes in source assessment or new interpretations may yield an *additional or updated hypothesis* or can *change the probability of one or more hypotheses* or *the reliability of the visualization*. This may lead to a new conclusion (the hypothesis that has the highest probability). In this process a detailed *tracking* of the updates is needed. This is not only a technical issue. A *consensus* amongst the investigators is required during the implementation of changes to the 3D visualization, and they need to be validated by experts. As pointed out before, this is normally an iterative process that requires the involvement of several specialists. They may not share the same working space or meet daily, therefore an online tool and interactive platform is required for effective collaboration. It may be that specialists do not agree on a certain conclusion, that there is too little evidence to favour one interpretation over another, or that an update is not endorsed by all the specialists involved. In that case, there are *two or more solutions* that are treated *as equally probable*. Thorough consultation is needed before the decision can be made about the most probable interpretation and 3D visualization.

Considerable expertise is needed to interpret and visualize a site, or alter it subsequently. Everybody should be able to contribute to the interpretation of the sources, much as in *Wikipedia*, by following an agreed methodology and user authentication. However, to avoid the problem of 'vandalism' of the content faced by *Wikipedia*, and maintain the quality of the material, there should be an authorization and accreditation process for those who want to change the conclusions and make, or change, the 3D visualizations. The quality of a 3D visualization published online will be maintained if full transparency about the interpretation process is maintained. All paradata derived from the creation and updating, as well as implementation software (see below) and its associated data (typically a variety of documents integrated in a database) also require maintenance and should eventually be migrated to new file formats to prevent the original files becoming obsolete.

Reliability of the Hypotheses

Due care should be taken about the reliability of the visualization that results from the most probable hypotheses. Although it is difficult to put a number on the reliability of each structural element of a visualization, some estimation may be derived from the reliability of the sources (see *source assessment* and *source correlation*) and the number of sources that are available for that specific element (see *source correlation*). In most cases, an indication of high, medium and low reliability is sufficient. If sources are unreliable or when there is only one source, the visualization will be of low reliability. If multiple, reliable sources are available, the visualization will be considered highly reliable.

In the same way, if a hypothesis conforms to all available sources, the visualization can be considered as highly reliable. However, when the sources reflect poorly on a hypothesis but a better one is not possible, the visualization should be considered unreliable (even if the hypothesis is considered most probable).

Unlike some other specialists in the field of 3D visualization,[5] the author prefers not to quantify reliability but assess the reliability as *low, medium or high*. Other authors use a similar methodology. Peter Sterckx uses the same system for the visualization of the historical development of Horst castle in Belgium (see Plate 17),[6]

---

5   Sorin Hermon, Franco Niccolucci and Andrea D'Andrea, 'Some Evaluations of the Potential Impact of Virtual Reality on the Archaeological Scientific Research', *Proceedings of VSMM 2005*, pp. 105–114.

6   Peter Sterckx, *Digitale reconstructie en architectuurhistorische studie van het kasteel van Horst, te Holsbeek* (Leuven, 2007).

while Han Vandevyvere uses four categories (low, medium, high and very high) for Mariemont castle,[7] as does Matt Jones in his visualization of Southampton in 1454.[8]

Whether unreliable parts of the visualization should be visualized at all is a serious issue. From a scholarly point of view, it is better not to visualize unreliable parts. From a presentation point of view, one needs to show a *consistent* image of the visualized structure, so the unreliable parts then tend to be shown after all.

In the case of Ename abbey around 1070 (see Plate 18, bottom) the reliability of the visualization has been indicated through colour coding: green indicates high reliability of the 3D visualization, yellow is medium reliability, red is low reliability.

Two areas are marked in red: the doorway in the abbey gate house and the field next to the abbey farm on the right-hand side of the picture. The doorway has a low reliability because that area has not been excavated, and the location of this entrance has been derived from a single drawing and a topological analysis of a seventeenth-century map. Considerable archaeological information is available for the area marked with red on the right-hand side, showing many remains of wooden buildings. All these traces are highly incomplete or disturbed by later phases, so it is nearly impossible to define the size and exact location of the buildings.

In this study case, the *scholarly visualization* should refrain from showing wooden buildings as no final conclusions can be made from the available archaeological data. No other source gives more information about the possible presence of wooden buildings or their function, except for some archaeological traces of iron casting. Frequent rebuilding and reshaping of such wooden buildings is considered by the archaeologists as normal.

The *public visualization* however (see Plate 19) shows some wooden buildings, because it is known from other sites that an abbey had all kinds of utility outbuildings such as a forge, brewery or bakery. To give a consistent visualization of that phase of the abbey, some wooden buildings of appropriate size have been included in the area where the archaeological traces exist. In a later phase, these buildings are shown rebuilt in stone. Wooden buildings in the earlier phases suggest continuity in their use, even though this is not confirmed by the available sources.

The public must be informed that this particular visualization contains less reliable parts because the archaeological evidence is inconclusive. However, the visualization works better if the wooden buildings are shown rather than left out.

---

7   Han Vandevyvere, Herman Neuckermans and Krista De Jonge, 'Digital Historical Reconstruction: Case Studies of an Interdisciplinary Task', *International Journal of Design Sciences and Technology*, 1, 13 (2006): 51–65, available at <http://www2.asro.kuleuven.ac.be/asro/english/HOME/Hvdv/Reconstruction/Digital historical reconstructionFormatted.pdf>.

8   Matt Jones, *Southampton in 1454: A Three-Dimensional Model of the Medieval Town*, 3DVisa Student Award Essay <http://3dvisa.cch.kcl.ac.uk/student_award_3.html> and Chapter 9 in this volume.

Dealing with Multiple Hypotheses with the Same Level of Probability

If one hypothesis is clearly more probable than the others, the *conclusion* will put this hypothesis forward as the most probable interpretation of the available sources. However, if two or more hypotheses are more or less equally probable, the conclusion needs to reflect the ambiguous nature of the interpretation. In that case, all probable alternatives have to be expanded, that is have sub-hypotheses and developed virtual models. If the alternatives are not significantly different, one hypothesis can be chosen as the *representative conclusion* for public presentation, subject to making the information about the other equally probable alternatives available to the viewer. This may be illustrated through the visualization of a Roman watchtower, built towards the end of the third century, whose foundations were found on the top of Goudsberg hill in Valkenburg, the Netherlands (see Plate 20).

No such a tower is known to have survived and there is little iconography available. From a scholarly point of view, several designs for such structures are equally possible. For presentation, however, only one alternative is used (see Plate 20 bottom), even though two alternative designs are equally possible (see Plate 20 top) and are made available to the visitors through interactive exploration of the tower features. In this way, the interested visitor may find out that there are multiple possible ways to visualize this tower and discover the process and issues involved in 3D visualization.

Ways of Expressing Uncertainty

In the Goudsberg watchtower project the surrounding landscape was also visualized. A detailed study was carried out of the geology and hydrography, which yielded information about possible vegetation and land use, yet there was very little archaeological evidence. It was therefore necessary to find a way to *express the uncertainty* of the resulting visualization of landscape.[9] We were reluctant to create the landscape, vegetation and animals in 3D, as the cost of work to ensure a sufficient visual quality was high. A graphic artist painted the Roman landscape in watercolour on the basis of in-depth research and a panoramic view taken of the site as it is today (see Plate 21, bottom). The tower was visualized in panoramic mode and 'downgraded' from a 3D rendering to a watercolour, which better expresses the uncertainty of the visualization than sharp, well-defined 3D images.

---

9   Nick Halper, Mara Mellin, Christoph S. Herrmann, Volker Linneweber and Thomas Strothotte, 'Towards an Understanding of the Psychology of Non-Photorealistic Rendering', in Jochen Schneider, Thomas Strothotte and Winfried Marotzki (eds), *Proceedings of the Workshop on Computational Visualiztics, Media Informatics and Virtual Communities*, Magdeburg 4–5 April 2003 (Wiesbaden, 2003), pp. 67–78.

Other ways to express uncertainty is to reduce 3D visualization to line drawings or even sketches, or to use black-and-white or sepia images.[10] For public presentation however, it is important to ensure the imagery has sufficient aesthetic quality.

Visualizing Historical Development

The aim of visualizing the historical development of a structure, or part of it, is to explore it from all sides and see it from the most appropriate angle (see Plate 22). Several technical solutions have the potential to do that, but a QuickTime VR object is a simple and very powerful technique. QuickTime VR (QTVR) is the part of QuickTime software that may be used to visualize panoramic and spherical images and interactive objects. Interactive objects consist of a matrix of images that can be visualized interactively and dragged horizontally or vertically in a viewer.

When a 360-degree rotation of the object is placed in the horizontal rows of the matrix, and the historical development over time in the vertical columns of the matrix, a *4D visualization tool* is obtained for showing objects interactively in 4D (space and time, that is evolution). Hence, when the cursor is moved horizontally or the left/right arrow keys are used, the viewpoint changes. Moving the cursor vertically or using the up/down arrow keys, the historical development of the object is visualized from a particular point of view. Alongside QuickTime, other technologies such as Flash and Java exist to turn a set of images, structured as a 4D matrix, into such an interactive 4D object. The major advantage of most of these tools is that *hyperlinks* can be added to the interactive object so that it can be integrated into hyperlink-based tools.

The London Charter

The methodology proposed here implements The London Charter (version 1.1). In particular, this methodology addresses the following points:

- valid for 3D visualization in all cultural heritage domains;
- appropriateness to the aims;
- based on identification and evaluation of relevant sources;
- makes the 3D outcomes transparent in relation to the sources;
- documentation of the 3D visualization process allows repeatability of the interpretation process and reuse of the outcomes, and creates a scientific dialogue and understanding;
- uses standards and ontologies approved by the community;
- sustainability;
- improved access to cultural heritage.

---

10   Ibid.

The tool presented here may support a wide range of applications and serve different goals. The concept of assessing sources before they are used in the interpretation process and the method of correlating sources to reveal common characteristics are generally applicable. The concept of building a hypothesis tree allows work in both directions, bottom-up and top-down. The methodology presented here can be used for research, as well as for communication purposes.

Tool Structure

EPOCH, as the Network of Excellence for the use of ICT in cultural heritage, has created tools for the cultural heritage community to support specific tasks.[11] A tool based on the methodology explained here has been created for 4D visualization, and is freely available. The tool has five major functionalities: a source database, source assessment, source correlation, a hypothesis tree with conclusions and a 4D visualization page. It is based on wiki technology that implements not only the hyperlinking but also the discussion forum and the consensus process that is needed to communicate and discuss research results and update them when necessary. Resulting 3D models or derived products (such as still images and animations) can be stored in a data repository and hyperlinked to the 4D visualization page.

The Source Sheet

The *source database* should refer to the sources used in the interpretation. Source records are needed to facilitate location of the documents, but in practice the interpretation process is better served if the actual sources are stored in digital form and are readily accessible. For example, when iconographic sources are available as high-resolution images, this is of course more practical than a lot of printouts and photographs. In other words, appropriate viewers, tools to find the right sources and good management of multiple windows are important. The use of *annotated images* is particularly helpful. In this way, transcriptions or comments may be added to certain areas of the image and appear when the cursor moves over the annotated area (see Figure 7.6).

Every source is recorded on a *source sheet* that also contains the *source assessment* that records the context, quality and interpretation of the source itself. *Primary sources* are used in the interpretation process, while *secondary sources* are only used for the source validation and do not themselves require validation or images. Should a reliability issue concerning secondary sources arise, a source assessment section can be added.

---

11   EPOCH Network of Excellence <http://www.epoch.eu/>.

huus vanden heere van Voorda omme watert van den Schelden
house of the lord of Voorde surrounded by the water of the river Scheldt

Figure 17.6   Iconographic   source   annotated   with   transcription   and translation of the medieval text

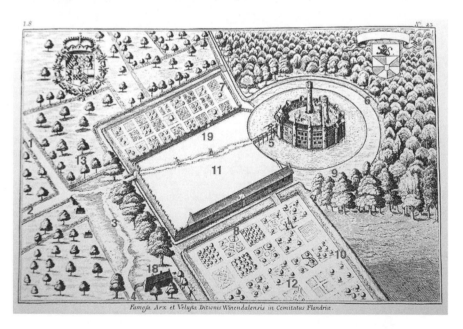

Figure 17.7   Bird's eye view of Wijnendale castle by Sanderus (1641). Numbers indicate features matching with Figure 17.8

Source Correlation Sheet

The *source correlation sheet* documents the correlation process between information provided by sources. By numbering matching features in iconographic sources (see Figure 17.7) elements with a higher reliability can be extracted and used in the visualization process. In the case of the Wijnendale castle (see Figures 17.7 and another source illustrated in Plate 14 top, and visualized in Plate 14 bottom), elements from the historic drawing are not only considered reliable enough to be used for visualization when appearing in multiple sources, but are also essential for proper dimensions and georeferencing when correlated with a cadastral map (see Figure 17.8).

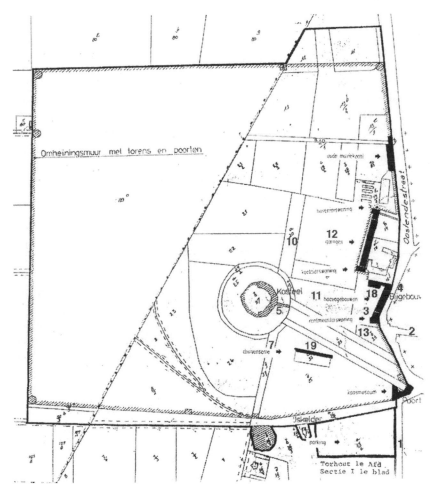

Figure 17.8   Cadastral plan of Wijnendale castle. Numbers indicate features matching with Figure 17.7

When there are significant differences between sources, a more elaborate technique for matching features (see Plate 13 top) may rely on features colour marked (for example, green – good match, red – no match; yellow – possible match. Based on such an analysis, a detailed description should be recorded in the source correlation sheet, showing not only the matching features but also the differences, and reasons for the differences observed. For example, further correlation of feature 10 in Plate 13 (top) with other secondary sources for the rebuilding of the abbey from 1596 onwards leads to the conclusion that the sources in Plate 13 do not date from the same time. In this process, the secondary contextual sources are recorded in the source database. The source correlation is captured in text with hyperlinks referring to the sources and annotations accompanying the images, transcriptions or interpretations.

Hypothesis Sheet

The *hypothesis tree* provides a simple way to decompose the interpretation of a structure (building, landscape etc.) into a set of branching hypotheses, and broken further down into sub-hypotheses. At each level of the hypothesis tree, conclusions are made, based upon the probability of the possible hypotheses. If a hypothesis has little probability, one can choose not to generate sub-hypotheses.

It is proposed to build this hypothesis tree as a set of hyperlinked pages called *hypothesis sheets* (see Ename case study). This tree structure is flexible and can be altered easily. A common problem in historical interpretation is the assumption of certain conditions or elements. To remove the assumption made at a certain level and replace it with an interpretation, an extra level of sub-hypotheses is needed in the middle of the tree, and this can be done by changing a few hyperlinks.

Archaeologists are dependent on what has been excavated already and favour a bottom-up approach to data, rather than top-down. They can make hypothesis sheets that deal with parts of structures and later link them with overarching hypotheses once the excavations have progressed or finished. The flexibility of creating and modifying a hypothesis tree through new or modified hyperlinks makes the approach described here applicable in many different cases and contexts.

The structure of the hypothesis tree also reflects the logical structure of the object to be visualized (as has been discussed in 'Making a hypothesis tree showing conclusions'). As Vatanen points out, only hyperlinked structures can provide the necessary flexibility and interlinking to represent 3D or 4D structures which may display a complex development pattern.[12] If one hypothesis is clearly more probable than the others, the *conclusion* will put this hypothesis forward as

---

12   Isto Vatanen, 'Deconstructing the (Re)Constructed: Issues in Conceptualising the Annotation of Archaeological Virtual Realities', in *Martin Doerr and Apostolos Sarris (eds), The Digital Heritage of Archaeology, Proceedings of the 30th CAA Conference, Computer Applications and Quantitative Methods in Archaeology, Heraklion, Crete, April 2002* (Athens, 2003), pp. 69–74.

the most probable interpretation of the available sources. Each conclusion is linked to the *resulting virtual model* and appropriate tools refer to its parts, linked to each sub-hypothesis (see Ename case study). If two or more hypotheses are more or less equally probable, the conclusion will reflect the ambiguous nature of the interpretation. In that case, all probable alternatives will be expanded, that is will have sub-hypotheses and developed virtual models. Nevertheless, one hypothesis may be chosen as a *representative conclusion* for public presentation, provided that information is available about the other equally probable alternatives.

Each conclusion should also estimate the reliability of the most probable hypothesis. This depends on the number and quality of sources and the match between the hypothesis and the sources, as discussed above. Although parts of a structure can have a low reliability, one may choose to visualize those parts to maintain the consistency of the visualization. The decision to visualize or not to visualize depends very much on the purpose of the visualization. The preference in scholarly practice is not to visualize unreliable parts.

3D/4D Visualization Page

In most cases the interpretation of a structure (building, landscape etc.) is concerned with the historical development of that structure through a certain period. A potential user interface to show this development could be *4D visualization* using QuickTime VR, where both time and 3D viewpoint can be changed. In this way, links can be made to the interpretation pages. Clicking on the reconstructed element refers to the discussion of this element's structure on the hypothesis tree. If the visualization contains no historical development, this page simply shows the reconstructed element from all sides (3D visualization).

Advantages of a Wiki Implementation

To enable collaborative work on a reconstruction, allowing for the necessary discussion and consensus mechanisms, the use of *wiki technology* with predefined templates, revision control and consensus mechanisms is proposed for constructing the three components outlined above: a source database, source correlation and hypothesis tree. Four-dimensional visualization tools embedded into a wiki provide the fourth component. User registration, authentication and authorization on different levels (edit, conclusions, 3D model creation and edit) can use common wiki tools. The update of 3D models is triggered by a change in the conclusions, therefore a change in conclusion and a change of the virtual models can only be decided by authorized contributors.

Data preservation is another important aspect. The record of interpretation process and the actual virtual models should both be maintained (kept up to date to reflect new knowledge) and preserved safely in the long term, together with all related files, such as textures and animation scripts, and other derived files (images, animations, interactive applications, etc). In this way, a *central public repository* is implemented so that the investment in making the virtual model is secured. As 3D model files can have a variety of file types, it is important to provide long-term maintenance of those files by translating them into open file formats, and avoid their obsolescence and preserve data by migrating these files to new formats.

As the majority of virtual reconstructions are funded by public money, it is conceivable to request that 3D models are published and maintained in such a way, thus safeguarding the financial and intellectual investments and ensuring public access. It is hoped that appropriate structures can be established, and training provided to ensure that these concepts are widely accepted and influential over national policies.

Other Approaches

The Architectural History and Conservation Research group and the CAAD research group at the University of Leuven have defined a metafile approach for documenting 3D visualizations of historical buildings.[13] This metafile has the form of a spreadsheet. It provides information about the logical structures within the object to be visualized (rows), as well as the facts, written and iconographical sources, inspection reports, reliability data and comments (columns). This metafile also breaks down the different major elements into a tree structure through a numbering system of the rows.

However, the application of this approach to complex structures, such as Horst castle in Belgium, shows insufficient flexibility to represent numerous links between the elements and the extensive descriptions and interpretations that are required for each of them.[14] There are no means to record hypotheses which transgress the facts column (where they definitely do not belong) and the comments column. Especially the interlinking between the different hypotheses gets somewhat lost in the limited area that each fact or comment cell provides. The assessment of the sources is not systematic as it ends up in the comment column, separated from the different source columns. Most sources are not subjected to assessment and there is nearly no source correlation. There is only a text link to the sources, which results in considerable manual browsing and searching.

Most projects where the metafile approach has been applied are concerned with extant buildings for which a detailed resolution of interpretation issues is the most important. The metafile approach works quite well for this kind of projects, but is less satisfactory for when only ruins or archaeological remains survive, or when

---

13   Han Vandevyvere, Herman Neuckermans and Krista De Jonge, 'Digital historical reconstruction: Case studies of an interdisciplinary task', *International Journal of Design Sciences and Technology*, 13/1 (2006): 51 – 65, available at <http://www2.asro.kuleuven.ac.be/asro/english/HOME/Hvdv/Reconstruction/Digitalhistorical reconstructionFormatted.pdf> .

14   Sterckx, Peter, *Digitale reconstructie en architectuurhistorische studie van het kasteel van Horst, te Holsbeek*, Thesis KU Leuven, 2007.

significant rebuilding took place. In this case, significantly different hypotheses need to be compared to each other.

Joyce Wittur has adopted a different approach to the study of the methodology of the Lorsch Abbey Reconstruction and Information System.[15] Lorsch abbey is a major eighth-century abbey and a UNESCO World Heritage Site near Mannheim in Germany. The site consists of a few buildings and major archaeological remains. This approach uses *argumentation networks* that link sources with interpretations and in this respect are similar to the approach proposed here. These networks are built of interlinked primary data, comparisons, observations and interpretations. The major difference, however, is that there are no phases in the interpretation process, for example source assessment, source correlation and hypothesis building, and that hypothesis building does not require a tree structure.

The example shown in Figure 17.9 is closely related to the text-based source correlation process described here. The left-hand-side network, for instance, can be described as follows: 'the clerestory consists of small, roughly hewn stones and

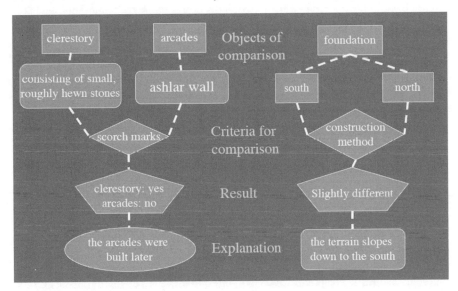

Figure 17.9   Argumentation network after Joyce Wittur

Source: Joyce Wittur, *Argumentation Networks*, Seminar 3D-Virtualisierung am Beispiel des Klosters Lorsch, University of Heidelberg, 2007 <http://www.iwr.uni-heidelberg. de/groups/ngg/Lorsch/aims.php?L=E>, including Lorsch Abbey Reconstruction and Information System.

---

15   Joyce Wittur, *Argumentation Networks*, Seminar 3D-Virtualisierung am Beispiel des Klosters Lorsch, University of Heidelberg, 2007 <http://www.iwr.uni-heidelberg. de/groups/ngg/Lorsch/aims.php?L=E>, including Lorsch Abbey Reconstruction and Information System.

has scorch marks while the arcades consist of ashlar masonry and show no scorch marks; the conclusion is that the arcades were built later than the clerestory'.

Every element in the argumentation network can be linked to data such as images and text. This is very similar to the hyperlink approach used here and offers efficient means of linking and structuring the data. Although there are no formal phases of source assessment, source correlation or hypothesis construction, all these elements are present in these argumentation networks. On the one hand, the network approach allows the flexibility needed to describe all kinds of different interpretation processes, but, on the other hand, it lacks the rigour and the step-by-step approach and workflow promoted here.

At present, the argumentation networks do not consider the reliability of sources, probability of hypotheses or the update process, yet these elements are crucial for good interpretation management. This approach has also been promoted by Vatanen but without consideration for the history of the interpretation process and updating.[16] Argumentation networks represent well the way we think, but look somewhat complex and daunting at first. This could influence negatively the take-up by the 3D visualization community, so the use of plain text is promoted in a first phase to describe the arguments. As Vatanen points out, the first goal of documenting interpretation should be peer communication within the community. Nevertheless, argumentation networks are a good basis for structured storage of the interpretation process.

Wiki Template

This section provides a detailed proposal for the structure of different types of wiki page (sources with their assessment, source correlation, hypothesis tree, 4D visualization, overview). The source database is implemented as a set of *source pages*, which provide references to physical sources and contain digital images that may facilitate interpretation and validation of these sources. The aim of source assessment is to ascertain the level of reliability of the source and its eligibility to support interpretation; to reveal the interpretation processes that have already taken place during the creation of the source so that trusted elements can be defined and unreliable ones discarded. A source page contains:

- a short description of the source;
- a conclusion (of the validation/assessment process) at the top of the page;
- a correct and complete reference to the source, and a URL if online;

---

16   Isto Vatanen, 'Deconstructing the (Re)Constructed: Issues in Conceptualising the Annotation of Archaeological Virtual Realities', in Martin Doerr and Apostolos Sarris (eds), *The Digital Heritage of Archaeology, Proceedings of the 30th CAA Conference, Computer Applications and Quantitative Methods in Archaeology, Heraklion, Crete, April 2002* (Athens, 2003), pp. 69–74.

- images (plus details if necessary) related to the source, for practical reference and for supporting the reconstruction process;
- a detailed description of the source;
- a detailed description of the context of the source (who made it, why, etc.), this can require links to other sources (both primary and secondary);
- a validation and assessment of the source itself concerning its context and reliability (both through primary and secondary sources).

A source correlation page groups a number of sources that have something in common, and records the correlation process between all these sources, yielding conclusions that can be drawn about that group of sources. In this way, archaeological sources are compared and correlated with iconographic and other sources. A source correlation page contains:

- one or more conclusion(s) at the top of the page;
- a list of related sources that document a certain structure, area or period; each source is identified through a hyperlink to its own source page (a source can appear in more than one list);
- a comparison of the listed sources, using correlation techniques and based upon the source assessment, trying to assess similarities (are they really similar?), differences (why is there a difference?), omissions (why is a certain structure missing in a certain source?) or interpretations by other authors in relation to all available sources; each source is hyperlinked for easy reference;
- drawing conclusions from the correlation process: if all sources depict the same feature in the same way, the conclusion is that the sources show a reliable feature, if the sources show different and non-consistent depictions of a certain feature, we can conclude that we have little to no evidence for that feature.

The *hypothesis tree* is implemented by a set of hyperlinked hypothesis pages and each page covers one branch of the hypothesis tree. All hypothesis pages are linked with each other through hyperlinks to form a tree. A hypothesis page contains:

- one or more conclusion(s) at the top of the page, linked to the 3D/4D visualization page if available;
- all hypotheses concerning a certain structure or part of a structure, each hypothesis links to its sub-hypotheses;
- a written description of the argumentation, pros and cons of a certain hypothesis, linked to the appropriate source and source correlation pages.

A *3D/4D reconstruction* page shows the resulting virtual reconstruction in an interactive way and includes links to the related hypothesis pages. If a development over time is available, the model can be 4D. Techniques such as Flash or QuickTime

VR can visualize such 4D models. Plate 22 shows such a 4D model in which, for example, one can click on the bell tower to arrive at the page that explains why a bell tower of this kind is the most probable interpretation.

Finally, access to all these pages are provided through one or more overview pages that give access to the hypotheses for the object to be visualized. An *overview page* can contain multiple objects (for example, a list of buildings). The overview pages can be organized in a tree-like structure for large and complex sites. As primary and secondary source pages, source correlation pages and 3D/4D visualization pages are referenced from hypothesis pages, they do not need to be listed explicitly on the overview page.

Benefits

This methodology has several benefits for different stakeholders involved in a 3D visualization process.

First, there is little standardization available about how to conduct and document 3D visualization research, and this methodology helps to *structure and rationalize the interpretation process.* Currently, the interpretation process behind a 3D visualization project is in most cases a black box with certain inputs and outputs, but little transparency concerning the process itself. A commonly accepted methodology will be beneficial for mastering the process and its quality.

Second, by recording the interpretation process via an online tool, other scholars or 3D visualization specialists can understand the process and contribute their knowledge via wiki mechanisms for discussion and consensus. This creates not only *scientific transparency* but also stimulates *interdisciplinary collaboration.* Specialists in certain domains (such as structural engineers or architectural historians) can be invited to contribute. Hence, the proposed tool provides a *collaboration platform* for bringing together all the necessary specialism into heritage research and/or for public presentation through 3D visualization.

By hosting this tool on a single server, and managed by a central cultural heritage organization in each participating country or region, the 3D visualization processes can be fully *recorded and preserved*, while the organization itself can take care of backup and *long-term storage* of the resources created and knowledge yielded by publicly funded 3D visualization projects that would otherwise disappear, ensuring also *general availability of 3D visualization results* to interested communities and re-use in other projects. When new information becomes available, the underlining database can be updated. Specialists may be invited to integrate new findings into the 3D visualizations, so no outdated 3D visualizations are used or distributed.

Conclusion

The focus of 3D visualization of historical structures is not 3D modelling or creating stunning images, but an in-depth, systematic study of the sources, their assessment and correlation, proposition of most probable hypotheses, documentation of this interpretation process in a structured way, to finally produce visualization according the requirements and context for its use.

The methodology proposed here is, on the one hand, flexible and capable of dealing with a wide range of subjects and goals, and, on the other, provides a standardized workflow for 3D visualization of historical structures that is documented and repeatable, transparent and publicly accessible. In other words, this methodology for interpretation management establishes a sound framework for creating and publishing the results of 3D or 4D visualizations, for improving their quality and preservation of the investments and intellectual effort that go into such projects. This unique InMan tool, based on wiki technology, has been realized to support this process and guarantee safeguarding of the resulting data.

St Saviour Church in Ename, Belgium: A Case Study

This case study of St Saviour church, excavated at the archaeological site of Ename (see Plate 23), shows how the interpretation management tool is applied in practice. We show two source sheets (one for iconography and one for archaeological results), one source correlation sheet, one hypothesis sheet and one 4D visualization sheet. The hyperlinks to the corresponding pages are underlined (not all linked pages are shown in this case study).

The *source sheets* use a different approach per type of source. For the archaeological source sheet, an existing excavation report can be used, with hyperlinks referring to the appropriate paragraphs in the relevant excavation report, so that it is not necessary to cut and paste the excavation report into different source sheets.

On the *correlation sheet*, we have listed several correlations between sources. Most correlations are between two sources, but some use a two-stage reasoning scheme (bullets 6, 7 and 8) that first correlates two sources and then correlates the result with a third source. Clicking a hypothesis on the *hypothesis sheet* gives the subsequent sub-hypothesis in the hypothesis tree. As you can see below on this sheet, hypothesis 3 has no further branches, as it has no hyperlink (because its probability is low).

The hyperlinks in the conclusion of the hypothesis tree link to the *4D visualization sheet*, where the 3D visualization is shown in a 4D way. The appropriate phase and structure is highlighted, but the user can explore that structure from all sides and check phases before and after. The hyperlink in the 'Description' part of the 4D visualization sheet links back to the corresponding hypothesis.

The *overview page* lists the hypotheses for the different buildings and structures of the Ename archaeological site (where the abbey buildings were), the hyperlinks of the hypotheses bring the user to the 4D visualization of each building, to the source correlations that feed the hypotheses and to the primary sources used (secondary sources are referenced in the source assessment of the primary sources). The overview page of the Ename site can be further referenced in an overview page of Ename, where all other elements of the village are listed.

Source Sheet 1

Short description
Depiction of the Ename abbey in the *Viel Rentier*

Conclusion
This drawing depicts the Ename abbey, probably a long time before 1275

Reference
Viel Rentier, Royal Library of Belgium, Brussels, Manuscript Dept. 1175, f8r
(see <http://lucia.kbr.be/multi/ms_1175Viewer/imageViewer.html>)
Published in L. Verriest, *Le polyptique illustré dit 'Viel Rentier' de Messire Jehan de Pamele-Audenarde*, Brussels

Description

Figure 17.10 *Viel Rentier*, reproduced with kind permission from the Royal Library of Belgium, Brussels, MS 1175, f 8r

This seems to be the oldest depiction of the abbey of Ename, It shows – from left to right – the abbey church (St Saviour), the abbey buildings, a wall of the enclosure and a gate. The document is dated around 1275.

Context
This book lists all the properties of knight Jehan de Pamele-Audenarde, and all the benefits he received for renting these properties to third parties. The text is illustrated by two different illustrators who have added drawings that were related to the text. In the case above, the text talks about the rent to be paid by the abbot of Ename ('abbas eham', see lower left in the picture above). Due to the illustrative nature of the drawings, scholars believe that the depicted buildings belong to the abbey of Ename.

Analysis

The drawing always has been interpreted (see for example <u>Berings, 1989</u>, p. 147) as the Ename abbey around 1275. We are convinced however that the drawing does not need to be contemporary, but can depict an older phase of the abbey. This is also the case for example for the <u>Pamele Church</u> which is depicted in *le Viel Rentier* in its first phase as chapel (1110–1235), while that phase was replaced already by the current Gothic church in 1275 (building activities started in 1235, and were finalized in 1300), which is of substantial size. As the illustrators had to make many drawings, it is possible that they did not go on site but copied older iconography that is unknown today.

Source Sheet 2

Short description
Excavation plan of structure S15 in Ename

Conclusion
Shows the structure and building phases of S15/Ename

Reference
(Ref. No. for an archaeological drawing)

Description

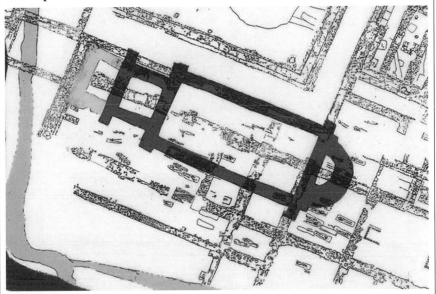

Figure 17.11 Excavation plan of the church of St Saviour in Ename

Traces of the foundations of S15 church show a building consisting in a first phase (in red, see Plate 15) of a round east apse, a nave and a square structure on the west side, which was extended in a second phase (yellow), which is younger than the oldest abbey buildings, based on stratigraphic analysis.

Context
Excavations seasons 1986–1988

Analysis

The structure of the building and its later extension is quite well defined although most of the foundations only left a negative groundtrace. The foundations of the first phase show typical underground extensions at the west side, at the connection of the west apse to the nave, and at the connection of the nave to the east apse. These extensions are nearly not present in the second phase.

All foundations of the first phase have about the same width, except for the foundations of the east apse which are significantly wider. The foundations of the second phase are wider and more irregular, except for the northern part.

Source Correlation Sheet

Conclusion correlation analysis
The abbey depicted in the Viel Rentier is the first phase of the Ename abbey (about 1070 – about 1160) and the church depicted is the first phase (about 1005–1139) of the St Saviour church of Ename.

Correlated sources
- Depiction of the Ename abbey in the 'Viel Rentier'
- Excavation plan of structure S15 in Ename
- Excavation plan of the St Laurence church in Ename
- Roof structure analysis and dating of the St Laurence church in Ename
- Excavation report A. Vande Walle of the St Saviour church
- Excavation report on the palace building in Ename
- Excavation report on the first abbey in Ename

Correlation analysis

- in the Viel Rentier drawing, the roofing consists of Roman *tegulae* and wooden tiles, both have been found in layers of the first abbey (1070–1160) during the excavation, while other types of roof tiles where found in the layers that can be associated with the period around 1275.
- in the excavation plan, we see that the ratio of the length of the archaeological remains of the west structure against the nave of the building of the first phase is 1:3, which fits perfectly with the structure (4 equal parts) of the church depicted in the Viel Rentier drawing, while the remains of the second abbey church cannot be correlated with this drawing.
- the west extension (phase 2 of S15, build before the second abbey church in 1139) does not fit with the Viel Rentier drawing, the drawing could precede the extension – the abbey buildings depicted on the Viel Rentier drawing fit with the excavation results of the first abbey, from left to right we see the abbots house (with entrance), the guest rooms, the refectory and the dormitorium
- from the analysis of the foundations of the St Laurence church, which is build around the same time, we see that there is a strong correlation between the foundation structure of S15 and the St Laurence church, one of the typical features is the presence of underground extensions of the foundations where arch structures are present
- having the same foundation structure, and as the St Laurence church has no visible buttresses, we can deduce that S15 had no visible buttresses too, which fits with the absence of buttresses in the Viel Rentier drawing
- from the analysis of the foundation structure, we deduce that there is a wall (probably with an arch) between the west structure and the nave, and that such

a wall extends to the roof (see <u>roof structure of the St Laurence church</u>), this fits very well with place of the small bell tower in the <u>Viel Rentier drawing</u>
- when analysing the <u>foundation structure of S15</u>, and taking into account that there is a clear relationship between foundation width and the height of the walls on that foundation (see the analysis of the foundation structure of both the <u>St Laurence church</u> and the <u>palace building</u> in Ename), we have to conclude that the west structure should be of similar height as the nave, as both structures have a similar foundation width, this fits with the depiction of the St Saviour church in the <u>Viel Rentier drawing</u> as a building of constant height over its entire length.

Hypothesis Sheet

Conclusions

Figure 17.12 Computer visualization of the St Saviour church in Ename around 1020, 1065, 1070 and 1100

The excavated structure S15 can be identified most probably as the first phase (about 1005–1139) of the <u>St Saviour church of Ename, consisting of a nave, west apse and east apse</u>. The extension (phase 2) of structure S15 can be identified as an <u>extension of the west apse of the church</u>, while being abbey church, dated between 1070 and 1139.

Hypotheses
1. <u>The excavated structure S15 is the St Saviour church of Ename, consisting of a nave, east apse and tower.</u>
2. <u>The excavated structure S15 is the St Saviour church of Ename, consisting of a nave, east apse and west apse (most probable).</u>
3. The excavated structure S15 is a palace building that has been converted into a church (least probable).

Analysis
- from the similar foundation width of the west structure and the nave of the building, hypothesis 2 is most probable, as a tower (hypothesis 1) would need a wider foundation on the west side, while a palace building (hypothesis 3)

would need a smaller foundation on the west side (as a camera on the west side in palace buildings is typically one floor while the nave is typically two floors, see for example foundation structure of the Ename palace building).
- the structure S15 was surrounded by a ditch, which is typical for a church, demarcating the holy ground and cemetery, such a ditch is unusual for a palace building – the phase preceding S15 was also surrounded by a similar ditch, so it is much more probable that S15, and its predecessor, have been churches, with no relation to a palace building (the palace building has been found archaeologically 200 m north of S15)
- a text source states clearly that Ename had two churches, St Saviour at the portus (that becomes abbey site) and St Laurence at the village; with St Laurence still standing, no other potential site than S15 is known today to be St Saviour.
- the St Laurence church is most probably a church with west and east apse without tower, the St Saviour church, built in the same period under the same rulers, has most probably also the same structure
- the correlation between the Viel Rentier drawing and all archaeological related sources is high, so we accept this drawing as a depiction of S15 as the St Saviour church with a nave, west apse and east apse.

4D Visualization Sheet

Description
4D visualization of the <u>St Saviour church of Ename, consisting of a nave, a west apse and an east apse</u>, for the approximate dates 1020, 1065, 1070 and 1100. The church has been found probably in 1005 and was replaced by a much larger abbey church in 1139.

3D models
<u>saint_saviour_church_Ename_1020.3ds</u> (3D model representing the 1020 phase)
<u>saint_saviour_church_Ename_1065.3ds</u> (3D model representing the 1065 phase)
<u>saint_saviour_church_Ename_1070.3ds</u> (3D model representing the 1070 phase)
<u>saint_saviour_church_Ename_1100.3ds</u> (3D model representing the 1100 phase)

Derived results
<u>saint_saviour_church_Ename_QTVR.mov</u> (4D interactive object)
<u>saint_saviour_church_Ename.mov</u> (animation)
<u>saint_saviour_church_Ename_1020.jpg</u> (high resolution still image)

Ename Archaeological Site Overview

St Saviour Church
The first phase of the St Saviour church of Ename (about 1005–1139) consists of a double apse church with later extension of the west apse.
The second phase of the St Saviour church of Ename (about 1149–1578) consists of a Hirschau type of Romanesque church.
The St Saviour church of Ename has been destroyed and dismantled during the Protestant revolt (1578–1582) and plundered by the local community until 1596.
The St Saviour church of Ename has been rebuilt from 1596 to 1607.
The third phase of the St Saviour church of Ename (1607–1795) has the same structure as the second phase with a later addition of an Our Lady chapel.

St Saviour Central Abbey buildings
The Ename abbey has been founded in 1063 in the palace building at the Ename castrum
The first phase of the St Saviour abbey buildings (about 1070 – about 1160) have been build with the reused stones and tiles of the Ename keep.

PART IV
Conclusion

Chapter 18

Processual *Scholia*: The Importance of Paradata in Heritage Visualization

Anna Bentkowska-Kafel

This book emphasizes the importance of making the process of digital visualization of cultural heritage transparent. The records of this process, or paradata, should be made a standard, integral part of heritage visualization practice. It is only then, the contributors argue, that computer-based visualization of cultural heritage can be recognized as a valid scholarly method for studying and presenting cultures of the past.

The chapters included in this volume offer an insight into research in this area conducted internationally in recent years. The contributors show how their approach – of ensuring conceptual transparency of the process through which visualization is conceived and created – has evolved from initial theoretical and practical propositions to methodological solutions and scholarly practice guided by The London Charter for the Computer-based Visualisation and Communication of Heritage. The focus here is on visualization of material culture exemplified by archaeological sites and architecture, movable artefacts and palaeontological heritage. The same care for safeguarding intellectual transparency is being advocated for visualization applied to the study and preservation of intangible or living heritage and abstract cognitive processes.[1] Each of these fields carries the inheritance of discrete research philosophies and practices. Benefiting from the interaction between established conventions and the ever more sophisticated digital techniques, visualization of cultural objects, theories and phenomena emerges as a pursuit of unprecedented capacity for interdisciplinary enquiry.

What this new interdisciplinary research entails in arts and humanities computing is an interesting question in its own right. Drawing on some pertinent points raised by the contributing authors, this conclusion tries to demonstrate that, in the context of modern methodologies for historical research, computer-based visualization, if conducted with scholarly rigour and according to restoration ethics, may serve as an important investigative tool that enhances our knowledge of cultural heritage and its significance. Stable preservation and

---

1   See definitions and resources available on the UNESCO Intangible Heritage website at <http://www.unesco.org/culture/ich/index.php?pg=00002> and <http://whc.unesco.org/en/glossary>. (All URLs active at the time of writing.)

effective communication are necessary conditions for successful dissemination of visualization-based research.

Heritage Visualization as a Research Method

This volume is part of the Ashgate series 'Digital Research in the Arts and Humanities'. The first volume, *The Virtual Representation of the Past*, addressed issues in digital scholarship across a broad range of historical studies, and included an introduction to the principles of The London Charter for Computer-based Visualisation.[2] Recognizing the problematic nature of any representation of the past, the book's co-editor, Mark Greengrass argues:

> The historical accounts through which we try to reconstruct [the past] are representations, framed by the window and obscured by the glass through which we try to view it. Both the window and the glass stand in the way of any realistic, let alone objective, picture that we are able to make of it. But the picture is, nevertheless, structured, capable of being understood, and full of meaning. And it is constrained in every pixel by the evidential remains of the past. Archaeologists equally see themselves as reconstructing the past into a believable story, necessarily partial and always subject to revision.[3]

The contributors to this volume take heritage visualization beyond the constraint of pixels and outside the frame of computer 'glass', while agreeing on representations of the past being subjective and not fixed. The frequent inevitability of leaving findings of historical investigation open-ended has been recognized across academic research, whether conducted by traditional or digital means. In a radio interview, the classicist Mary Beard – author of *The Roman Triumph*, in which she pieces together elusive traces of this important ancient ceremony – marvels at 'that wonderful paradox' in historical research that makes one less certain the more one knows. She criticizes some authors of popular books about the ancient world for trying to impose 'their truth'. They are thus:

> slightly talking down to the reader. It's assuming that the reader hasn't got the brain that takes something in. Most readers want to explore the way you know about it. They want their uncertainties, their doubts shared with, not Tipp-Exed.[4]

---

2   Richard Beacham, '"Oh, to make boards to speak! There is a task!" Towards a Poetics of Paradata', in Marc Greengrass and Lorna Hughes (eds), *The Virtual Representation of the Past* (Aldershot, 2008), pp. 171–7.

3   Ibid., p. 1.

4   Mary Beard in conversation with Fi Glover, *Saturday Live*, BBC Radio 4, 29 August 2009, 9am, 5:50–6:10. *The Roman Triumph* was published by Harvard University Press, 2007.

Processual *scholia* are therefore important if one is to avoid giving the impression that a proposed representation of the past is the only possible or correct one. Various digital tools – visual, textual, computational and others – have been developed across historical disciplines to convey incomplete, uncertain or ambiguous readings of the past. Many such multimedia tools are well suited for comparative presentation of information and its sources. The choice as to how to interact with and explore this material may be left at the discretion of the user. A system developed by Andrej Ferko et al. (see Chapter 4) allows the user of an urban visualization to examine individual phases in the development of the city and assess the level of certainty of historical information about each phase. Matt Jones ensures similar transparency by accompanying his computer model of Southampton – which shows how this city might have looked in 1454 – with a descriptive assessment of reliability of the individual architectural features (see Chapter 9 and Table 9.1). Donald Sanders's visualization of an ancient Egyptian model of a ship goes even further and empowers the user with the tools for historical exploration, as advocated by Mary Beard. The user is presented with virtual surrogates of the individual parts of the ship for self-assembly on screen and can make his or her own reconstructive decisions (see Chapter 5).

In 2002, Karen M. Kensek, Lynn Swartz Dodd and Nicholas Cipolla presented a methodology for making ambiguity in historical visualization 'dynamically' transparent to a user.[5] This methodology also covers the evaluation of the quality of evidence, as well as alternative reconstructions and their critique. The significance of this approach in pedagogy has been demonstrated, among others, by John Pollini, whose students in classics (Nicholas Cipolla and others) have been using 3D visualization to study ancient monuments.

> Students [...] became acutely aware that the presentation of antiquity grows out of choices made in the present, which can include the decision to represent a particular moment in time or the decision to privilege one piece of evidence over another. [...] For [teachers], the investment of time has been fruitful because of the extended interaction with the ancient place – albeit a virtual ancient place. Whatever the cautions in creating virtual models and worlds, the goal of our research is to create new ways of allowing scholars, students, and the general public to experience and consider antiquity in all its complexity.[6]

---

5   Karen M. Kensek, Lynn Swartz Dodd and Nicholas Cipolla, 'Fantastic Reconstructions or Reconstructions of the Fantastic? Tracking and Presenting Ambiguity, Alternatives, and Documentation in Virtual Worlds', paper presented at the 2002 Conference of the Association for Computer Aided Design in Architecture in Pomona, California, published in *Automation in Construction*, 2, 13 (2004): 175–86.

6   John Pollini, Lynn Swartz Dodd, Karen Kensek and Nicholas Cipolla, *Problematics of Making Ambiguity Explicit in Virtual Reconstructions: A Case Study of the Mausoleum of Augustus*, in Anna Bentkowska-Kafel, Trish Cashen and Hazel Gardiner (eds), *Theory and Practice,* proceedings of 21st Conference of Computers and the History of Art

Although heritage visualization is judged primarily on the basis of the final 3D virtual model, scholars employing visualization tools consider the actual process of visualization as the most enlightening stage of investigation. In the digital humanities a similar recognition of the process has been offered by Willard McCarty. Commenting generally on the 'computational emphasis on process rather than product', he argues that 'computational models, however finely perfected, are better understood as *temporary states in a process of coming to know* rather than fixed structures of knowledge'.[7] The realization of how beneficial such a cognitive process can be has led to the development of a variety of techniques and methodologies for recording paradata digitally. Both automated and manual tools for tracking and recording the operator's actions and commentary are in use. Standard annotations include the popular 'hot spot' pop-ups that rely on text or audio and are placed within the computer model. Other tools work in a similar way to 'Track Changes' in word-editing programmes or scripts for recording and replicating actions during imaging work that are proprietary to Adobe's Photoshop software. Various methods for recording processual data may be emulated from disciplines as diverse as literary and linguistic studies, finance and investment risk analysis, cognitive sciences and information management. A variety of approaches is proposed here, ranging across such disciplines as philology, psychology and computer science, some of which have been tested and proved useful to visualization-based research. Although critical of the use of the term 'paradata' in this context, Mark Mudge argues for the advantages of keeping a lab notebook, which has traditionally been employed by archaeologists (see Chapter 15).

The aim of both automated and semantic methods for paradata capture is to make the process of heritage visualization transparent, traceable, replicable and correctable. Examples of implementation not discussed in the preceding chapters (but discussed elsewhere in the same Ashgate series) include e-Science projects such as the eCurator, eSAD and eDance.[8] The e-Science and Ancient Documents (eSAD) project (2008–11) is concerned with the recording, decipherment and interpretation of ink and stylus tablets discovered in the Roman fort of Vindolanda in Britain, and other ancient documents. The transcription of the Latin text is often difficult owing to the poor condition of the tablets and missing fragments, which makes their reading ambiguous and fragmentary. A number of digital techniques are used to support the work of expert epigraphers, including the 3D imaging

---

(CHArt), British Academy, London, November 2005, available at <http://www.chart.ac.uk/chart2005/papers/pollini.html>.

7   Willard McCarty, *Humanities Computing* (2005), pp. 26–7.

8   See e-Science and Ancient Documents (eSAD) <http://esad.classics.ox.ac.uk/>; eCurator: 3D colour scans for remote object identification and assessment <http://www.museums.ucl.ac.uk/research/ecurator/>; eDance: Relocating Choreographic Process <http://projects.kmi.open.ac.uk/e-dance/>, respectively. For brief introduction to the aims and methodologies of these projects, bibliography and links, see case studies compiled by Anna Bentkowska-Kafel for the Arts and Humanities e-Science Support Centre, UK, available at <http://www.ahessc.ac.uk/initiative-projects>.

of tablets in Polynomial Texture Mapping (PTM). A Decision Support System (DSS),[9] based on an interpretative tree model, has been developed to accommodate records of alternative readings of the text, allowing for subsequent corrections, if and when possible. As a result of the eCurator project (2007–2008) virtual 3D records of a variety of museum objects – a small Egyptian scarab, a woven tribal mask from Papua New Guinea and an oil painting, among others – were acquired using an Arius3D colour laser scanner. A methodology for tracing the process of creating 3D records (which does not involve modelling) was developed so that the procedures could be analysed and repeated on the same object with the same results by different operators. The 3D records are now available for viewing and editing within a collaborative virtual environment. The eDance project (2007–2009) puts at the disposal of performers and researchers a number of digital tools for choreographing, staging and documenting dance. Dancers can perform and improvise in hybrid (real and virtual) environments. Various ephemeral forms of expressions may simultaneously be recorded, annotated and interpreted.

Novelty and experimentation are major attractions of digital technology. A London Charter principle is only to apply computer-based visualization if its potential for the discovery of new knowledge can be demonstrated. It has been argued, elsewhere, that visualization should be seen 'as part of a continuum of established academic practice rather than something that is in some way new, "revolutionary", or lacking in rigorous scholarly value'.[10] The insistence on a scholarly approach to digital visualization of cultural heritage, and on the importance of this process being duly documented and made visible, is accepted quite naturally by researchers and practitioners versed in the principles of physical archaeology and conservation of heritage, but may be of secondary interest to those who come to digital visualization from other backgrounds. There is a balance to be struck between interpretative and reconstructive processes that are based on the philological principles of *recensio*, *examinatio*, and *divinatio* (see Chapter 4) and the elimination of discovery in the process of verification and proof which, according to Henry Mehlberg, is the gist of the scientific method (see Chapter 3).

Computer-based visualization is a global pursuit aimed at an international audience. It needs to employ principles and practices that can be universally understood and accepted. The London Charter is a step in this direction. 'There is a need to reconcile heritage visualization with professional norms of research, particularly the standards of argument and evidence,' argues Hugh Denard (see Chapter 6). As has been demonstrated, there is no single understanding of what professional norms involve in heritage visualization. Establishing conceptual, ethical, methodological and pedagogical connections between the physical and virtual preservation of heritage may offer a way forward, benefiting practices

---

9   The eSAD Decision Support System was originally called 'Interpretation Support System' (ISS) as reflected in the project literature up to October 2009.

10   Martyn Jessop, 'Digital Visualization as a Scholarly Activity', *Literary and Linguistic Computing*, 3, 23 (2008): 281.

in both these domains so that no virtual heritage looks synthetic, or resorts to a multiplication of features that contradicts the uniqueness of man-made artefacts. The charters published by the International Council on Monuments and Sites (ICOMOS), a non-governmental, world-wide organization of heritage professionals, are of critical significance for the establishment of a methodological consensus for heritage visualization across disciplines.[11] The *ICOMOS Principles for the Preservation and Conservation of Wall Paintings*, for example, address many issues highlighted in this volume. The relevance of these principles to digital visualization can be illustrated with two articles concerning the level of required complexity of investigation and its detailed and permanent documentation:

Article 2: Investigation

All conservation projects should begin with substantial scholarly investigations. The aim of such investigations is to find out as much as possible about the fabric of the structure and its superimposed layers with their historical, aesthetic and technical dimensions. This should encompass all material and incorporeal values of the painting, including historic alterations, additions and restorations. This calls for an interdisciplinary approach.

The methods of investigation should be as far as possible non-destructive. [...]

Article 3: Documentation

In agreement with the Venice Charter, the conservation-restoration of wall paintings must be accompanied by a precise program of documentation in the form of an analytical and critical report, illustrated with drawings, copies, photographs, mapping, etc. [...] Furthermore, *every stage* [my emphasis] of the conservation-restoration, materials and methodology used should be documented. [...][12]

The ICOMOS *Charter for the Interpretation and Presentation of Cultural Heritage Sites* is specific in insisting on making the interpretation implicit together with its

---

11   It should be noted that ICOMOS charters are not legal documents and have received mixed international reception, depending on local conservation practices. ICOMOS charters and associated documents on cultural heritage policies are readily available online from, among other resources, <http://www.international.icomos.org/centre_documentation/chartes_eng.htm>, <http://www.getty.edu/conservation/research_resources/charters.html>, and <http://www.enamecharter.org/links.html>.

12   *ICOMOS Principles for the Preservation and Conservation of Wall Paintings*, October 2003, available at <http://www.international.icomos.org/charters/wallpaintings_e.htm>.

sources and variants. The Charter also makes it clear that presentation specifically denotes the carefully planned communication of interpretive content.

Principle 2: Information sources

Visual reconstructions, whether by artists, architects, or computer modelers, should be based upon detailed and systematic analysis of environmental, archaeological, architectural, and historical data, including analysis of written, oral and iconographic sources, and photography. The information sources on which such visual renderings are based should be clearly documented and alternative reconstructions based on the same evidence, when available, should be provided for comparison.

Interpretation and presentation programmes and activities should also be documented and archived for future reference and reflection.[13]

Recognized charters of best practice in physical preservation and The London Charter advocate complex and systematic documentation of meta- and paradata. The implementation of these principles in digital visualizations of heritage is still an exception rather than the norm.

Heritage Visualization as Reconstruction

'The term "virtual reconstruction" is not used here, because the main goal is not to reconstruct the past – this is something one simply cannot do – but to bring together all available sources of information and visualize this process with 3D technology.' By putting forward this argument (see Chapter 17), Daniel Pletinckx represents many practitioners of heritage visualization. Matt Jones (see Chapter 9) refers to Maurizio Forte's preference for the generic term 'representation', rather than the more widely used 'reconstruction'. Drew Baker (see Chapter 14) goes as far as to suggest that the shift 'away from the idea of "reconstruction" – trying to recreate a site or building based on the evidence – in favour of a move towards a process of "visualization"' is needed if such attempts are to gain scholarly credibility. More secure but narrower is Sven Havemann's use of the term '3D modelling' of surviving heritage as 'the process of creating a digital replica' of a real artefact (see Chapter 13).

The wide range of case studies referred to in this volume demonstrates the complexity of computer-based visualization of heritage. It may involve digital reconstruction or restoration, reproduction or simulation; it can take the form of an

---

13   *ICOMOS Charter for the Interpretation and Presentation of Cultural Heritage Sites,* October 2008, pp. 2 and 5, available at <http://www.international.icomos.org/charters/interpretation_e.pdf>.

accurate replica or approximate copy; it can be a product of precise laser scanning or an artistic impression. An *anastylosis*, discussed by Maurizio Forte and Sofia Pescarin (see Chapter 16) in the context of virtual archaeology, is a method of repair (sometimes referred to as resurrection). It consist of returning fallen pieces of a monument to their original position, or 'connecting all points and traces found on the ground and by reproducing shapes of any artefacts' through digital processes. Both physical and virtual *anastylosis* may be combined with reconstruction of missing parts, typically unevenly worn out edges of stone. Bearing in mind the very different subject areas and epistemological conventions represented within the 3D visualization community, the lack of common understanding of critical vocabulary and evaluation criteria is not surprising.

Physical reconstruction of historic artefacts (objects, buildings and sites) following their partial or total destruction or damage has inevitably also been based on fragmentary evidence and the very same incomplete knowledge of the past. The historical validity and ethics of material reconstruction have also been questioned on many occasions, just as virtual heritage. It may therefore be helpful to look at computer-based visualization of heritage within the context of established principles and vocabularies of conservation and restoration of monuments and sites, and to keep bringing these terms to the attention of visualization practitioners. This language, and its associated theoretical literature, may prove not only a source of guidance, but also offer reassurance of methodological credibility.

The *International Charter for the Conservation and Restoration of Monuments and Sites*, a key document of 1964 known as the Venice Charter, stipulates 'The conservation and restoration of monuments must have recourse to *all the sciences and techniques* [my emphasis] which can contribute to the study and safeguarding of the architectural heritage.'[14] According to the Venice Charter, the main purpose of conservation and restoration is to enhance the significance of a monument. Historical research that has recourse to virtual heritage is generally guided by the same aim and would benefit from a wider emulation of the principles and terminology of ICOMOS charters. The Burra Charter, for example, clarifies the definition of reconstruction, meaning returning a site or object to a known historic state which involves introduction of new material into the fabric.[15] Importantly, reconstruction returns the structure to a known historic state of greater significance by removing accretions or by reassembling existing components.

The decision on what constitutes 'greater significance' is usually highly arbitrary and influenced by current fashion and taste. In physical restoration, this kind of decision has on some occasions been perceived abusive to the substance and interpretation of the original structure. Although there is no risk of material

---

14   See Article 2 of the Venice Charter, <http://www.icomos.org/venice_charter. html>.

15   *The Burra Charter*, Australia International Council on Monuments and Sites, November 1999, <http://www.icomos.org/burra_charter.html>.

abuse in virtual restoration, visualization is not free from similar controversy.[16] Much negative criticism of visualization products will be pre-empted if the selection of sources and the decision-making process during execution are made transparent and fully documented. A greater emulation of traditional restoration techniques for making the differences between the original and reconstructed (or newly introduced) features will contribute to greater credibility of virtual heritage, while a terminological consensus between contributing subject areas will make the communication of computer models more effective. Mark Carnal argues (see Chapter 8) that in CGI reconstructions 'full transparency cannot be presented without undermining the illusion of "reality"'. When it is important to maintain this illusion of a 'perfect' reconstruction, an alternative 'transparent' viewing may be offered.

As new techniques for 3D recording in near real time (such as colour 3D laser scanning or structured light recording) become more readily available alongside rapid prototyping (or 3D printing) and other manufacturing processes, the distinction between documentation, visualization and replication is losing its critical edge. Good understanding of the variety of technological processes and techniques now available to arts and humanities researchers is needed to ensure that the nature of our mixed-reality heritage is duly explained in paradata records.

Heritage Visualization as Experience

Increasingly, visualization projects explore the potential of digital media for recreating the experience of cultural heritage. There are significant differences in the perception and phenomenology of the approaches proposed, depending on the level of knowledge about a site, artefact or other cultural phenomenon, as well as the nature of relationships between a visualization and its creator or user. No two experiences of heritage can ever be the same and no technology to date has been capable of capturing and representing the complexity of what it means, or has meant in the past, to 'be there'. However, Mark Greengrass's view that visualizations are representations 'framed by the window and obscured by the glass' is too narrow.[17] Today's hybrid virtual worlds employ augmented reality and multimedia, immersion and haptics. They provide dynamic environments in which the real experience of cultural heritage may be approximated.

The potential for simulating human experience in such environments is different and – as many will argue – much greater than in many familiar surrogate representations achieved though more traditional means. A museum display is a striking example of an inadequate yet common means of exploring cultural

---

16   See, for example, the discussion on the veracity and authenticity of computer-based visualization in *3DVisa Bulletin*, issues 1–4 (2006–2008), <http://3dvisa.cch.kcl.ac.uk/bulletin.html>.

17   See note 3.

heritage. The experience of religious painting offered by museums, for instance, demonstrates that even when the actual artefact is present, its experience is disconnected from the original spiritual, physical, socio-physical and historical contexts.

Virtual simulation solves some but not all problems. Technology mediates between the present and the past, but the claim, made by some visualization projects, of 'bringing to life' heritage sites and cultural phenomena is premature. The year 1454 was chosen for the visualization of Southampton (see Chapter 9) because 'there is good documentary evidence for the town's structure and commercial activity during this period', but to what extent does the computer model reflect this activity? Interactive, immersive and haptic computer-mediated environments in three or four dimensions respond to the age-long quest for a total experience of art. Eugène Fromentin, for example, wrote in 1876 about Dutch seventeenth-century landscape painting: 'We live in the picture, we walk about in it, we look up into its depths, we are tempted to raise our heads to look at its sky.'[18] This description reads like an invitation for spatial visualization of a pictorial space and indeed many such attempts have been undertaken. The interaction with virtual objects and tools typically illustrates how much can be learnt about human perception and cognitive processes as one tries to 'teach' a machine to simulate real-life experiences.

As one goes about interpreting the characteristics of a digital object one also detects its *affordances*, exploring its functions and uses (see Chapter 16). Anyone who doubts the level of engagement with the artefact that can be stimulated by the process of its visualization need look no further than Ryan Egel-Andrews's experience of scrutinizing the evolution of Piet Mondrian's Neo-Plastic space (see Chapter 10). Mondrian's signature geometrical compositions emerge as contemplation pieces that convey the artist's concerns with – in his own words – the 'abstract real' space and visual expression of anthroposophy to which he adhered.

The creator's interaction with visualization throughout its conception, design and execution is paramount. Like other forms of research, visualization is a creative pursuit and to some extent also artistic. A stringent scholarly framework and technical standards advocated here for heritage visualization must not curtail creativity and individuality. Transparent tools are required for demonstrating where one ends and the other begins. These tools can partly be modelled on those used in physical restorations. No two brushstrokes or chisel marks are ever the same, resulting in the individuality of every hand-made object. In computer visualization, the tendency is to create a single feature and replicate or mirror it.

---

18   Eugène Fromentin, *Les Maitres d'Autrefois* (6th edn, Paris, 1890), p. 183: '[La peinture hollandaise] On l'habite, on y circule, on y regarde au fond, on est tente de relever la tête pour mesurer le ciel. Tout concourt a cette illusion: la rigueur des perspectives aériennes, le parfait rapport de la couleur et des valeurs avec le plan que l'objet occupe.' English translation after *The Masters of Past Time: Dutch and Flemish Painting from van Eyck to Rembrandt* (London and New York, 1948), p. 103.

A tool that 'will allow users to pick details from a digital library of architectonic parts to complete a volumetric reconstruction, validated according to the principles of statics', is presented in this very volume (see Chapter 4) not as 'science fiction' but 'a near future'. Virtual pieces of historic furnishings are already sourced from online shops even in academic visualizations. This is not what the real historic fabric looks like. When working in traditional media, '[...] in all art, the artist instinctively keeps the marks which reveal how a thing was done', the architect Louis I. Kahn is known to have said.[19] This is not the case with digital media, which tend to conceal such marks:

> Artists keep sketches and notebooks and use graphic packages to play with ideas, but do not have a tradition of recording this process as it relates to a given work. Writers work on personal computers with a word processor. The result is one final perfect copy without any evidence of process. Poets move words around the screen to find the best pattern. Once found this process is lost when the 'save' button is pressed.[20]

It is therefore even more important to create and keep a record of these processes. In arts computing, the need for a critical apparatus for revealing the life cycle of the image has been apparent right from the inception of bitmap graphics.[21] Many solutions have been proposed to compensate for the loss of the authenticity of the image, and this continues to be the subject of debate. Recently, ArtLog, 'a software solution to be used in any situation where process is as important as product', has been proposed for digital artists.[22] Paradata records – advocated by every contributor to this volume – fulfil similar requirement in scholarly visualization. Bearing in mind the open-ended nature of heritage visualization and the ever-changing human interaction with digital media, a record of a particular historical interpretation – that can be questioned and improved – conditions an academic debate. If academic visualization fails to establish credible criteria for differentiating itself from garish mass-produced edutainment it will not be taken seriously, nor deserve to be.

---

19   Louis I. Kahn, 'Toward a Plan for Midtown Philadelphia. 1953', in Alessandra Latour (ed.), *Louis I. Kahn: Writings, Lectures, Interviews* (New York, 1991), pp. 45–6.

20   Yvonne Desmond, 'ArtLog: An Electronic Archive of Artistic Process', *Object and Identity in a Digital Age: Proceedings of the CHArt 25th Conference*, Birkbeck, University of London, 12–13 November 2009, forthcoming at <http://www.chart.ac.uk>.

21   See my discussion in: 'Moving Images, Shifting Notions. Who can Trust the Digital Image?', in Anna Bentkowska-Kafel and John Sunderland (eds), *Visual Culture and the New Millennium* (2001), <http://www.chart.ac.uk/chart2000/papers/toc.html>.

22   ArtLog (2008–12) is a collaborative project between the Library Services and Digital Media Centre of Dublin Institute of Technology and the Tyrone Guthrie Centre. See Desmond, 'ArtLog'.

Heritage Visualization as Diffusion of Knowledge

'Work in the humanities has no value to anyone other than yourself until it can be communicated [...]' is the advice offered to students pursuing postgraduate studies at the Centre for Computing in the Humanities of King's College London. This truism is worth reiterating in the context of visualization-based scholarship because the practice shows that dissemination of research in this form is far from satisfactory. Despite the frequent assurance that proposed visualizations will be freely and easily available online, the reality of Open Access is cause for concern. Although Open Access requirements increasingly condition funding for visualization projects, and technical means for the wide dissemination of virtual heritage of the highest quality are available, a short animation is often all that is available for demonstration. The eCurator project is one of many to have demonstrated that an online resource no longer needs to be limited to low-resolution graphics.

Research into past visualization projects shows that most projects have a worryingly short life cycle.[23] The neglect of resources created, rather than their technological obsolescence, seems a single major reason for this situation, which jeopardizes the validity of visualization as a scholarly method. Even when fully functional and usable, computer models created in the past are relatively quickly superseded by demand for more accurate rendering techniques, enhanced interaction and integration of complex digital tools. Despite acute awareness of this problem, even the contributors to this volume have not been able to ensure the longevity and reuse of their own visualizations. A computer model of the presumed tomb of the Etruscan king Porsenna is cited in the subject literature (and referred to twice here: see Chapters 3 and 4) but illustrated in only small and rather inferior still images (see Figure 3.2).

The source for this ancient monument is a first-century description by Pliny the Elder. The monument has fascinated artists and scholars ever since. In manuscript notes for his unpublished *Discourse on Architecture*, the eminent seventeenth-century architect Christopher Wren says that 'Pliny took his description of this extraordinary Pilo from the measures set down by Varro, *a diligent and therefore credible author* [my emphasis].'[24] Donald H. Sanders mentions trust as an important criterion and Daniel Pletinckx emphasizes the extent of specialist skill

---

23   In 2006–2007, the Visualisation in the Arts Network (3DVisa), funded by the UK Joint Information Systems Committee, conducted a survey of 3D visualization projects in the arts and humanities. The resulting *3DVisa Index of 3D Projects*, ed. Anna Bentkowska-Kafel, continues to be maintained and augmented with records of new projects, see <http://3dvisa.cch.kcl.ac.uk/projectlist.html>. For most projects, access to actual visualization products of the 1980s, 1990s and more recent years, proved impossible beyond surrogate material such as a short animation, still images or a publication.

24   Christopher Wren Jr, *Parentalia, or, Memoirs of the family of the Wrens* (1750), p. 12.

required in visualization work, yet in our modern times trust or 'diligence' alone do not suffice to recognize scholarly excellence. 'Reuse and repurposing are a fundamental test for digital information', argues Mike Mudge (see Chapter 15). The same can be argued about scholarship if its value is to be maintained. If the claim – that the intellectual content of visualization constitutes its greatest benefit for research and education – is to be substantiated, long-term preservation and diffusion of this content need to be ensured.[25] Emphasis on the importance of the process of visualization should not be taken as justification for restricted access to the products of such research. Although such digital resources age less 'gracefully' than material outputs, more needs to be done to prevent their neglect or loss.

'Digital resources can have lasting value and therefore constitute a heritage', recognizes the UNESCO Programme on E-Heritage, adding 'Not all digital materials are of enduring value, but those that are require active preservation approaches if continuity of digital heritage is to be maintained,' and 'The digital heritage consists of unique resources of human knowledge and expression.'[26] Many computer-based scholarly visualizations created for the purpose of research in the arts and humanities fall into this category. These should be proactively maintained and preserved beyond the lifespan of the technology, software and hardware, used in their creation. Very few projects have this goal embedded in their original plan. Projects funded by short-term grants often generate a large volume of digital resources but have no means to implement a strategy for their long-term preservation. By contributing and maintaining more web content of the highest scholarly quality it might become possible to counterbalance the view of the internet as 'a charlatan's playground' and an ideal 'delivery system for pseudohistorians and pseudoscientists of all stripes'. It might also be possible to prove wrong those who, by so dubbing the net (not without a reason), fear modern media as 'a threat to the standards of "objective" history'.[27]

In Ron Howard's film, *A Beautiful Mind*, John F. Nash, the scientist and the 1994 Nobel Prize winner in Economic Sciences, played by Russell Crowe, says:

---

25   Source <http://www.cch.kcl.ac.uk/legacy/teaching/av1000/howto/essay-report.doc>.

26   See *UNESCO E-Heritage Programme* website at <http://portal.unesco.org/ci/en/ev.php-URL_ID=24268&URL_DO=DO_TOPIC&URL_SECTION=201.html>. *UNESCO Charter on the Preservation of the Digital Heritage*, 2003 available at <http://portal.unesco.org/ci/en/ev.php-URL_ID=13367&URL_DO=DO_TOPIC&URL_SECTION=201.html>. I discuss long-term preservation of digital heritage in the wider context of digital culture in 'The Fix v. the Flux. Which Digital Heritage?', in Dieter Daniels and Günther Reisinger (eds), *netpioneers 1.0 – archiving, representing and contextualising early netbased art* (Berlin and New York, 2009), pp. 55–72.

27   Ronald H. Fritze, *Invented Knowledge. False History, Fake Science and Pseudo-Religions* (2009). Quotations after the review article by Vincent Crapanzano, 'How to Fake Science, History and Religion. An Investigation into the Invented Histories of Atlantis, pre-Ice Age Civilizations and Cosmic Catastrophes', *The Times Literary Supplement*, 5 August 2009, <http://entertainment.timesonline.co.uk/tol/arts_and_entertainment/the_tls/article6739960.ece?&EMC-Bltn=CFME6B>.

'To triumph we need results – publishable, applicable results.'[28] This is still true of academic research in general. An academic without publications is a 'nobody'. Publications remain the key measure of academic excellence, and impact greatly on the level of research funding. Computer visualizations and project websites still compete with books and journal articles published by prestigious houses for equal recognition. Here is another book illustrated with still images even though this format is not suitable for interactive multimedia material. While the commentary offered in paper publications is still critically important, The London Charter community believes that the much greater visibility of academic visualization products will eventually contribute to the recognition this method deserves. ICOMOS recognizes this need in one of its charters on restoration, stipulating that, *regardless of the technique used*, full documentation of every stage of the process should be made widely available to the interested public, kept in public archives and *in situ*.

> It is also recommended that the results of the work should be published. This documentation should consider definable units of area in terms of such investigations, diagnosis and treatment. Traditional methods of written and graphic documentation can be supplemented by digital methods. However, regardless of the technique, the permanence of the records and the future availability of the documentation is of utmost importance.[29]

There are, therefore, many reasons for virtual heritage to be maintained, disseminated and preserved for the future. If adopted widely, the approach proposed by The London Charter will ensure good understanding of the importance of keeping paradata accessible and usable in the long term, thus demonstrating that, if accurately recorded, a process of creation may also constitute a means of communication.

It seems only apt to end with an observation about digital scholarship in the arts and humanities in general.

> Abundant experience throughout digital scholarship shows that the twin imperatives of computing, absolute consistency and total explicitness, pitted against the rich ambiguities of human knowledge, challenge us not only to rethink interpretative structures but also to explain *how we know what we know*. That, Lorraine Daston has pointed out elsewhere, is a high priority for the humanities of the twenty-first century.[30]

---

28   *A Beatiful Mind*, Universal Pictures and DreamWorks Pictures, USA 2001.

29   'Article 3: Documentation', *ICOMOS Principles for the Preservation and Conservation of Wall Paintings*, October 2003, available at <http://www.international. icomos.org/charters/wallpaintings_e.htm>.

30   Willard McCarty, Guest Editorial, *Interdisciplinary Science Review*, 30, 2 (June 2005): 97–8; Lorraine. Daston: 'Whither CI?', *Critical Inquiry*, 30 (2004): 363.

Within this broader framework, the challenge is – one is reminded in Chapter 5 – to apply computer-based visualization, 'this now-not-so-leading-edge technology, in ways that innovate, educate and elucidate'.[31]

---

31   See Donald H. Sanders, Chapter 5 this volume, p. 42.

Glossary of Terms

This glossary includes definitions of terms used within The London Charter for the Computer-based Visualisation of Cultural Heritage which are not intended to be prescriptive beyond that function.

affordance   A term used in psychology of visual perception, referring to the onlooker's interpretation of the characteristics of an object (for example, 'this is a comfortable armchair so I'll sit down and relax'). The term was coined by J.J. Gibson[1] to replace 'values', which he considered overburden with philosophical meaning.

anakyklosis   A cycle; the term is mainly known from the writings of Polybius and in relation to forms of government.

anastylosis   A simple form of repair of a collapsed monument, such as a Classical temple, by placing the fallen pieces to their original position.

computer-based visualization   In The London Charter this term denotes the process of graphically representing information in three dimensions.

computer-based visualization method   In The London Charter this term is used to indicate the systematic application, usually in a research context, of computer-based visualization in order to address identified aims.

computer-based visualization outcome   In The London Charter this term is used to denote an outcome of computer-based visualization, including but not limited to models, still images, animations, physical models.

cultural heritage   The London Charter adopts a wide definition of this term, encompassing all domains of human activity that are concerned with the understanding of communication of the material and intellectual culture. Such domains include, but are not limited to, museums, art galleries, heritage sites,

---

1   James J. Gibson, 'How Perception Really Develops: A View from Outside the Network', in Davide L. LaBerge and S. Jay Samuels (eds), *Basic Processes in Reading: Perception and Comprehension* (Hillsdale, NJ and London: Erlbaum, 1977), pp. 155–73. James J. Gibson, *The Ecological Approach to Visual Perception* (Boston, MA: Houghton Mifflin, 1979).

interpretative centres, cultural heritage research institutes, arts and humanities subjects within higher education institutions, the broader educational sector and tourism.

data artefact   Data recorded and attributed to a data object as a product of human conception or agency.

data load   The amount of data artefacts created and assigned to a data object. A low data load suggests that little is recorded about the data object. Conversely, a high data load suggests that there is a large number of data artefacts associated with it.

data object   A material object, perceptible by one or more of the senses, about which data are held.

dependency relationship   In The London Charter this term is used to indicate a dependent relationship between the properties of elements within digital models, such that a change in one property will necessitate change in the dependent properties. (For instance, a change in the height of a door will necessitate a corresponding change in the height of the doorframe.)

intellectual transparency   In The London Charter this term is used to indicate the provision of information, presented in any medium or format, to allow users to understand the nature and scope of 'knowledge claim' made by a computer-based visualization outcome.

machinima   A film genre which involves making films and other works using in-game engines and some post-processing software.

paradata   The London Charter defines 'paradata' as information about human processes of understanding and interpretation of data objects. Paradata is thus constantly being created, irrespective of whether they are systematically recorded or disseminated. Examples of paradata include a note recording method in a laboratory report, descriptions stored within a structured dataset of how evidence was used to interpret an artefact, or a comment on methodological premises within a research publication. Paradata differ in emphasis from 'contextual metadata': whereas the latter tends to focus upon how an object has been interpreted, the central focus of paradata tends to be the processes of interpretation through which understanding of objects or communicated is sought.

processualism   According to the *Oxford English Dictionary,* 'a theoretical approach based on a methodological and often comparative analysis of processes; advocacy of such an approach. Processual methods are used in social sciences, archaeology, anthropology and other fields.'

research   The London Charter adopts the definition of research given in the British Arts and Humanities Research Council's *Research Funding Guide* (2005) which stipulates that research should: 'address clearly-articulated research questions or problems, set in a clear research context, and using appropriate research methods'. It stipulates, in addition, that the chosen research methods should constitute 'the most appropriate means by which to answer the research questions'. This definition therefore recognizes that 'the precise nature of the outputs of the research may vary considerably, and may include, for example, monographs, editions or articles; electronic data, including sound or images; performances, films or broadcasts; or exhibitions. Teaching materials may also be an appropriate outcome from a research project provided that it fulfils the definition above.'[2]

research sources   The London Charter defines research sources as all information, digital and non-digital, considered during, or directly influencing, the creation of the computer-based visualization outcomes.

subject community   In The London Charter this term denotes a group of researchers generally defined by a discipline (for example, archaeology, Classics, Sinology, Egyptology) and sharing a broadly-defined understanding of what constitute valid research questions, methods and outputs within their subject area.

sustainability strategy   A strategy to ensure that some meaningful record of computer-based visualization processes and outcomes is preserved for future generations.

---

2   Source: *AHRC Research Funding Guide* (2005), pp. 15–16. <http://www.ahrc. ac.uk/ahrb/website/images/4_96278.pdf>, accessed, 3 March 2006.

Selected Bibliography

Includes publications on The London Charter not referred to in the preceding chapters. All URLs active at the time of writing.

Websites

3DVisA, JISC 3D Visualisation in the Arts Network, UK <http://3dvisa.cch.kcl. ac.uk>.
AHeSSC, Arts and Humanities e-Science Support Centre, UK <http://www. ahessc.ac.uk>.
AHRC ICT Methods Network, UK <http://www.methodsnetwork.ac.uk>.
ArcheoVirtual <http://www.vhlab.itabc.cnr.it/archeovirtual/eng/index.html>.
Bodleian Library, University of Oxford <http://www.bodley.ox.ac.uk/dept/ scwmss/wmss/medieval/mss/lat/misc/e/086.htm>.
Body and Mask in Ancient Theatre Space Project <http://www.kvl.cch.kcl.ac.uk/ masks/>.
Building Virtual Rome <http://www.itabc.cnr.it/buildingvirtualrome/stampa.htm> (October 2010).
CHARISMATIC Project <ftp://ftp.cordis.europa.eu/pub/ist/docs/ka3/iep_ charisma.pdf> (October 2010).
CHArt, Computers and the History of Art <http://www.chart.ac.uk>.
Contact VRML viewer <http://www.blaxxun.com>.
Cortona VRML viewer <http://www.parallelgraphics.com>.
CREW, Collaborative Research Events on the Web <http://www.crew-vre. net/?page_id=8>.
DICOM, Digital Imaging and Communications in Medicine <http://medical. nema.org/>.
Dublin Core <http:/www.dublincore.org>.
eCurator: 3D colour scans for remote object identification and assessment <http:// www.museums.ucl.ac.uk/research/ecurator/>.
eDance: Relocating Choreographic Process <http://projects.kmi.open.ac.uk/e-dance/>.
EPOCH Network of Excellence <http://www.epoch-net.org>, <http://www.epoch. eu/>.
eSAD, e-Science and Ancient Documents <http://esad.classics.ox.ac.uk/>.
Europeana <http://www.europeana.eu/portal/>.
ICOMOS <http://www.icomos.org>.

Institute for the Visualization of History, Inc. <http://www.vizin.org/>.

Learning Sites, Inc. <http://www.learningsites.com/>.

London Charter <http://www.londoncharter.org>.

London Charter in Second Life project <http://iu.di.unipi.it/sl/london/>.

Lorsch Abbey Reconstruction and Information System <http://www.iwr.uni-heidelberg.de/groups/ngg/Lorsch/>.

Making Space Project <http://www.kvl.cch.kcl.ac.uk/makingspace/index.html>.

Meshlab <http://www.meshlab.sourceforge.net>.

Mondrian's Paris studio at 5 rue Coulmiers <http://slurl.com/secondlife/Digital%20Humanities/25/187/31/> and <http://mondrian.wikispaces.com>.

myExperiment, a Virtual Research Environment for finding, using and sharing scientific workflows and research Objects <http://myexperiment.org/>.

NuME Nuovo Museo Elettronico, 4D visualization of Bologna <http://www.storiaeinformatica.it/nume/english/ntitolo_eng.html>.

NuME, Nuovo Museo Elettronico, Centro Gina Fasoli, University of Bologna <http://www.centrofasoli.unibo.it/nume/english/home_eng.html>.

Octaga VRML viewer <http://www.octaga.com>.

OpenSceneGraph <http://www.openscenegraph.org>.

QuickTime VR <http://www.apple.com/quicktime/technologies/qtvr/>.

Research Computing Services <http://www.rcs.manchester.ac.uk/>.

Roman Villa at Oplontis Visualisation Project <http://www.kvl.cch.kcl.ac.uk/oplontis.html>.

Rome Reborn 1.0 <http://www.romereborn.virginia.edu/>.

Theatron 3 Project <http://www.english.heacademy.ac.uk/explore/projects/archive/technology/tech23.php>.

UNESCO <http://whc.unesco.org>.

UNESCO E-Heritage Programme <http://portal.unesco.org/ci/en/ev.php-URL_ID=24268&URL_DO=DO_TOPIC&URL_SECTION=201.html>.

UNESCO Glossary <http://whc.unesco.org/en/glossary>.

UNESCO Intangible Heritage <http://www.unesco.org/culture/ich/index.php?pg=00002>.

Via Appia Project <http://www.appia.itabc.cnr.it>.

Virtual Museum of the Ancient Via Flaminia <http://www.vhlab.itabc.cnr.it/flaminia/>.

Virtual Museum of the Scrovegni Chapel <http://www.vhlab.itabc.cnr.it/giotto/>.

Virtual Museums Transnational Network (V-MUST) <http://virtual-museum-transnational-network.meetup.com/>.

Virtual Research Environment Programme, a UK initiative funded by JISC, 2006 <http://www.jisc.ac.uk/programme_vre.html>.

Virtual Terrain Project <http://www.vterrain.org>.

VisTrails 2007, Visualization workflow software, Release v1.0 University of Utah <http://www.vistrails.org/>.

vizNET, UK Visualization Support Network <http://www.viznet.ac.uk>.

Publications in Print and Online

Ackoff, Russel L., 'From Data to Wisdom', *Journal of Applied Systems Analysis*, 16 (1989): 3–9.

Alcock, James A., Burns, Jean and Freeman, Anthony (eds), 'PSI Wars: Getting to Grips with the Paranormal', *Journal of Consciousness Studies*, special double issue, 6–7 (2003).

Andrews, Patrick R., Blackledge, Jonathan M. and Turner, Martin J., *Fractal Geometry in Digital Imaging* (San Diego, London, Boston: Academic Press, 1998).

Annunziato Mauro and Piero Pierucci, 'Emergenza e biodiversità della forma: l'estetica dello scambio tra vita reale ed artificiale', in *Proceedings of the Second Italian Workshop of Artificial Life*, Rome, 2–5 March 2005, available at <http://www.plancton.com/papers/emergenc.pdf>.

Annunziato, Mauro, Lucchetti, Matteo, Orsini Giuseppe and Pizzuti Stefano, 'Artificial Life and Online Flows Optimisation in Energy Networks', in *Proceedings of the IEEE Swarm Intelligence Symposium*, Pasadena (CA), USA, June 2005 (Rome: SIS, 2005), pp. 412–15.

Arnold, David, 'Economic Reconstructions of Populated Environments: Progress with the Charismatic Project', in Franco Niccolucci (ed.), *Virtual Archaeology*, Proceedings of the VAST Euroconference, Arezzo, 24–25 November 2000, Bar International Series 1075 (Oxford: Archaeopress, 2002), pp. 203–208.

Arqueologia Mexicana, special monographic issues on Calakmul, 42 (2000) and 5 (2005).

Attardi, Giuseppe, Betrò, Marilina, Forte, Maurizio, Gori, Roberto, Imboden, Silvano and Mallegni, Francesco, '3D Facial Reconstruction and Visualization of Ancient Egyptian Mummies Using Spiral CT Data Soft Tissue Reconstruction and Texture Application', in Juan A. Barceló, Maurizio Forte and Donald H. Sanders (eds), *Virtual Reality in Archaeology*, BAR International Series 843 (Oxford: Archaeopress, 2000), pp. 79–86.

Attenborough, David, *Life on Air* (London: BBC Books, 2003).

Bani, Marco, Genovesi, Francesco, Ciregia, Elisa et al., 'Learning by Creating Historical Buildings', in Judith Molka-Danielsen and Mats Deutschmann (eds), *Learning and Teaching in the Virtual World of Second Life* (Trondheim: Tapir Academic Press, 2009).

Barceló, Juan A., 'Visualizing What Might Be: An Introduction to Virtual Reality Techniques in Archaeology', in Juan A. Barceló, Maurizio Forte and Donald H. Sanders (eds), *Virtual Reality in Archaeology*, BAR International Series 843 (Oxford: Archaeopress, 2000), pp. 9–36.

Bateson, Gregory, *Steps to an Ecology of Mind* (San Francisco: Chandler Press, 1972).

—, *Mind and Nature: A Necessary Unit* (New York: Dutton, 1979).

BBC News, '*Entertainment Ratings Record for Dino Saga*', <http://news.bbc.co.uk/1/hi/entertainment/480284.stm> (accessed October 1999).

Beacham, Richard, '"Oh, to make boards to speak! There is a task!" Towards a Poetics of Paradata', in Marc Greengrass and Lorna Hughes (eds), *The Virtual Representation of the Past* (Aldershot: Ashgate, 2008), pp. 171–7.

Beacham, Richard, Denard, Hugh and Niccolucci, Franco 'An Introduction to the London Charter', in Marinos Ioannides et al. (eds), *The e-volution of Information Communication and Technology in Cultural Heritage*, Proceedings of VAST 2006, (Budapest: Archaeolingua, 2006), pp. 263–9.

Bentkowska-Kafel, Anna, 'Moving Images, Shifting Notions. Who Can Trust the digital image?', in Anna Bentkowska-Kafel and John Sunderland (eds), *Visual Culture and the New Millennium*, Proceedings of the 16th Annual CHArt Conference, Courtauld Institute of Art, London, 1–2 September 2000 (London: Computers and the History of Art, 2001), <http://www.chart.ac.uk/chart2000/papers/toc.html>.

—, 'The Fix v. the Flux. Which Digital Heritage?', in Dieter Daniels and Günther Reisinger (eds), *netpioneers 1.0 – archiving, representing and contextualising early netbased art* (Berlin and New York: Sternberg Press, 2009), pp. 55–72.

— (ed.), *3DVisA Index of 3D Projects*, <http://3dvisa.cch.kcl.ac.uk/projectlist.html>.

Berners-Lee, Tim, Hendler, James and Lassila, Ora, 'The Semantic Web', *Scientific American*, 284, 5 (2001): 34–43.

Berns, Roy S., Frey, Franziska S., Rosen, Mitchell R. et al., *Direct Digital Capture of Cultural Heritage: Benchmarking American Museum Practices and Defining Future Needs* (Rochester, NY: Rochester Institute of Technology, 2005), <http://msc.mellon.org/research-reports/Direct%20Digital%20Capture%20of%20Cultural%20Heritage.pdf/view>.

Beynon, Meurig, 'Computational Support for Realism in Virtual Environments', in *Proceedings of the 11th International Conference on Human-Computer Interaction (HCII 2005)*, vol. 10, *Internationalization, Online Communities and Social Computing: Design and Evaluation*, Las Vegas, NV, 22–27 July 2005 (CD), also available at <http://www2.warwick.ac.uk/fac/sci/dcs/research/em/publications/papers/084/>.

Binford, Lewis R., *In Pursuit of the Past. Decoding the Archaeological Record* (London: Thames and Hudson, 1983).

Blau, Eve and Kaufman, Edward (eds), *Architecture and Its Image: Four Centuries of Architectural Representation. Works from the Collection of the Canadian Centre for Architecture* (Montreal: Canadian Centre for Architecture, 1989).

Blotkamp, Carel, *Mondrian. The Art of Destruction* (London: Reaktion Books, 1994).

Bocchi, Francesca, 'The Long Road of Nu.M.E. (Nuovo Museo Elettronico, Bologna virtuale): Criteria and Methods', in *Proceedings of the 6th Virtual Reality International Conference*, 11–16 March 2004, Laval, France.

Boëda Eric, Geneste, Jean-Michel and Meignen, Liliane, 'Identification de chaînes opératoires lithiques du Paléolithique ancien et moyen', *Paleo*, 2 (1990): 43–80.

Burgess, Lawrence Arthur (ed.), *The Southampton Terrier of 1454* (London: HMSO, 1976).

Callebaut, Dirk, 'The Experiences of the Ename 974 Project with New Media: Where and How Do Virtual Reality and Interactivity Fit in?', in Franco Niccolucci (ed.), *Virtual Archaeology*, Bar International Series 1075 (Oxford: Archaeopress, 2002), pp. 179–86.

Callebaut, Dirk, van der Donckt, Marie-Claire and Pletinckx, Daniel, 'Projekt Ename 974: Neue Technologien in der Erbgutpräsentation', in *Archäologie virtuell: Projecte, Entwicklungen Tendenzen seit 1995*, Schriften zur Bodendenkmalpflege in Nordrhein-Westfalen 6 (Bonn: Habelt, 2002), pp. 50–56.

Callebaut, Dirk, Pletinckx, Daniel and Silberman, Neil A., 'Why Multimedia Matter in Cultural Heritage: The Use of New Technologies in the Ename 974 Project', in Franco Niccolucci and Sorin Hermon (eds), *Multimedia Communication for Cultural Heritage* (Budapest: Archaeolingua, 2002), pp. 65–72.

Calori, Luigi, Camporesi, Carlo, Forte, Maurizio and Pescarin, Sofia, 'Interactive Landscapes Reconstruction: A Web 2D and 3D Open Source Solution', in Mark Mudge, Nick Ryan and Roberto Scopigno (eds), *VAST 2005. The Sixth International Symposium on Virtual Reality, Archaeology and Cultural Heritage. Short Presentations* (2005), available at <http://www.cineca.it/stdoc/VAST2005_PescarinCamporesi.pdf>.

Calori, Luigi, Diamanti, Tiziano, Felicori, Mauro et al., 'Databases and Virtual Environments: A Good Match for Communicating Complex Cultural Sites', in *SIGGRAPH Educators' Program* (New York: ACM, 2004), p. 30.

Calori, Luigi, Camporesi, Carlo, Forte, Maurizio, Imboden, Silvano and Pescarin, Sofia, 'Open Heritage: An Open Source Approach to 3D Real-time and Web-based Landscape Reconstruction', in Hal Thwaites (ed.), *VSMM 2005. Atti dell XI International Conference su Virtual Systems and Multimedia: Virtual Reality at Work* (Budapest, 2005), pp. 313–20.

Champa, Kermit Swiler, *Mondrian Studies* (Chicago and London: University of Chicago Press, 1985).

Cicero, *Paradoxa Stoicorum*, 5.38.2, in *On the Orator*, trans. Harris Rackham, Loeb Classical Library, vol. 349 (Cambridge, MA: Harvard University Press, 2004).

Clarke, Arthur C., 'Hazards of Prophecy: The Failure of Imagination', in *Profiles of the Future* (New York, 1962).

Cleveland, Harlan, 'Information as a Resource', *The Futurist*, 12 (1982): 34–9.

Collingwood, Robin G., Outlines of a Philosophy of Art (Oxford, 1924).

— *Speculum Mentis* (Oxford, 1924).

Craik, Kenneth, *The Nature of Explanation* (Cambridge: Cambridge University Press, 1943).

Cull, Grant, Cioffi, George A., Dong, Jim et al., 'Estimating Normal Optic Nerve Axon Numbers in Non-human Primate Eyes', *Journal of Glaucoma*, 12, 4 (August 2003): 301–306.

D'Andrea, Andrea and Niccolucci, Franco, 'An Ontology for 3D Cultural Objects', in David Arnold, Marinos Ioannides, Katerina Mania and Franco Niccolucci (eds), *Proceedings of VAST2007, the Seventh International Symposium on Virtual Reality, Archaeology, and Intelligent Cultural Heritage* (Aire-La-Ville: Eurographics Publications, 2003), pp. 203–10.

Dante, *Divine Comedy*, Princeton Dante Project Italian-English edition, trans. Robert and Jean Hollander (Princeton University, 1997–1999) <http://etcweb. princeton.edu/dante/pdp/>.

Denard, Hugh, '"At the foot of Pompey's Statue": Reconceiving Rome's *Theatrum Lapideum*', in Alan K. Bowman and Michael Brady (eds), *Images and Artefacts of the Ancient World* (Oxford: Oxford University Press, 2005), pp. 69–76.

—, 'Making 3D Visual Research Outcomes Transparent': A Report on the Seminar Held at the British Academy on 23–25 February 2006', in L. Hughes (ed.), *The AHRC ICT Methods Network,* (Office for Humanities Communication, 2008), p. 39; also available at <http://www.methodsnetwork.ac.uk/activities/ act1.html>.

Denard, Hugh, Salvatori, Erica and Simi, Maria, 'Learning by Building in Second Life: Reflections on Interdisciplinary and International Experiences', in Giovanni Vincenti and James Braman (eds), *Multi-User Virtual Environments for the Classroom: Practical Approaches to Teaching in Virtual World* (IGI Global, 2011), pp. 134–58.

Desmond, Yvonne, 'ArtLog: An Electronic Archive of Artistic Process', *Object and Identity in a Digital Age. Proceedings of the CHArt 25th Conference*, Birkbeck, University of London, 12–13 November 2009 (London: Computers and the History of Art), forthcoming at <htttp://www.chart.ac.uk>.

Devlin, Kate, Chalmers, Alan and Brown, Duncan, 'Predictive Lighting and Perception in Archaeological Representations', *UNESCO World Heritage in the Digital Age 30th Anniversary Digital Congress* (2003).

Devlin, Kate, Chalmers, Alan and Reinhard, Erik, 'Displaying Digitally Archived Images', in Franziska Frey and R. Buckley (eds), *Proceedings of IS&T Archiving Conference, Society for Imaging Science and Technology* (2004), pp. 157–62.

Devlin, Kate, Chalmers, Alan, Wilkie, Alexander and Purgathofer, Werner, 'Tone Reproduction and Physically Based Spectral Rendering', in Dieter Fellner and Roberto Scopignio (eds), *State of the Art Reports (STAR)* (Eurographics Association, 2002), available at <http://www.cs.bris.ac.uk/Publications/ Papers/1000662.pdf>.

Dilke, Oswald Ashton Wentworth, *Mathematics and Measurement* (London: British Museum Press, 1987).

Dodge, Martin, McDerby, Mary J. and Turner, Martin, Geographic Visualization: Concepts, Tools and Applications (Chichester: Wiley Publications, 2008).

Doerr, Martin, 'The CIDOC Conceptual Reference Module: An Ontological Approach to Semantic Interoperability of Metadata', *AI Magazine*, 24, 3 (2003): 75–92.

Doerr, Martin and LeBoeuf, Patrick, 'Linking CIDOC-CRM and FRBR', *Proceedings of the Conference on Intelligent Access to Digital Heritage*, National Library of Estonia, Tallin, 18–19 October 2007, available at <http://conference2007.kul.ee/failid/LeBoef_Linking_CIDOC_CRM_and_FRBR.pdf>.

Doerr, Martin and Sarris, Apostolos (eds), *The Digital Heritage of Archaeology*, Proceedings of the 30th CAA Conference, Computer Applications and Quantitative Methods in Archaeology, Heraklion, Crete, April 2002 (Athens: Hellenic Ministry of Culture, 2003).

Dorrell, Peter G., *Photography in Archaeology and Conservation* (2nd edn, Cambridge: Cambridge University Press, 1994).

Earl, Graeme P., 'At the Edge of the Lens: Photography, Graphical Constructions and Cinematography', in Patrick Daley and Thomas L. Evans (eds), *Digital Archaeology: Bridging Method and Theory* (London: Routledge, 2006), pp. 191–209.

Ekstrom, Ruth B., French, John W. and Harman, Harry H., *Manual for Kit of Factor-Referenced Cognitive Tests* (Princeton: Educational Testing Service, 1976).

Fairchild, Mark D., *Color Appearance Models* (Reading, MA: Addison-Wesley, 1998).

Feijs, Leo, 'Divisions of the Plane by Computer: Another Way of Looking at Mondrian's Nonfigurative Compositions', *Leonardo*, 37, 3 (2004): 217–22.

Felicori, Mauro, Guidazzoli, Antonella, Liguori, M.C. and Pescarin, Sofia, 'Integration and Communication of Cultural Contents: The Experience of the Certosa Virtual Museum', in *Proceedings of ICHIM* (2005).

Feller, Joseph. and Fitzgerald, Brian, *Understanding Open Source Development* (Reading: Addison-Wesley, 2001).

Ferko, Andrej, Grabner, Markus, Schwann, Günter et al., 'Navigation Functionality for Virtual Archaeology', in Jarek Rossignac and Vaclav Skala (eds), *Proceedings of the 11th International Conference in Central Europe on Computer Graphics, Visualization and Computer Vision* (WSCG 2003)*, 3–7 February 2003, University of West Bohemia, Plzen, *Journal of WSCG*, 1 3, 11 (2003): [1–4], available at <http://wscg.zcu.cz/wscg2003/Papers_2003/J97.pdf>.

Ferwerda, James A., 'Three Varieties of Realism in Computer Graphics', *in Proceedings of SPIE Human Vision and Electronic Imaging '03* (2003), pp. 290–97.

Forte, Maurizio, 'About Virtual Archaeology: Disorders, Cognitive Interactions and Virtuality', in Juan A. Barceló, Maurizio Forte and Donald H. Sanders (eds), *Virtual Reality in Archaeology*, BAR International Series 843 (Oxford: Archaeopress, 2000), pp. 247–59.

Forte, Maurizio and Pescarin Sofia, 'The Virtual Reconstruction of the Archaeological Landscape', in Jean-François Berger, Frédérique Bertoncello, Frank Braemer et al. (eds), *XXVe rencontres internationales d'Archéologie et d'Histoire d'Antibes: temps et espaces de l'homme en société, analyses et modèles spatiaux en archéologie* (Antibes: Editions APDCA, 2005), pp. 55–66.

Forte, Maurizio and Siliotti, Alberto (eds), *Virtual Archaeology: Great Discoveries Brought to Life through Virtual Reality* (London: Thames and Hudson, 1997).

Forte, Maurizio, Pescarin, Sofia and Pietroni, Eva, 'The Appia Antica Project', in *The Reconstruction of Archaeological Landscapes through Digital Technologies*, Atti del II Convegno Italia-USA, BAR International Series 1379 (Oxford: Archaeopress, 2005), pp. 79–95.

Frischer Bernard, Niccolucci, Franco, Ryan, Nick and Barcelò, Juan A., 'From CVR to CVRO: The Past, Present, and Future of Cultural Virtual Reality', in Franco Niccolucci (ed.), *Virtual Archaeology*, Proceedings of the VAST Euroconference, Arezzo, 24–25 November 2000, Bar International Series 1075 (Oxford: Archaeopress, 2002), pp. 7–18.

Fritze, Ronald H., *Invented Knowledge. False History, Fake Science and Pseudo-religions* (London: Reaktion Books, 2009).

Fromentin, Eugène, *Les Maitres d'Autrefois* (6th edn, Paris, 1890).

—, *The Masters of Past Time: Dutch and Flemish Painting from van Eyck to Rembrandt* (London and New York, 1948)

Gamble, C., *Archaeology: The Basics* (London: Routledge, 2001).

Gibson, James J., 'How Perception Really Develops: A View from Outside the Network', in Davide L. LaBerge and S. Jay Samuels (eds), *Basic Processes in Reading: Perception and Comprehension* (Hillsdale, NJ and London: Erlbaum, 1977), pp. 155–73.

Gibson, James J., *The Ecological Approach to Visual Perception* (Boston, MA: Houghton Mifflin, 1979).

Glassner, Andrew S., *Principles of Digital Image Synthesis* (San Francisco: Morgan Kaufmann, 1995).

Globus, AL and Raible, Eric, '14 Ways to Say Nothing with Scientific Visualization', *IEEE Computer*, 27, 7 (1994), pp. 86–8 Al Globus and Eric Raible, '14 Ways to Say Nothing with Scientific Visualization', *IEEE Computer*, 27/7 (1994): 86–8, available at <http://www.arsc.edu/~cskills/14ways.pdf>.

Goodman, Nelson, *Languages of Art* (Indianapolis: Hackett Publishing Company, 1976).

Goodrick, Glyn and Gillings, Mark, 'Constructs, Simulations and Hyperreal Worlds: The Role of Virtual Reality (VR) in Archaeological Research', in Gary Lock and Kayt Brown (eds), *On the Theory and Practice of Archaeological Computing* (Oxford: Oxford University Committee for Archaeology, Institute of Archaeology, 2000), pp. 41–58.

Greengrass, Marc and Hughes, Lorna (eds), *The Virtual Representation of the Past*, (Aldershot: Ashgate, 2008).

Grenville, Jane, *Medieval Housing* (Leicester: Leicester University Press, 1997; 2nd edn, 1999).

Grout, Catherine, Purdy, Phill, Rymer, Janine et al., *Creating Digital Resources for the Visual Arts: Standards and Good Practice* (Oxford: Oxbow Books, 2000).

Guidazzoli, Antonella, Pescarin, Sofia, Forte, Maurizio et al., 'From GIS to Landscape Virtual Museums', in M. Forte (ed.), *Archaeological Landscapes through Digital Technologies*, Proceedings of the Second Italy–United States Workshop, Rome, Italy, 3–5 November 2003 and Berkeley, USA, May 2005, British Archaeological Reports S1379 (Oxford: Archaeopress, 2005).

Gutierrez, Diego, Sundstedt, Veronica, Gomez, Fermin and Chalmers, Alan, 'Dust and Light: Predictive Virtual Archaeology', *Journal of Cultural Heritage*, 8/2 (2007): 209–14.

Haegler, Simon, Müller, Pascal, Wonka, Peter et al., 'Procedural Modeling of Buildings', in *Proceedings of ACM SIGGRAPH 2006/ACM Transactions on Graphics*, 25, 3 (New York: ACM Press, 2006), pp. 614–23.

Hague, Barry N. and Loader, Brian D. (eds), *Digital Democracy: Discourse and Decision Making in the Information Age* (Cambridge, UK and New York: Routledge, 1999).

Haines, Tim, *Walking With Dinosaurs: A Natural History* (London: BBC Worldwide Limited, 1999).

Halper, Nick, Mellin, Mara, Herrmann, Christoph S. et al., 'Towards an Understanding of the Psychology of Non-photorealistic Rendering', in Jochen Schneider, Thomas Strothotte and Winfried Marotzki (eds), *Proceedings of the Workshop Computational Visualiztics, Media Informatics and Virtual Communities*, 4–5 April 2003, Wiesbaden (Wiesbaden: Deutscher Universitäts-Verlag, 2003), pp. 67–78.

Happa, Jassim, Mudge, Mark, Debattista, Kurt et al., 'Illuminating the Past: State of the Art', *Virtual Reality*, 14, 3, (2010): 155–82, <http://www.springerlink.com/content/d0472051303777n0/?p=38c05227cf864b7ca15c87e10c147cae&pi>.

Havemann, Sven, *Generative Mesh Modeling*, PhD thesis, Institute of Computer Graphics, Faculty of Computer Science, Technische Universität Braunschweig, Germany, November 2005.

Havemann, Sven and Fellner, Dieter, 'Seven Research Challenges of Generalized 3D Documents', *IEEE Computer Graphics and Applications*, special issue on 3D documents, 27, 3 (2007): 70–76.

Hegarty, Mary, 'Diagrams in the Mind and in the World: Relations between Internal and External Visualizations', in Alan F. Blackwell, Kim Mariott and Atsushi Shimojima (eds), *Diagrammatic Representation and Inference. Lecture Notes in Artificial Intelligence*, vol. 2980 (Berlin: Springer-Verlag, 2004), pp. 1–13.

Henkels, Herbert, 'Mondrian in his Studio', in *Mondrian. From Figuration to Abstraction,* (London: Thames and Hudson, 1988).

Henshũshitsu, Akurosa, *'Sekai Shōhin no Tsukurikata: Nihon Media ga Sekai o Sesshita hi'* (Tokyo: Parco Shuppan, 1995) pp. 41–2.

Hermon, Sorin, 'Reasoning in 3D: A Critical Appraisal of the Role of 3D Modelling and Virtual Reconstructions in Archaeology', in Bernard Frischer and Anastasia Dakouri-Hild (eds), *Beyond Illustration: 2D and 3D Digital Technologies as Tools for Discovery in Archaeology*, BAR International Series

1805 (Oxford: Archaeopress, 2008), pp. 36–45, available at <http://www.iath. virginia.edu/~spw4s/Beyond/BAR/Hermon.pdf>.

Hermon, Sorin and Fabian, Peter, 'Virtual Reconstruction of Archaeological Sites: Some Archaeological Scientific Considerations', in Franco Niccolucci (ed.), *Virtual Archaeology*, Proceedings of the VAST Euroconference, Arezzo 24–26 November 2000. British Archaeological Reports International Series 1075 (Oxford: Archaeopress, 2002), pp. 103–108.

Hermon, Sorin and Niccolucci, Franco, 'A Fuzzy Logic Approach to Reliability in Archaeological Virtual Reconstruction', in Franco Niccolucci and Sorin Hermon (eds), *Beyond the Artifact. Digital Interpretation of the Past* (Budapest: Archaeolingua, 2006), pp. 11–17.

Hermon, Sorin, Niccolucci, Franco and D'Andrea, Andrea, 'Some Evaluations on the Potential Impact of Virtual Reality on the Archaeological Scientific Research', in *VSMM 2005. Proceedings of the Eleventh International Conference on Virtual Systems and MultiMedia* (Ghent, Belgium, 2005), pp. 105–14.

Herodotus, *Histories*, trans. George Rawlinson (London: Wordsworth, 1996).

Hodder, I., Reading the Past. Current Approaches to Interpretation in Archaeology (3rd edn, Cambridge: Cambridge University Press, 2003).

Holtzman, Harry and James, Martin S. (eds.), *The New Art – The New Life: Collected Writings of Piet Mondrian* (London: Thames and Hudson, 1987).

ICOMOS Burra Charter, Australia International Council on Monuments and Sites, November 1999, <http://www.icomos.org/australia/burra.html>.

ICOMOS Charter for the Interpretation and Presentation of Cultural Heritage Sites, October 2008, available at <http://www.international.icomos.org/ charters/interpretation_e.pdf>.

ICOMOS Principles for the Preservation and Conservation of Wall Paintings, October 2003, available at <http://www.international.icomos.org/charters/ wallpaintings_e.htm>.

ICOMOS Venice Charter, <http://www.icomos.org/venice_charter.html>.

Jablonka, Peter, Kirchner, Steffen and Serangeli, Jordi, 'Troia VR. A Virtual Reality Model of Troy and the Troad', in Martin Doerr and Apostolos Sarris (eds), *The Digital Heritage of Archaeology,* Proceedings of the 30th CAA Conference, Computer Applications and Quantitative Methods in Archaeology, Heraklion, Crete, April 2002 (Athens: Hellenic Ministry of Culture, 2003), pp. 13–20, available at <http://homepages.uni-tuebingen.de/jordi.serangeli/Articoli/ Jablonka%20et%20al%202003.pdf>.

Jessop, Martyn, 'Digital Visualization as a Scholarly Activity', *Literary and Linguistic Computing*, 3, 23 (2008): 281–93.

Johnson, Matthew, *Archaeological Theory: An Introduction* (Oxford: Blackwell, 1999).

Jones, Matt, *Southampton in 1454: A Three-Dimensional Model of the Medieval Town*, 3DVisA Student Award Essay, 2007 <http://3dvisa.cch.kcl.ac.uk/ student_award_3.html>.

Joosten, Joop M. and Welsh, Robert P., *Piet Mondrian Catalogue Raisonné*, vol. 2 (Blaricum: V+K Publishing, 1998).

Kaiser, Peter K., *The Joy of Visual Perception: A Web Book*, 2006–2009, <http://www.yorku.ca/eye/thejoy.htm>.

Kahn, Louis I., 'Toward a Plan for Midtown Philadelphia.1953', in Alessandra Latour (ed.), *Louis I. Kahn: Writings, Lectures, Interviews* (New York: Rizzoli, 1991), pp. 29–87.

Kandel, Eric R., Schwartz, James H. and Jessell, Thomas M. (eds), *Principles of Neural Science* (4th edn, New York: McGraw-Hill, Health Professions Division, 2000).

Kantner, John, 'Realism vs. Reality: Creating Virtual Reconstructions of Prehistoric Architecture', in Juan A. Barceló, Maurizio Forte and Donald H. Sanders (eds), *Virtual Reality in Archaeology*, BAR International Series 843 (Oxford: Archaeopress, 2000), also available at <http://www.sarweb.org/kantner/SAA00/index.html>.

Kensek, Karen M., Dodd, Lynn Swartz and Cipolla, Nicholas, 'Fantastic Reconstructions or Reconstructions of the Fantastic? Tracking and Presenting Ambiguity, Alternatives, and Documentation in Virtual Worlds', *Automation in Construction*, 2, 13 (2004): 175–86.

Korzybski, Alfred, *Science and Sanity: An Introduction to Non-Aristotelian Systems and General Semantics* (Lakeville, CT: International Non-Aristotelian Library Publishing Co., 1933).

Ledda, Patrick, Chalmers, Alan, Troscianko, Tom and Seetzen, Helge, 'Evaluation of Tone Mapping Operators using a High Dynamic Range Display', *ACM Transaction on Graphics*, 24/3 (2005), pp. 640–48.

Lemagny, Jean-Claude and André Rouillé (eds), *A History of Photography: Social and Cultural Perspectives*, trans. by Janet Lloyd (Cambridge: Cambridge University Press, 1987).

Lemonnier, Pierre, 'The Study of Material Culture Today: Towards an Anthropology of Technical Systems', *Journal of Anthropological Archaeology*, 5 (1986): 147–86.

Leong-Hong, Belkis W. and Plagman, Bernard K., *Data Dictionary/Directory Systems: Administration, Implementation and Usage* (New York: ACM, 1974).

Leroi-Gourhan, André, *Le geste et la parole. I – Techniques et langage* (Paris: Albain Michel, 1964).

Leroi-Gourhan André, Bailloud Gérard, Chavaillon, Jean and Laming-Emperaire, Annette, *La Prehistoire* (Paris: PUF Nouvelle Clio, 1966).

Lévi-Strauss, Claude, *Structural Anthropology* ([1958]; New York: Basic Books, 1976).

London Charter for the Computer-based Visualisation of Cultural Heritage, The, version 2.1, February 2009, <http://www.londoncharter.org>.

Ludel, Jacqueline, *Introduction to Sensory Processes* (San Francisco: W.H. Freeman and Co., 1978).

Maas, Paul, *Textual Criticism*, trans. Barbara Flower (Oxford: Clarendon Press, 1958).

McCarty, Willard, *Humanities Computing* (Basingstoke: Palgrave, 2005).

McDerby, Mary J., *Introduction to Scientific Visualization*, training notes (Manchester: University of Manchester Research Computing Services, 2007).

McGowan, Christopher, *The Dragon Seekers* (London: Abacus, 2003): 150–53.

Martill, David and Naish, Darren, *Walking with Dinosaurs: The Evidence* (London: DK Adult, 2001).

Maturana, Humberto and Varela, Francisco, 'Autopoiesis and Cognition: The Realization of the Living', in Robert S. Cohen and Marx W. Wartofsky (eds), *Boston Studies in the Philosophy of Science*, vol. 42, (Dordecht, Holland: D. Reidel Publishing Co., 1980).

Mauss, Marcel, 'Les Techniques et la technologie', *Journal de psychologie normale et pathologique*, 41 (1941): 71–8.

Mehlberg, Henry, 'The Range and Limits of the Scientific Method', *The Journal of Philosophy*, 51, 10 (1954): 285–94.

Meyer, Gary W., Rushmeier, Holly E., Cohen, Michael F. et al., 'An Experimental Evaluation of Computer Graphics Imagery', *ACM Transactions on Graphics*, 5, 1 (1986), pp. 30–50.

Meyers, Eric (ed.), *The Oxford Encyclopaedia of Archaeology in the Near East* (Oxford: Oxford University Press, 1997).

Mondrian, Piet, *Natural Reality and Abstract Reality: An Essay in Trialogue Form*, trans. Martin S. James (New York: George Braziller, 1995).Mudge, Mark, 'Cultural Heritage and Computer Graphics Panel', in *SIGGRAPH 2004 Conference Presentations, Web Graphics/Special Sessions/Panels* (2004).

Mudge, Mark, Ashley, Michael and Schroer, Carla, 'A Digital Future for Cultural Heritage', in A. Georgopoulos and N. Agriantonis (eds), *Anticipating the Future of the Cultural Past XXI CIPA International Symposium* (Athens, 2007), pp. 521–6.

Mudge, Mark, Malzbender, Tom, Chalmers, Alan et al., 'Image-based Empirical Information Acquisition, Scientific Reliability, and Long-Term Digital Preservation for the Natural Sciences and Cultural Heritage', *Eurographics 2008: Tutorial Notes* (Eurographics, 2008), <http://homepages.inf.ed.ac.uk/rbf/CVonline/LOCAL_COPIES/MUDGE/EG-mudge-tutorial-notes-final.pdf>.

Mudge, Mark, Malzbender, Tom, Schroer, Carla and Lum, Marlin, 'New Reflection Transformation Imaging Methods for Rock Art and Multiple-viewpoint Display', in *VAST2006 The e-Volution of Information Communication Technology in Cultural Heritage* (Budapest: Archaeolingua, 2006).

National Electrical Manufacturers Association, *Digital Imaging and Communications in Medicine (DICOM) Part 14: Greyscale Standard Display Function* (2003), <http://medical.nema.org/dicom/2004/04_14PU.pdf>.

Niccolucci, Franco, 'Virtual Reality in Archaeology: A Useful Tool or a Dreadful Toy?', *Proceedings of the Medi@terra Symposium* (Athens, 1999), pp. 238f.

— (ed.), *Virtual Archaeology*, Proceedings of the VAST Euroconference, Arezzo, 24–25 November 2000, Bar International Series 1075 (Oxford: Archaeopress, 2002).

Niccolucci, Franco and Cantone, Francesca, 'Legend and Virtual Reconstruction: Porsenna's Mausoleum in X3D', in Martin Doerr and Apostolos Sarris (eds), *The Digital Heritage of Archaeology*, CAA 2002, Proceedings of the 30th Conference of Computer Applications and Quantitative Methods in Archaeology, Heraklion, Crete, April 2002 (Athens: Hellenic Ministry of Culture, 2003), pp. 57–62.

Nielsen Report, *Video Gamers in Europe – 2008* (London, 2008).

Oakhill, Jane and Garnham, Alan (eds), *Mental Models in Cognitive Science* (Mahwah, NJ: Lawrence Erlbaum Associates, 1996).

Osterberg, G., 'Topography of the Layer of Rods and Cones in the Human Retina', *Acta Ophthalmol*, suppl. 6 (1935): 1–103.

Oyster, Clyde W., *The Human Eye: Structure and Function* ([1999]; Sunderland, MA: Sinauer Associates, 2006).

Palmer, Stephen E., *Vision Science. Photons to Phenomenology* (Cambridge, MA: MIT Press, 1999).

Parola, Rene, *Optical Art: Theory and Practice* (New York: Dover Publications, 1996).

Pásztor, Emília, Juhász, Ákos, Dombi, Miklós and Roslund, Curt, 'Computer Simulation of Stonehenge', in Juan A. Barceló, Maurizio Forte and Donald H. Sanders (eds), *Virtual Reality in Archaeology*, BAR International Series 843 (Oxford: Archaeopress, 2000), pp. 111–14.

Pelegrin, Jacques, 'Reflection sur le comportement technique', in *L'Apport des sols d'habitat a l'étude de l'outillage technique*, ed. M. Otte (Oxford: British Archaeological Reports, 1985), pp. 72–91.

—, 'Les savoir – faire: une très longue histoire, *Terrain*, 16 (1991) : 106–13.

Pelegrin, Jacques, Karlin, Claudine and Bodu, Pierre, 'Chaînes opératoires: un outil pour le préhistorien', in J. Tixier (ed.), *Technologie Lithique* (Paris: CNRS, 1988) pp. 55–62.

Pescarin, Sofia, 'GIS Contribution to Urban History and to the Reconstruction of Ancient Landscape', in Goran Burenhult (ed.), *Archaeological Informatics: Pushing the Envelope*, Proceedings of the 29th CAA Conference, Gotland, April 2001, BAR International Series 1016 (Oxford: ArchaeoPress), pp. 125–8.

Pigeot, Nicolle, 'Technical and Social Actors: Flint Knapping Specialists and Apprentices at Magdalenian Etiolles', *Archaeological Review from Cambridge*, 9 (1990): 126–41.

— 'Réflexions sur l'histoire technique de l'homme: de l'évolution cognitive a l'évolution culturelle', *Paleo*, 3 (1991): 167–200.

Platt, Colin and Coleman-Smith, Richard (eds), *Excavations in Medieval Southampton, 1953–1969* (Leicester: Leicester University Press, 1975).

Pliny the Elder, *The Natural History*, trans. John Bostock and Henry T. Riley (London: H.G. Bohn, 1857).

Pollini, John, Dodd, Lynn Swartz, Kensek, Karen and Cipolla, Nicholas, *Problematics of Making Ambiguity Explicit in Virtual Reconstructions: A Case Study of the Mausoleum of Augustus*, in Anna Bentkowska-Kafel, Trish Cashen and Hazel Gardiner (eds), *Theory and Practice*, Proceedings of 21 Conference of Computers and the History of Art (CHArt), British Academy, London, November 2005, available at <http://www.chart.ac.uk/chart2005/papers/pollini.html>.

Postma, Frans, *26 Rue du Départ, Mondrian's Studio Paris 1921–1936* (Berlin: Ernst and Son, 1995).

Proceedings of Indo–US Science and Technology Forum, November 2005, Mussoorie, India, forthcoming.

Quine, Willard Van Orman, *Word & Object* (Cambridge, MA: MIT Press, 1964).

Quiney, Anthony, *Town Houses of Medieval Britain* (New Haven: Yale University Press, 2003).

Rabinowitz, Adam, Schroer, Carla and Mudge, Mark, 'Grass-roots Imaging: A Case-study in Sustainable Heritage Documentation at Chersonesos, Ukraine', *Proceedings of the CAA Conference March 22–26, 2009 Williamsburg Virginia* (Oxford: Archaeopress, 2010), pp. 320–28.

Ranke, Leopold von, *Geschichte der romanischen und germanischen Völker von 1494 bis 1514* (Leipzig, 1874).

Raymond, Eric S., *The Cathedral and the Bazaar: Musings on Linux and Open Source by an Accidental Revolutionary* (rev. edn, Beijing: O'Reilly, 2001).

Reilly, James and Frey, Franziska, 'Recommendations for the Evaluation of Digital Images Produced from Photographic, Microphotographic, and Various Paper Formats', Report to the Library of Congress (1996).

Reilly, Paul, 'Towards a Virtual Archaeology', in K. Lockyear and S. Rahtz (eds), *Computer Applications in Archaeology*, BAR International Series 565 (Oxford: Archaeopress, 1990), pp. 133–9.

Reinhard, Erik, Ward, Greg, Pattanaik, Sumanta and Debevec, Paul, *High Dynamic Range Imaging: Acquisition, Display, and Image-Based Lighting* (San Francisco: Morgan Kaufmann, 2005).

Reynolds, Craig W., 'Description and Control of Time and Dynamics in Computer Animation', in the notes for the SIGGRAPH '85 course, Advanced Computer Animation (ACM SIGGRAPH, 1985).

—, 'Steering Behaviors for Autonomous Characters', in *Proceedings of Game Developers Conference 1999* (San Francisco: Miller Freeman Game Group, 1999), pp. 763–82.

—, 'Interaction with Groups of Autonomous Characters', in *Proceedings of Game Developers Conference 2000* (San Franciso: 2000), pp. 449–60.

Roberts, Jonathan C. and Ryan, Nick S., 'Alternative Archaeological Representations within Virtual Worlds', in Richard Bowden (ed.), *Proceedings of the 4th UK Virtual Reality Specialist Interest Group Conference*, Brunel University, Uxbridge, Middlesex, November 1997, pp. 179–88, <http://www.cs.kent.ac.uk/people/staff/nsr/arch/vrsig97/vrsig.html>.

Roussou, Maria and Drettakis, George, 'Photorealism and Non-Photorealism in Virtual Heritage Representation', in David Arnold, Alan Chalmers and Franco Niccolucci (eds), *Proceedings of VAST 2003 Fourth International Symposium on Virtual Reality, Archaeology and Intelligent Cultural Heritage* (Aire-La-Ville: Eurographics Publications, 2003), pp. 51–60.

Ruiz-Rodarte, Rocio, 'Augmented Reality for Museum Exhibits', *Proceedings of the* Seventh *International Workshop. PRESENCE 2004* (Spain: ISPR, the International Society for Presence Research and MedICLab/UPV, 2004), pp. 317–20.

—, 'Museo Virtual de Calakmul', *Gaceta de Museos*, 33 (October 2004–January, 2005): 22–7.

Rushkoff, Douglas, *Open Source Democracy* (2003), <http://www.gutenberg.org/files/10753/10753.txt>.

Rushmeier, Holly, Ward, Greg, Piatko, Christine et al., 'Comparing Real and Synthetic Images: Some Ideas about Metrics', in *Proceedings of the Eurographics Rendering Workshop* (1995).

Ryan, Nick, 'Computer-based Visualization of the Past: Technical "Realism" and Historical Credibility', in Peter Main, Tony Higgins and Janet Lang (eds), *Imaging the Past: Electronic Imaging and Computer Graphics in Museums and Archaeology*, British Museum Occasional Papers No. 114 (London: British Museum, 1996), pp. 95–108.

—, 'Documenting and Validating Virtual Archaeology', *Archeologia e Calcolatori*, 12 (November 2001): 245–73.

Sanders, Donald H., *Behavior and the Built Environment: An Interpretive Model for the Analysis of Architecture in an Archaeological Context and Its Testing on Material from the Aegean Bronze Age Site of Myrtos, Crete*, PhD dissertation, Columbia University [1984], Ann Arbor: University Microfilms International [#85-06,031] (1985).

—, 'Architecture: The Neglected Artifact', in Elizabeth B. French and Kenneth A. Wardle (eds), *Problems in Greek Prehistory: Papers Presented at the Centenary Conference of the British School of Archaeology at Athens, Manchester, April 1986* (Bristol: Bristol Classical Press, 1988), pp. 489–98.

—, 'Archaeological Publications Using Virtual Reality: Case Studies and Caveats', in Juan A. Barceló, Maurizio Forte and Donald H. Sanders (eds), *Virtual Reality in Archaeology*, BAR International Series 843 (Oxford: Archaeopress, 2000), pp. 37–46.

Scagliarini Corlàita, Daniella, Coralini, Antonella, Guidazzoli, Antonella et al., 'Archeologia virtuale e supporti informatici nella ricostruzione di una domus di Pompei', in *Archeologia e Calcolatori*, 14 (2003): 237–4.

Schroeder, Will, Martin, Ken and Lorensen, William, *The Visualization Toolkit* (2nd edn, New Jersey: Prentice Hall, 1998).

Sekuler, Robert and Blake, Randolph, *Perception* (New York: McGraw-Hill, 1994).

Seneca, *Epistulae Morales*, 88.22, in *Epistles*, trans. Richard M. Gummere, Loeb Classical Library, vol. 76 (Cambridge, MA: : Harvard University Press, 1991), p.349.

Staley, David J., *Computers, Visualization and History: How New Technology Will Transform Our Understanding of the Past* (Armonk, NY: M.E. Sharpe, 2002).

Stallman, Richard, *Free Software, Free Society: Selected Essays of Richard M. Stallman*, ed. Joshua Gay, with an introduction by Lawrence Lessig (Boston: GNU Press, 2002).

Sterckx, Peter, *Digitale reconstructie en architectuurhistorische studie van het kasteel van Horst, te Holsbeek*, thesis, KU Leuven (2007).

Stuart, James and Revett, Nicholas (eds), *The Antiquities of Athens* (London: John Haberkorn, 1762).

Szalavári, Zsolt and Gervautz, Michael, 'Using the Personal Interaction Panel for 3D Interaction', *Proceedings of the Conference on Latest Results in Information Technology* (Budapest, 1997), <www.cg.tuwien.ac.at/research/vr/pip/sembud97.pdf>), pp. 3–6.

Theodoridou, Maria, Tzitzikas, Yannis, Doerr, Martin et al., 'Modeling and Querying Provenance by Extending CIDOC CRM', *Distributed and Parallel Databases*, 27, 2 (2010): 169–210.

Thompson, Richard F., *The Brain: A Neuroscience Primer* (3rd edn, New York: Worth, 2000).

Troy, Nancy, *The De Stijl Environment* (Cambridge, MA: MIT Press, 1985).

Tufte, Edward R., *The Visual Display of Quantitative Information* (2nd edn, Cheshire, CT: Graphics Press, 2001).

UNESCO Charter on the Preservation of the Digital Heritage <http://portal.unesco.org/ci/en/ev.php-URL_ID=13367&URL_DO=DO_TOPIC&URL_SECTION=201.html>.

Vandevyvere, Han, Neuckermans, Herman and De Jonge, Krista, 'Digital Historical Reconstruction: Case Studies of an Interdisciplinary Task', *International Journal of Design Sciences and Technology*, 13, 1 (2006): 51–65, available at <http://www2.asro.kuleuven.ac.be/asro/english/HOME/Hvdv/Reconstruction/Digital historical reconstructionFormatted.pdf>.

Vatanen, Isto, 'Deconstructing the (Re)Constructed: Issues in Conceptualising the Annotation of Archaeological Virtual Realities', in Martin Doerr and Apostolos Sarris (eds), *The Digital Heritage of Archaeology*, Proceedings of the 30th CAA Conference, Computer Applications and Quantitative Methods in Archaeology, Heraklion, Crete, April 2002 (Athens: Hellenic Ministry of Culture, 2003), pp. 69–74.

Vergauwen, Maarten and Gool, Luc van, 'Web-based 3D Reconstruction Service', *Machine Vision and Applications*, 17, 6 (2006): 411–26.

Vitruvius, *The Ten Books on Architecture*, trans Morris Hickey Morgan (New York: Dover Publications, 1960).

Ward, Gregory, 'The RADIANCE Lighting Simulation and Rendering System' in Andrew Glassner (ed.), *Proceedings of SIGGRAPH '94*, Computer Graphics Proceedings, Annual Conference Series (1994), pp. 459–72.

Williams, Tennessee, *A Streetcar Named Desire* (New York: New Directions Books, 1947).

Wittgenstein, Ludwig, *The Blue and Brown Books* (New York: Harper and Row, 1965).

Wittur, Joyce, *Argumentation Networks*, 3D-Virtualisierung am Beispiel des Klosters Lorsch (seminar), University of Heidelberg, 2007, <http://www.iwr. uni-heidelberg.de/groups/ngg/Lorsch/aims.php?L=E>.

Wren Jr, Christopher, *Parentalia, or, Memoirs of the Family of the Wrens* (1750).

Zeleny, Milan, 'Management Support Systems: Towards Integrated Knowledge Management', *Human Systems Management*, 7, 1 (1987): 59–70.

—, 'Human Systems Management: Integrating Knowledge, Management and Systems', *World Scientific*, 9 (2005): 15–16.

Zhao, Jun, Goble, Carole, Greenwood, Mark et al., 'Annotating, Linking and Browsing Provenance Logs for e-Science', in *Proceedings of Second International Semantic Web Conference (ISWC 2003) Workshop on Retrieval of Scientific Data* (Florida, 2003), pp. 158–76.

Zuk, Torre, Carpendale, Sheelagh and Glanzman, William D. 'Visualizing Temporal Uncertainty in 3D Virtual Reconstructions', in Mark Mudge, Nick Ryan and Roberto Scopigno (eds), *Proceedings of VAST 2005, The 6th International Symposium on Virtual Reality, Archaeology and Cultural Heritage* (Aire-La-Ville: Eurographics Publications, 2003), pp. 99–106.

Film

Beowulf, dir. Robert Zemeckis, DVD (ImageMovers and Shangri-La Entertainment, 2007).

Dinosaur, dir. Eric Leighton and Ralph Zondag, DVD (Walt Disney Pictures, 2000).

Final Fantasy VII: Advent Children, dir. Tetsuya Nomura and Takeshi Nozue, DVD (Square Enix Company and Square US, 2006).

Gladiator, The, dir. Ridley Scott (US, 2000).

Ice Age, dir. Chris Wedge and Carlos Saldanha, DVD (Blue Sky Studios, 2002).

Jurassic Park, dir. Steven Spielberg, based on the novel by Michael Crichton, DVD (Universal Pictures, 1993).

Scipio Africanus, dir. Carmine Gallone (US/Italy, 1937).

Sea Monsters: A Prehistoric Adventure, dir. Sean MacLeod Phillips (Day's End Pictures and National Geographic Giant Screen Films, 2007).

Toy Story, dir. John Lasseter, DVD (Walt Disney Pictures and Pixar Animation Studios, 1999).

Machinima

Borg War, dir. Geoffrey James (Starbase 28, 2006).
Diary of a Camper, dir. Matthew Van Sickler.
Quake demo recording (United Ranger Films, 1996).
Red vs. Blue: The Blood Gulch Chronicles, dir. Burnie Burns and Matt Hullum, DVD (Rooster Teeth Productions, 2003).

Television Programmes and Series

The Ballad of Big Al, writ. Kate Bartlett and Michael Olmert, DVD (British Broadcasting Corporation, BS Asahi, Discovery Channel, Pro 7 and TV Asahi, 2001).
Dinotopia, dir. Marco Brambilla, DVD (Hallmark Entertainment, Mat I, Mid Atlantic Films and RTL, 2002).
Doctor Who series 4, prod. Phil Collinson and Susie Liggat, DVD (BBC, 2007).
Dragnet, dir. Jack Webb, US TV series from 1951; see <http://en.wikipedia.org/wiki/Dragnet_(series)>.
Last Dragon, The, dir. Justin Hardy, DVD (Darlow Smithson Productions, 2004).
Life in Cold Blood, exec. prod. Sara Ford, DVD (BBC and Animal Planet, 2008).
Prehistoric Park, DVD (Impossible Pictures, 2006).
Primeval, prod. Cameron Mcallister and Tim Haines, DVD (Impossible Pictures, 2007).
Reboot, exec. prod. Jay Firestone (Mainframe Entertainment, 1994).
Rome, dir. Michael Apted, Allen Coulter, Alan Poul et al., DVD (HD Vision Studios, BBC, Home Box Office, 2005)
Roughnecks: Starship Troopers Chronicles, dir. Andre Clavel, DVD (Adelaide Productions, 1999).
Walking with Beasts, dir. Nigel Patterson, DVD (BBC, Discovery Channel, TV Asahi, BS Asahi and ProSieben, 2001).
Walking with Cavemen, DVD (BBC, Discovery Channel, Evergreen Films LLC and ProSieben Television, 2003).
Walking with Dinosaurs, dir. John Lynch, DVD (BBC, Discovery Channel and TV Asahi, 1999).
Walking with Monsters, dir. Tim Haines and Chloe Leland, DVD (Impossible Pictures, 2005).

Video Games and Virtual Worlds

Dinosaur World, <http://www.bbc.co.uk/sn/prehistoric_life/games/dinosaur_world/>.
Foldit, <http://fold.it/portal/> (University of Washington, 2008).

Google Earth, <http://earth.google.com/> (Google, 2008).

Google SketchUp, PC and Mac, <http://sketchup.google.com/index.html> (Google, 2008).

Pokémon Diamond, Nintendo DS (Game Freak, 2006).

Pokémon Pearl, Nintendo DS (Game Freak, 2006).

Sea Monsters: A Prehistoric Adventure, Nintendo Wii, Nintendo DS and PlayStation 2 (DSI Games, 2008).

Second Life, <http://secondlife.com/> (Linden Lab, 2003).

Spore <http://www.spore.com/ftl> (Electronic Arts Inc., 2008).

Index